# LOOK TO THE  EARTH

D0146891

# LOOK TO THE EARTH

*Historical Archaeology*

*and the American*

*Civil War*

*Edited by Clarence R. Geier, Jr. and Susan E. Winter*

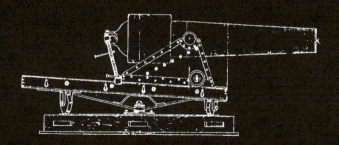

THE UNIVERSITY OF TENNESSEE PRESS / KNOXVILLE

Copyright © 1994 by The University of Tennessee
Press / Knoxville.
All Rights Reserved. Manufactured in the
United States of America.
First Edition.

The paper in this book meets the minimum
requirements of the American National Standard for
Permanence of Paper for Printed Library Materials.
∞
The binding materials have been chosen
for strength and durability.

Library of Congress Cataloging-in-Publication Data

Look to the earth: historical archaeology and the
    American Civil War / edited by Clarence R. Geier,
    Jr. and Susan E. Winter.
            p.   cm.
    Includes bibliographical references and index.
    ISBN 0-87049-857-6 (cloth: alk. paper)
    1. United States—History—Civil War, 1861–1865—
    Antiquities. I. Geier, Clarence. R. II. Winter, Susan E.
    E646.5.L66      1994                    94-15587
    973.7—dc20                               CIP

# CONTENTS

# FIGURES

# TABLES

# FOREWORD

With the 125th anniversary of the American Civil War, the nation reaffirmed its continuing fascination with that event through television productions, movies, reenactments, publications both fictional and factual, and renewed concern for preserving battlefields and other sites of the period. As part of the commemoration, a day-long session on Civil War archaeology was organized and presented as part of the twenty-fourth annual meeting of the Society for Historical Archaeology, appropriately held in Richmond, Virginia, the capitol of the Confederacy, in January 1991. The purpose of this special session was to draw attention to the role that historical archaeology can play in the study of the Civil War, on local, regional, national, and even international levels. The chapters of this book are, for the most part, revised and expanded versions of papers presented at that conference.

While this book is the first published compilation of historical archaeology research devoted solely to Civil War period sites, it is viewed by the authors and editors as an exploratory study. Its goals are modest. The first is to make people aware of the contributions that archaeology can make toward understanding the Civil War, an event that profoundly influenced the contours of American culture and society from the mid-nineteenth century to the present. Together with historical documentation, archaeology can verify or dispute events recounted in folk, popular, and academic histories. It also can suggest physical details of events that may not be available in written reports and discussions.

In the absence of historical records, archeological remains preserved in the earth may furnish the only documentation of particular events and effects of the war. Historical archaeology also makes it possible for us to listen anew to those segments of society who were affected by the war and its aftermath but whose voices, for the most part, have been lost in the filtering process of history. Such groups of society include freed slaves, poor whites, farmers whose fields and homes were ravaged and destroyed, rural millers whose "factories" were destroyed, and a host of others. It is these people who comprise the fabric of the communities which benefited from, or were ravaged by, the dynamics of war. Yet their lack of prestige and social status made them of little interest to the creators of traditional history.

The second goal of this book is to look beyond the Civil War as a strictly military event and examine its impact on the larger cultural landscape. This aim parallels the recent trend in social historical research to view the war within a broader societal context (see, for example, Vinovskis 1990b; Clinton and Silber 1992). Consistent with modern initiatives in reenactment, in popular and social history, and in anthropology, the authors include themes and sites set apart from traditional military histories and studies of battlefield tactics.

Material culture, the primary focus of archaeological research, can be an extremely sensitive indicator of cultural and social change. As a result, the discipline of archaeology, particularly when combined with historical research, is well placed to contribute new insights into the tremendous changes that occurred across American society due to the war. The wide range of sites and topics included in this volume reflects this perspective, as the repercussions of the war extended beyond the military sphere and into the domestic and industrial spheres.

Not surprisingly in a book of this nature, the essays included represent diverse theoretical backgrounds and perspectives. The editors have encouraged these different perspectives, without favoring one over another.

Given the goals of the text, the editors are frustrated to some degree by the book's limitations. While the Civil War was both national and international in scope, a large number of articles deal only with the war's eastern theater. Further, while the authors and editors are convinced that historical archaeology can play an important role in illuminating the Civil War, to date the majority of archaeological work carried out on Civil War–period sites has resulted from federally mandated compliance or preservation projects. As a result, research is often limited by some "project boundary or right-of-way" that has no historical meaning. Such work, rather than being part of a larger, more inclusive social history project, has been limited to the recovery of material artifacts within a portion of a site threatened with loss or destruction.

In effect, the place of historical archaeology within the study of Civil War history is in the process of being established. This book is designed to help point the way.

The book is organized into four parts. Part 1, "Introduction and Directions," includes chapters that discuss and illustrate the importance of combining a study of historical records and archaeological remains to provide an accurate understanding of Civil War events. Part 2, "Battlefield Analysis and Reconstruction," provides examples of the use of archaeological method in the analysis and reconstruction of events occurring as part of military engagements. Part 3, "Fortifications, Encampments, and Camp Life," illustrates the role of archaeology in supplying information demanded by the growing ranks of reenactors and historians interested in daily life at military facilities and encampments. Part 4, "Other Directions," presents chapters illustrating applications of historical archaeology to diverse military and domestic issues. Topics include changing regional agricultural patterns, battlefield impact on domestic life, munitions manufacture and espionage, the study of underwater archaeological sites of military ships and merchantmen, and symbolic landscapes.

*Clarence R. Geier, Jr.*
*Susan E. Winter*

# ACKNOWLEDGMENTS

L ike many complex undertakings, this book's conception began simply, over a casual beer with friends at a Middle Atlantic Archaeological Symposium in Rehobeth Beach, Maryland. Subsequent events generated a core of staunch and dedicated professionals who recognized the essential role that historical archaeology must play in the study of the American Civil War. Initially this group encouraged and then organized a one-day symposium held at the 1990 meetings of the Society for Historical Archaeology in Richmond, Virginia. From this commitment emerged the groundwork and, in part, the contents of this book. Given this dedicated effort, we are pleased to acknowledge the contributions of Dr. Stephen Potter, regional archaeologist, National Capital Region, National Park Service; Christopher Calkins, park historian, Petersburg National Battlefield Park; Dennis Frye, historian, Harpers Ferry National Historical Park; and Jan Townsend, county archaeologist, Prince William County.

# Part I.

## Introduction and Directions

The two chapters in this section introduce readers to the general nature and character of historical archaeology and illustrate past and possible applications of the discipline. Steven Smith examines the relationship that exists between written and archaeological records, and the role each type plays in understanding the events and implications of the Civil War. To archaeologists he points out the need to master the voluminous, often highly technical and detailed historical records, many of which have not been researched or previously interpreted. To others interested in the war, Smith stresses that artifacts and features in place in the ground have great value as critical and often unduplicated records of past actions of human beings. It is in blending the archaeological record with the archival-historical one that the full contribution of historical archaeology may be realized.

Continuing the theme of ways in which archaeological research can contribute to the interpretation of the Civil War, David Orr examines several studies conducted around Petersburg and City Point, Virginia. He illustrates how these studies can provide insights into the war's effects *upon its participants, both military and civilian, on an individual level. In addition, Orr gives examples of how the archaeological research can transcend or enhance the available historical record.*

# 1

*Steven D. Smith*

# ARCHAEOLOGICAL PERSPECTIVES ON THE CIVIL WAR
## *The Challenge to Achieve Relevance*

In the mid–1960s, the discipline of archaeology began to broaden its field of inquiry even as it strove to become more rigorous in its methodology. At the same time, American archaeologists began to specialize and to focus on the study of the historic period. Now, after some twenty-five years, historical archaeology is well established, although its influence upon other disciplines is still slight (Schuyler 1988: 37). Further, it is not yet clear what contribution historical archaeology can make to an understanding of America's historic past. From within the discipline and from such related disciplines as history and anthropology come increasingly loud voices, raising persistent, haunting questions. What has historical archaeology contributed? What *can* it contribute that cannot be derived from other sources? As historical archaeologists begin to address the Civil War, these voices will become clamorous, for certainly the Civil War already is one of the most well-examined phenomena in American history. Given such thorough coverage by military historians, social scientists, economic historians, and others, questions concerning historical archaeology's possible contribution loom large. What can historical archaeology contribute? How does it contribute? Who cares what it contributes?

This chapter examines these questions and points to the responsibility that historical archaeologists have to ensure that their discipline contributes new and relevant information to an understanding of the Civil War. The special problems of doing Civil War archaeology amplify the necessity for a cautious approach, for taking short, solid steps forward. Despite these challenges, it is argued herein that archaeology can make valuable contributions; in fact, archaeology *must* contribute.

## The Civil War's Place in the American Process

It would be difficult to overstate the impact and influence of the Civil War upon this country since 1865. Three million of our ancestors were members of armies in the war, over 1,000,000 were casualties, and 618,000 died (Patricia Faust 1986: 187; James Robertson 1988a: vii). These casualties may seem small compared with those in modern wars, but actually their impact was greater. If the United States in World War II had suffered in proportion to the casualties the South experienced during the Civil War, our nation would have incurred six million casualties by 1945 (McWhiney and Jamieson 1984: xiv). Of those aged thirteen to forty-three in 1860, approximately 6 percent of Northern white males and 18 percent of Southern white males died in the Civil War (Vinovskis 1990b: 7). The war also radically changed the lives of 3.5 million blacks, who gained freedom if not social equality as a result of the conflict (James Robertson 1988a: 30). The financial cost of the war to North and South together has been estimated at eight billion dollars (Patricia Faust 1986: 187). For half the nation, war's end brought the end of a society and the end of a way of life. The property and the economy of the southern half of the nation lay in ruins. As a result of four years of war, farm values in the South had fallen by 41 percent and the value of farm machinery by 38 percent (Gates 1965: 373). Recovery from the war was not only slow, it was confused, violent, and resentful, and arguably it is still in process. When Americans examine what the

South has been since 1861, the war holds a central place in their explanation.

The Civil War holds a central place not only in this nation's history but also in its basic ideology—an ideology that was conceived long before the Civil War. The concept of individual liberty, or, perhaps, the great experiment in individual liberty that began here in 1776, was severely tested in 1861 (Page Smith 1982: 993). The American Revolution began a process of defining liberty's linkage to nationalism, and the Civil War continued this process (Reid Mitchell 1988: 1–3; Fredrickson 1965: 53–64). Ironically, North and South shared this ideology, both paying allegiance to liberty, democracy, and individualism (Reid Mitchell 1988: 2; Jimmerson 1988: 2). Letters written home by soldiers attest time and time again to their commitment to liberty (Robertson 1988a: 10). But in 1776, liberty was not defined as applying to the large portion of the population that was enslaved. The Civil War extended liberty to all people. As long as the war is debated, its complex causes will be debated also. But no matter what actually caused the first shots to be fired at Fort Sumter, the war ended slavery in America.

Two visions of liberty clashed in the war: the Northern vision of strong nationalism and the Southern vision of state's rights (Burns 1982: 599). Civil War soldiers marched essentially as members of citizen armies, taking the war's destruction to a civilian population (Williams 1983a: 32; Hagerman 1988: xiii). As such, they were among history's first truly ideological armies (Keegan 1988: 191; Hagerman 1988). Thus, the study of ideology will form, quite appropriately, a context for our archaeological study of the Civil War and the American experience. But archaeologists must be aware of the power and responsibility of their scholarship. They must keep foremost in their minds the fact that throughout human history individuals have been willing to sacrifice themselves for an idea, especially if that idea is freedom. Ideas are powerful, and to ignore the power of liberty not only denigrates the human spirit but also misrepresents it.

The war has greatly influenced how Americans think and what Americans now think about. Discourse concerning the causes and effects of the Civil War has been described as a "'watershed' in [American] intellectual and literary history" (Fredrickson 1965: vii). T. Harry Williams (1983a: 36) has stated that the war "has sunk deeply into the national consciousness." Henry James asserted that it "marks an era in the history of the American mind" (Fredrickson 1965: 1). Page Smith has even declared that the war and Reconstruction "are the epic drama of American history, our Iliad, our War of the Roses, our Thirty Years' War, rolled into one" (1982: 994). The Civil War, in fact, has sunk so deeply into our national consciousness that the facts surrounding the events, causes, and effects of the war have been irrevocably confused in national myth (James O. Robertson 1980: 85–91).

The Civil War certainly has had a great deal of literary attention. It has been the "subject of more publications than any other episode of American history" (Nevins, Robertson, and Wiley 1970: v). It has been estimated that between eighty thousand and one hundred thousand volumes of publications exist for the thorough researcher to master, and that one hundred contributions are added every year (James I. Robertson 1988b: vii; Fowler 1986: xix). The intensity of the Civil War experience, described by both participants and pundits, has inspired some of America's finest examples of literary scholarship, including the writings of T. Harry Williams, Douglas Southall Freeman, Bruce Catton, and Shelby Foote.

The war is of enduring interest to all Americans, and this interest continues to grow. In 1986 the National Park Service reported that 3.5 million people visited the Civil War battlefields of Gettysburg, Antietam, and Vicksburg (U.S. National Park Service 1986: 10, 15, 22). Today as many as 150,000 to 200,000 Americans participate in Civil War reenactments (Jackson 1990: 56), and there is even a reenactment group in England specializing in the American Civil War. Popular magazines with combined circulations of over 235,000 readers now can be found at many newsstands (Manning 1990: 709, 713). When the PBS documentary *The Civil War* had its premier in 1990, 14 million people watched each night, making it the most widely viewed public television series to that date (Gerard 1990: 1).

Archaeologists who have excavated Civil War sites know just how popular these sites are with relic collectors. As a consequence of the invention of the portable metal detector, only a few Civil War sites remain untouched. Although these sites are not always totally destroyed by such activity (Legg and Smith 1989), archaeologists must deal with a continuing loss of information. Professional and avocational archaeologists will sadly note that the PBS documentary increased the value of Civil War relics on the antiquities market (Associated Press 1990: 2).

Quite simply, the Civil War has both defined the South as a region and, to a lesser but still crucial extent, defined this nation. The American public and academe know this and have an enduring fascination with every aspect of the war. Before the war, the nation debated the peculiar institution of slavery (Stampp 1956), and the industrial North sparred with King Cotton South. After the war, the South lived, and still lives, with the war's consequences. Anthropologically-oriented archaeologists will forever question the impact that particular events have on the evolution of culture (Kroeber 1917). But as archaeologists studying the historic period, we must acknowledge that nations are defined and shaped by historic events of the magnitude of the American Civil War.

## Why Archaeology?

The magnitude and scope of the Civil War, and the influence that it has had on our nation's past and on our very consciousness, makes it imperative that archaeologists investigate Civil War sites. Archaeologists cannot understand the nineteenth-century American experience without building an understanding not only of the four war years, but also of the events leading up to, and the impact of, those four years.

Archaeologists view themselves as scientists who seek out the patterns left by human behavior (Deetz 1967: 4–7; South 1977: 88). Explanations of these patterns are discussed within many contextual frameworks, such as systemic and ecological (Watson, LeBlanc, and Redman 1971), cognitive (Deetz 1977), ideological (Leone 1984), or even within the framework of basic culture history (Willey and Phillips 1958). The impact of an event as significant as the Civil War should be observable in the behavioral patterns discovered archaeologically. Thus, no matter what explanatory framework is used, it must account for the Civil War.

Furthermore, the public and scholarly communities' interest in and intensity of feelings about the war clearly imply that every bit of information, from whatever source, is precious, needed, and welcome. A subject of such demonstrated importance to understanding America must be studied from every possible viewpoint. No source can be overlooked, including material remains hidden beneath the American landscape. To ignore archaeological remains is to exercise a partiality researchers cannot afford. This is not to argue that all data are, in the final analysis, equal. Rather, all data are significant until proven insignificant. Careful archaeological excavation of Civil War sites must be conducted, if for no other reason than that the data must be collected until shown to be redundant (Legg and Smith 1989: 133). Furthermore, archaeologists, not others, must make this determination. It must not be left to others to dismiss or discover America's material past. Archaeological remains are so fragile, and analysis and interpretation so frustratingly difficult, that only a clear devotion to archaeological methods and principles can determine the data's value to an understanding of the Civil War.

Archaeologists must study the Civil War for other reasons, too. Historical archaeologists often point to the varied perspectives that can be obtained by combining information gathered through historical documents and archaeological excavation (William Adams 1977). Each discipline has its inherent biases (Seasholes 1990: 17–19; South 1977: 312; Williams 1983b: 188). Jointly, the two yield a more complete picture of the past than would a single perspective. The result of combining the data is a synergistic, or holistic, perspective on the past (William Adams 1977; Steven D. Smith 1991). Historians focus on the war's documentary history. Archaeology's reach can be much broader, because archaeologists are omnivorous in their attempts to get at the past. Archaeology's strength is that it is multievidential (Deegan 1988: 8–10; Schuyler 1977), using the benefits of such disciplines as physical anthropology, zoology, and geology to broaden its perspective, strengthen its conclusions, and provide new insight. Thus, in order to understand nineteenth-century America, archaeologists must understand the Civil War; in return, it is our unique perspective that other disciplines and the American public await.

## The Challenge

An archaeology of the Civil War must contribute pertinent new data, avoiding the trivial. This will not be easy. Hereafter are some thoughts and opinions on the challenges archaeologists face. To frame this discussion, the focus will be on those sites created during the four bloody war years. Primarily, these are defined as military sites: campgrounds, fortifications, entrenchments, wharves, and battlegrounds. Obviously, in building an understanding of the process of defining liberty, or the ideology of the nineteenth century, archaeologists must also study sites dating prior to and after the war. Northern industrial sites, such as textile mills, and Southern sites, such as those pertaining to the antebellum and postbellum plantation system, all may be studied and understood as part of processes leading up to and flowing from the Civil War. But as will be seen below, these broad processes cannot be examined without reference to those unique military sites created from 1861 to 1865. Further, it is the special nature and context of these sites that makes investigating them so challenging to archaeologists who attempt to contribute relevant information. Thus, the focus here is primarily on Civil War sites, and the issues raised here may or may not be pertinent to other areas of inquiry in historical archaeology.

There are serious methodological problems historical archaeologists must address before the discipline achieves relevance in Civil War studies. The most challenging is the nature of the documentary evidence. First, there is the vast amount of research previously conducted by historians. Before archaeologists can offer germane contributions, they have a responsibility to assimilate this effort to the extent possible, to gain a solid understanding of previous historical interpretations of the war (Seasholes 1990: 17–19; Schuyler 1988: 41). This task should not be viewed as a detriment or a limitation to the conduct of archaeology. Nor should it be seen as requiring archaeologists to become historians. Rather, the call is for archaeologists to enhance the relevance of archaeological work at Civil War sites by becoming historical archaeologists, defined here as scientists using and integrating the information provided by both documents and archaeology, rather than simply archaeologists excavating sites of the historic period. Such historical research not only should aid in developing a context for archaeological research, but also should stimulate the discipline toward asking questions that count (Cleland 1988: 16), questions that have not been asked before or at least not asked within the context of the archaeological record.

The second documentary challenge is the vast number of primary sources which still exist. The primary sources on the Civil War can overwhelm the researcher (Nevins, Robertson, and Wiley 1970: v). Archival material available for historians and archaeologists is often measured in feet. For instance, a sampling of a guide to the federal archival holdings on the Civil War finds that there are 60 feet of records pertaining to the arrival and disposition of exchanged or paroled Union prisoners, and 227 feet of records in the general file of Confederate Prisoners (Munden and Beers 1962: 321, 322).

While studying the lives of soldiers whose remains were excavated at General Edward Wild's "African Brigade" cemetery on Folly Island, South Carolina (Legg and Smith 1989), archaeologists conducted an archival reconnaissance of Record Group 94 at the National Archives. This record group, containing regimental descriptive books and morning reports, measures in at a mere 1,600 feet (Munden and Beers 1962: 404). The Manuscript Division of the Library of Congress has over forty million original items in ten thousand different collections (Sellers 1986: v). Beyond the federal archives, there are numerous state, historical, and university archives. Again during the Folly Island project, archaeologists were able to visit the archival holdings of the Massachusetts National Guard Supply Depot, in Natick, Massachusetts. Perhaps like many state archives, those in Natick contained box after box of records, many of them still folded and wrapped in red ribbon. The Civil War was a war of firsts, and one of these was that it was the first modern bureaucratic war. Historians and archaeologists also may be sure that, hidden away in attics across the country, are unpublished diaries and reminiscences awaiting discovery. These documentary resources offer the archaeologist a wealth of opportunity (Crass 1990: 118–19). The range of research topics open to us through historic military documents is extensive and already has been recognized by archaeologists (Babits 1988; Crass 1990). But the abundance of Civil War documentary data is both a blessing and a curse. While the documents pertaining to the war can be "incomplete, contradictory, and frequently inaccurate" (Williams 1983b: 188), archaeologists still need to examine them thoroughly. If archaeologists choose to work in isolation from the documents, they may find themselves conducting trivial investigations (Cleland 1988: 16). Would it not be dangerous, for instance, to make inferences based on an "artifact pattern" (South 1977) derived from the excavation of a Civil War regimental campground when detailed ordnance records and equipment lists are still available for that very regiment (Legg and Smith 1989: 99)? These records may well still exist.

On the other hand, knowing what is available in the archives and becoming familiar with methods for using and interpreting the documents allows the archaeologist to go beyond these resources. For instance, by deriving an artifact pattern from documentary sources and comparing it to what was found, one may shed light on procurement practices, the flow of contraband, or the value of sutlers' supplies during the Civil War. Appropriate use of primary records in conjunction with archaeological data could also offer a new perspective on the quality and quantity of Confederate versus Union army equipment, or on whether supplies from blockade runners actually made it to the Confederate front lines. Obviously, such documents are not always available and are often fragmentary when available. Furthermore, there are gaps in the overall historical record. However, historical archaeologists must thoroughly excavate Civil War archives, because the possibility that detailed primary sources exist is greater than in most areas of inquiry in historical archaeology. Thorough excavation of the archives also will uncover information gaps that archaeology can fill.

To further complicate the task before us, it is essential that archaeologists conduct archival research themselves (Schuyler 1988: 42). As argued above, it is critical to assimilate and understand the history of the Civil War, as researched and written by historians. But archaeologists must determine the kinds of archaeological questions that are relevant to ask when analyzing the primary sources. Furthermore, the appropriate use and integration of these data must be determined by archaeologists. Leone and Potter (1988: 14) have argued that the people who produced the documentary record usually were not the same individuals who created the archaeological record. However, as noted previously, archaeologists often may have an opportunity to analyze both records (day books, morning reports, regimental histories, and requisition forms) and archaeological remains from the same units. This makes the task of appropriately integrating historical documents and the archaeological record even more critical.

The abundance of Civil War archival material challenges us to find nontraditional methods of archaeological inquiry. Civil War sites in South Carolina illustrate this point and emphasize the necessity of thorough archival work. During the war, many of the coastal barrier islands around Charleston, Hilton Head, and Beaufort were occupied by the Union army. The army usually occupied its sites only for a few months. Traditional archaeological survey methods, primarily relying on systematic shovel testing, have missed these sites entirely or misrepresented their scope and value (Legg and Smith 1989: 132–33). At Folly Island, South Carolina, two different survey teams, using only a traditional level of presurvey documentary research, followed by shovel testing, failed to recognize the extensive nature of a Union campground. The relationship of isolated features to each other, as part of a large camp matrix, was not understood until formal excavations took place. At Bray's Island, South Carolina, another Civil War campground was missed altogether by shovel testing during an archaeological survey, only to be discovered later by resurvey using a metal detector (Robert Johnson, personal communication with author, 1989). Other surveys on Hilton Head, Seabrook, and Daufuskie Islands have overlooked similar occupations (Ramona Grunden, personal communication 1991).

In sum, after missing these sites, South Carolina archaeologists are learning that all routine National Historic Preservation Act compliance surveys on barrier islands should include an examination of the primary Civil War documents. In addition, these surveys should include a systematic metal detector survey along with the shovel testing. Many relic collectors have made good use of the primary documents and know the sites. As part of any survey, archaeologists should interview local collectors.

On South Carolina barrier islands, Civil War camps appear to be extensive across the landscape, but not dense. Features are single-point intrusions, widely separated yet associated with each other as part of occupations at the level of a regiment or a division and representing thousands of troops. This pattern has also been observed in North Carolina (Stine 1989). Such sites are difficult to find, but the rewards are high. These lessons might already have been learned in Virginia, where the physical aspects of the war are more evident on the landscape, but two points need to be re-emphasized. First, in compliance surveys in South Carolina, and perhaps elsewhere, Civil War military records are often overlooked. Second, traditional shovel testing alone often will fail to find these campgrounds, and if they do find an occasional feature, shovel testing alone will not reveal the archaeological value of such features.

Artifact studies constitute another realm in which archaeologists have an opportunity to move beyond the known and beyond traditional archaeological methods. Most of the military hardware of the Civil War, for example, already is well documented. Numerous sources, authored by technologists and collectors, are available detailing the military accouterments carried by both sides (Kerksis 1974; Lord and Wise 1970; Phillips 1974; Sylvia and O'Donnell 1978; Thomas 1981; Todd 1974). It may be useful in some cases to confirm the accuracy of these sources by examining the material culture recovered archaeologically, but it is doubtful that archaeology will contribute much new information about the hardware itself. Why bother with such work? Why bother, for instance, with traditional efforts to impose an archaeological artifact typology on Civil War materials? Typological studies, which have occupied prehistorians to a greater extent and historical archaeologists to a lesser extent, traditionally are conducted to understand and gain control of site and regional chronology. But the chronology of the Civil War is well documented, so typology diminishes in importance when excavating Civil War sites. Indeed, typological studies of Civil War artifacts may not always be necessary unless a specific question exists, the answer to which goes beyond the knowledge provided by technologists and collectors.

Further, since a soldier who discarded a given object did not directly modify nature to produce that object, the highly technological aspects of the object are of minimal importance to archaeologists seeking to understand the life of that soldier. More important is the impact that technology had on the soldier. Strictly from the viewpoint of military history, the war was a war of technological innovation, in keeping with the industrial revolution of the nineteenth century. This was the first war to make widespread use of railroads, armored ships, telegraph, photography, and balloons (Williams 1983a: 33; Luvaas 1988; Hagerman 1988; Stern 1959: 8). Historian T. Harry Williams (1983a: 34) asserts that "the explanation of what happened at Gettysburg and in other battles lay in technology and science." The power of rifled muskets and artillery to stop frontal assaults at Gettysburg was a costly lesson (McWhiney and Jamieson 1984). Obviously, technological innovations had a profound impact on the lives of the soldiers, and this impact is likely to be reflected in the material culture. Therefore, the research value of material culture in Civil War archaeology will lie not in what the material is, nor in the technological minutia of its production, but in the relationship of the artifacts to each other and to the people who used them.

## Archaeology's Contribution: A Culture History of the Civil War

The challenges of developing an archaeology of the Civil War, then, are great and complex. But the physical manifestations of the past, as seen in an archaeological assemblage, should focus attention firmly on what and how archaeology can contribute to an understanding of the Civil War. Archaeology's greatest and most unique asset is its ability to interpret the past using the physical remains of the past. After the documentary data have been mastered, archaeologists must step beyond them to the features and artifacts remaining in the ground. Otherwise, they are not doing archaeology. Below are some thoughts on the proper direction of Civil War archaeology.

One way archaeologists can contribute meaningfully to an understanding of the Civil War is by promoting public participation in excavation and handling of artifacts. Archaeologists often undervalue the power inherent in the simple concept that the past is real. Artifacts and features in the ground are real manifestations of the past actions of human beings. These artifacts and features are concrete examples of that past and allow both the public and the scholar to build a contemporary picture of that very real past.

Modern Americans increasingly experience the world through television and computer, depriving their senses of physical links and making their experience of the world, in the extreme, almost illusory. It has often been said that Civil War soldiers' letters bring the war experience alive. But archaeology can be equally powerful. Archaeology is not only multievidential, it is multisensory. Through archaeology, the past can be seen, touched, and held. Think of the Minié ball. Hefting a simple Minié ball for the first time, a single example among thousands that were buzzing through the ranks at Pickett's Charge, can be an emotional and thought-provoking experience. When people visit a site or participate in removing artifacts from the ground, they touch the past. When they visit a museum with well-executed interpretative displays, they are connected directly to the past. Archaeologists should not overlook the contributions they can make in using the physical manifestations of the past to provide an understanding of, and a link to, people living in past eras.

Beyond contributing to public understanding of the Civil War, archaeologists strive to make significant contributions to research. In studying military sites, archaeologists have a wonderful opportunity to refine many of their studies of status and ethnicity and to enhance their recognition of human behavioral patterns. For instance, South (1977: 125) has noted that historical documents can be used as a control to distinguish variations in human behavioral patterns seen in the archaeological record. Scientific control always has been a problem in testing hypotheses in historical archaeology. Often there are many cultural variables, including random behavior, that might explain the patterns seen archaeologically. However, military sites were created as a result of activities taking place within a closed cultural system, operating under strict rules. That system is well documented and well known. The system imposed on the culture a known control or norm, which should allow archaeologists to observe, under controlled conditions, variations in the patterns. For instance, the military settlement pattern of a regimental camp is expected because regulations were imposed (Legg and Smith 1989: D1–2). Variations in the expected settlement pattern are likely to be more visible in the archaeological record, and much less likely to be due to random behavior. Thus, in analyzing archaeological sites and artifact assemblages, comparisons can be made with greater confidence between Union and Confederate forces, say, or between white and black troops (Riordan 1985), or between the morale of soldiers in the early and late phases of the war (James I. Robertson 1988a: 43). Such visibility opens the door to studies of status and ethnicity, in a culture that perhaps imposed even greater control on its participants than antebellum plantation culture did (Otto 1977). Such studies can well yield relevant contributions.

Another area in which historical archaeology can contribute is in the study of battle. Here archaeologists face a skeptical audience. Anthropologists Rapoport and Turney-High have stated that examinations of material culture have only a secondary role to play in the study of war (Rapoport 1971: viii; Turney-High 1971: 5–6). Historian John Keegan (1976: 30) has noted that "it is not through what armies are but by what they do that the lives of nations and of individuals are changed." However, the excellent study of the Little Big Horn battlefield, using a controlled metal detector survey, has demonstrated how archaeologists can contribute to the study of battle (Scott and Fox 1987; Richard A. Fox 1993). To date, attempts to duplicate the Little Big Horn methods on Civil War battlefields have produced mixed results. At a battle site in Perryville, Kentucky, modern recreational use, including reenactments, appear to have masked the historical data which could be used to interpret the battle (Clay 1990: 3). These problems, and the sheer size and complexity of Civil War battles in the eastern theater, may preclude such studies at some of these battlefields. But at Mine Creek, Kansas, archaeologists have had better success (Lees 1990: 11; this volume). Furthermore, excavations at the Carter House at the Battle of Franklin in Tennessee have offered tantalizing insights into battlefield behavior (Samuel D. Smith 1991; this volume). These studies hold much promise for the future, as more Civil War sites are examined.

For the present, though, the most important way archaeology can contribute information germane to the study of the Civil War is by excavating sites in order to establish basic, but very necessary, archaeological facts (Courbin 1988: 110–49). Archaeological facts are established first through careful excavation and recording of the site being excavated. Archaeological facts seem mundane but actually are critical discoveries, such as where an artifact is found or the identity of a feature and its relationship to another (Courbin 1988: 112–13). Archaeological facts are those solid statements that are added to others to interpret a single site. The interpretations of that site then are tested against interpretations of other sites, and new archaeological facts are established. Through this tedious, time-consuming, but essential work, true patterns are seen, measured, and tested. From these patterns valid statements can be made concerning behavior.

By establishing facts, historical archaeology takes two critical steps. First, it provides historians as well as members of other disciplines with new information that can be absorbed into the general body of knowledge about the Civil War. In this manner, historical archaeology becomes a discipline that is noticed. Second, it provides the valid, relevant facts upon which to build an archaeology of the Civil War. These facts can build on the documentary history but also (and much more important) stand independent of the documentary history and go beyond it. Establishing facts is the first and most proper work of archaeological excavation of the Civil War period, and only through it can we build an independent body of data.

Establishing archaeological facts about the Civil War, as an immediate focus, certainly will be seen as restrictive or particularistic. Such an aim will fail to satisfy the yearning some have to establish general laws of anthropology (South 1977) or to create an explicitly scientific archaeology (Binford 1968) of the Civil War. Some will view this task as not worthy of their time, because they seek, now, to establish broad anthropological models. But it is suggested that these models may be premature. Further, the abundance of historic documents demands special attention. By necessity, a germane archaeology of the Civil War will be more document-oriented than other areas of archaeological inquiry. Courbin (1988: 131–32) most clearly has argued that "the establishment of facts . . . does not reduce anyone to a subordinate role, [it] brings into play all the archaeologist's knowledge, all his intelligence, all his imagination. And that is the key to everything that may follow." Such particularism provides the building blocks for any broader archaeological inquiry. For those whose interest is in the broadest interpretations of humanity, such facts may be less appropriate. But eventually such individuals will desire to test their theories and ideas against the hard reality

of the past, and these facts will emerge as necessary. This is not to advocate the abandonment of research designs prior to excavation, but it is
to suggest that anthropological models that are not constructed upon a
foundation of what is already known, or without reference to the facts
of excavation, ultimately will lack utility.

Not only will the focus on establishment of facts urged here be seen
as particularistic, but also it will appear to place an inordinate amount of
trust in historical documents, which archaeologists know to be sometimes inaccurate. In fact, archaeologists should mistrust the documents
as much as they should mistrust the archaeological data. It is the ability
to correctly interpret the historical documents that make the historian's
task so difficult. It is the ability to correctly interpret the archaeological
record that makes an archaeologist's task so difficult. Both of these difficult tasks require the intelligence, imagination, and experience that
Courbin finds so important in archaeology. In developing an archaeology of the Civil War, archaeologists simply face more documentary facts
than usually are available. These facts can create noise in any analysis,
masking the relevant data and demanding, for its discrimination, the expertise of a knowledgeable, experienced archaeologist. But these documentary facts also can prove the analysis wrong, making the correct
framing of archaeological questions more difficult and challenging. These
tasks, therefore, are not at all simple or unworthy of attention. In fact,
they make time and close attention essential. They make an archaeology
of the Civil War a very difficult undertaking, one worthy of the best
archaeological inquiry.

Previously, it was asserted that correct integration of these facts will
allow the development of an independent body of data, which has been
called an archaeology of the Civil War. In essence, what is called for is a
new culture history of the Civil War. This culture history (Willey and
Phillips 1958; Flannery 1974; Schuyler 1988: 42) will be based on the
facts established by archaeologists who have a control of the historical
documents and the archaeological record. It is a social history or, in the
term used by William H. Adams (1977: 126–46), an ethnoarchaeology,
which combines history, archaeology, and ethnohistory to create a holistic perspective broader than the one possible using a single source. It
will use the tests of both history and archaeology, with additional infor-

mation provided by physical anthropology and other disciplines as available and as constructed by archaeologists. From this culture history, archaeologists will develop an understanding of the war that will be new, insightful, critical, and pertinent. Glassie (1977: 32) has stated that "the past is too important to leave to historians. The human reality is too important to leave to novelists." At the present time, both the historian and the novelist have the upper hand when it comes to an understanding of the Civil War. Archaeologists can and must provide an understanding of the war built on archaeology. To gain that understanding will take time; it will take small solid steps, in the form of excavating sites, to establish archaeological facts and to establish a culture history. It is this kind of archaeology that other disciplines await.

A culture history of the Civil War as described above is similar to what Griffin, and very much what Schuyler, have urged us to create within the general discipline of historical archaeology (Griffin 1978; Schuyler 1988). Historical archaeologists have yet to construct this culture history. Within the context of the Civil War, it is even more important that they begin to do so very soon. A culture history, built on established archaeological facts, is the single best solution to the problems and challenges posed by the special nature of the documents and material culture created during the Civil War. A solidly established culture history of the war will also provide the basis for constructing and testing valid anthropological models. Regardless of the broad perspective taken to provide an explanatory context for the Civil War—ideological, technological, functional, or structural—archaeological facts are needed to provide the basis for the context.

## Discussion

The argument put forward here may be summarized as follows. The Civil War is the single most important historical event in nineteenth-century American history and a major milestone in American history since 1776. The Civil War continues to shape this nation even today. When the nation searches for its identity, it turns to the Civil War for answers. Historical archaeologists can add a valuable dimension to this understanding because of their unique approach.

The challenge, though, is to make a relevant contribution in an area which has been well covered by others, and in which primary documentary sources are abundant. This coverage provides both special challenges and special opportunities. Archaeologists must discover these opportunities and meet these challenges by first acquiring a thorough knowledge of what has come before. Then they must learn to use the primary documentary sources archaeologically, because what is already available offers tantalizing questions to test in the field. Archaeologists must also allow that their methods can be different from many current approaches.

There are many areas in which archaeologists can contribute a unique and valuable perspective. But it is suggested that the next priority should be to establish solid new facts about the Civil War through excavation and analysis. This means that, for immediate future, archaeologists should concentrate on excavation and solid reporting. But it also means that with these data, these facts, archaeologists can build, from integrated data, a solid culture history of the war that only they can provide. This culture history will be one of the most valuable contributions archaeologists can make. A discipline's seriousness and respectability are measured by what and how it contributes to the public and to other disciplines. Archaeology can contribute to the study of the Civil War. But to do so, it must take small, carefully researched steps until the data base is available for larger steps and grander statements.

# 2 David G. Orr

## THE ARCHAEOLOGY OF TRAUMA

*An Introduction to the
Historical Archaeology of
the American Civil War*

In January 1991, at its annual meeting in Richmond, Virginia, the Society for Historical Archaeology sponsored both regular and plenary sessions in the archaeology of the Civil War. The presentations made there reflected both a scholarly response to, and a public fascination with, the American Civil War and all its ramifications. Ambivalently, scholars have studied the Civil War for over a century, the great bulk of effort focusing on the events surrounding and leading up to military confrontation (Scott et al. 1989: 50). Anthropologically, this is surely fitting, war being one of the most ubiquitous yet least understood of all of our species' social institutions (Fussell 1991: 17–25). Only recently has the Civil War begun to stimulate analysis and discussion of other topics.

Social historians have given us a broad spectrum of approaches and issues: labor history, both slave and free; the growth of mercantile capitalism in the industrial North and South; the advance of communication networks through the railroad, a vital factor in determining the final Union victory; the role of merchant shipping, etc. We have now looked at the history and experience of blacks, women, children, and newly arrived immigrants, many of whom were "grafted into the army" (Work 1862). We have studied the incredible naïveté of the troops who at the advent of the conflict rushed out with the idea, voiced by many of the recruits, that the whole thing would be over in eight weeks. In addressing these and other aspects of social history, archaeology works as a great material metaphor in the organization and examination of evidence. The papers in this volume suggest the roles this discipline can play in the examination of this unfortunate conflict and its repercussions throughout American life.

Simply stated, the war was yesterday, and we are still participating in its agonies, its unresolved disputes, and its still smoldering divisions. Above all, there is the simple testimony of the war's victims: its dead, maimed, and displaced. William Butler Yeats speaks for many a Civil War soldier's experience, when he says, "and what if excess of love bewildered them till they died" (Rosenthal 1966: 87). The scars of this conflict are there for all to see and ponder. Its terrible memories are alive in the mass of primary source material: mountains of letters, diaries, regimental and unit histories, and, most important, photographic images. It was one of the first great conflicts to be so documented (Frassanito 1983). Edmund Wilson, in his brilliant anthology *Patriotic Gore,* posed this question:

> Has there ever been another historical crisis of the magnitude of 1861–65 in which so many people were so articulate? The elaborate orations of Charles Sumner, modeled on Demosthenes and Cicero; Lincoln's unique addresses, at once directives and elegies; John Brown's letters from prison and his final speech to the court; Grant's hard and pellucid memoirs; . . . the brilliant journal of Mary Chesnut. . . . Such documents dramatize the war as the poet or the writer of fiction has never been able to do.

The following brief case studies are presented to illustrate how archaeology can provide perspectives and matrices useful in understanding the social history of the Civil War. All the case studies presented here involved excavations carried out by the National Park Service under my direction. The cases also serve to introduce some of the concerns voiced in the essays that follow this chapter. Topics treated in the case studies include: (1) the experience of soldiers in combat, (2) the disruption of civilian domesticity by battle and siege, (3) the necessity of understanding the historical and archaeological evidence in terms of a larger cultural landscape encompassing both past and present, (4) the didactic value of sites and the great opportunities they present to communicate a challenging array of interpretive themes.

## Case Study 1: The Confederate Picket Line at the Crater, Petersburg, Virginia

The historical record relating to the occupation of the Confederate picket line near the site of the Crater in the Petersburg siege lines is extremely large and complex. The Union army under the command of Ulysses S. Grant arrived at Petersburg, Virginia, in mid-June 1864, after an arduous and bloody spring campaign. This campaign had begun in May with the crossing of the Rapidan River and the engagement of Robert E. Lee's army in a series of violent clashes. Petersburg represented the key to the taking of Richmond, the Confederate capital, mostly because of its situation on four railroad lines and on major roadways leading from Richmond to the south and west. In what constitutes the longest siege in American warfare (roughly ten months), the Union army slowly cut these supply lines and encircled Petersburg. This siege culminated in a final assault in early April 1865, which led to the surrender of Lee's army at Appomattox Court House a short time afterward.

Our excavation at the site of the Confederate picket line near the Crater was occasioned by the necessity to properly handle archaeological material to be displaced by the installation of a water line (fig. 2.1). Additionally, we needed to establish the condition of the earthwork and provide for its preservation. The test thus was extremely limited, so as to minimize adverse impact upon its integrity. The picket line was built following the Battle of the Crater, which began with the explosion of a large mine near this line on the morning of July 30, 1864. This explosion represented an attempt on the part of Federal forces to end the stalemate around Petersburg. The explosion produced a large crater, about

**Fig. 2.1.** *Confederate picket line near the Crater, Petersburg, Virginia. The area excavated is marked by the four stakes in front of the fence. Courtesy of the National Park Service.*

170 feet long, 60 feet wide, and 30 feet deep. Union troops attempting to exploit the hole made in the Confederate earthworks were unable to penetrate deeply into the Confederate position due to a number of factors, including the mistake many troops made of entering the crater instead of encircling it. As a result, they were stopped by a successful Confederate counterattack which resulted in more than four thousand Union casualties. The siege of Petersburg continued for an additional eight months.

The picket line earthworks were constructed in September 1864 and abandoned on the night of April 2–3, 1865. The mine explosion associated with the Battle of the Crater necessitated a great deal of reconstruction and realignment in the Confederate defenses (Blades 1981: 6). The new works included the "connection of the line of rifle pits from pickets" (Davis, Perry, and Kirkley 1896: 1287). Daily reports prepared by General Bushrod Johnson documented the probable construction methods used to build these works and also the concomitant problems of supply and exposure that plagued the Confederate troops (Blades 1981).

The data recovered during the 1978 National Park Service excavations of the picket line complement the historical record in important ways. The features left by the picket line combatants document their efforts to make life in the trenches more comfortable. A fire pit contained traces of three successive hearths in which coal was burned to provide heat (Blades 1981: 28–37). A ditch, constructed for drainage, lay in the center of the trench. Evidence of bullet recasting and the virtual absence of bullets from the occupation layers in the trench reflected the ammunition shortage within the Confederate army. While historical sources defined the general state of affairs, idiosyncratic solutions to the ennui and discomfort of trench occupation were revealed through archaeological excavation.

The seven-month stationary front at this picket line, with its rich archaeological data base, presents the potential to develop a trench ethnography of the material world of such warfare (Fussell 1975; Blades 1981: 10–20). The earthworks immediately adjacent to the picket line certainly contain material resources which would add to this small test in ways that would vividly illustrate this trench ethnography. An officer of the Seventeenth South Carolina summed up the physical evidence of our excavation: "The soldiers slept in the main trench. There were traverses, narrow ditches, cross ditches, and mounds over the officers' dens (burrows dug in the side of the ditches). One of the Federal Officers said the Quarters reminded him of the catacombs of Rome" (Edwards 1908: 394).

## Case Study Two: The Taylor and Hare House Sites in Petersburg, Virginia

Only a few hundred yards from the picket line stood the farm of William Byrd Taylor, destroyed in June 1864 as the Battle of Petersburg began. One summer's campaign of archaeological excavation located a dairy and a possible smokehouse which flanked the principal house of the farm complex (fig. 2.2). The brick foundations of the small outbuilding interpreted as a dairy had been robbed; the bricks, no doubt, were used to construct Federal works in the vicinity. The robbed

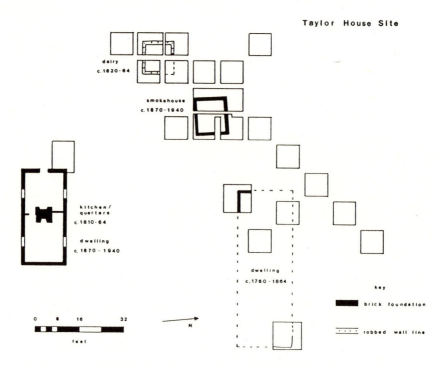

**Fig. 2.2.** *Plan of archaeological excavations at the Taylor House Site, Petersburg, Virginia. From Bevan et al. 1984. Reprinted by permission of the Society for Historical Archaeology.*

foundation contained military refuse from the siege, as well as a rich assemblage of Chinese Export porcelain.

Only one structure survived the engagement. The ruined quarter/ kitchen initially used by Taylor's slaves was occupied by him after the war. Today, this structure is marked by its centrally placed chimney and remnants of its foundation.

A ground-penetrating radar survey located the foundation of the main house, consisting of a brick-lined cellar measuring 55 feet by 19 feet (figs. 2.3 and 2.4; Bevan et al. 1984). Analysis of this structure indicates that it resembled a house owned by Taylor's neighbor, Augustus Hare, that also had been destroyed at the onset of hostilities (figs. 2.5 and 2.6; Blades and Cotter 1978). The Hare House cellar exists today as a "time capsule" of the advent of the siege, as its fill contained the remnants of its final domestic occupation. The Taylor House fill, on the other hand,

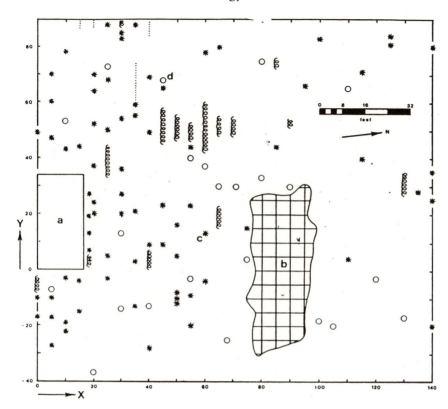

**Fig. 2.3.** *Plan of radar anomalies at the Taylor House Site, Petersburg, Virginia. Location of the kitchen/quarters is marked by "a." Original dwelling is the buried planar feature marked "b." From Bevan et al. 1984. Reprinted by permission of the Society for Historical Archaeology.*

indicates more disturbance; perhaps it was impacted by construction of the Federal earthworks in front of Fort Morton.

The Taylor and Hare sites constitute an important archaeological resource for the future study of the traumatic consequences of military occupation and civilian displacement. Both Taylor and Hare suddenly were deprived of house and property; the remainder of their lives was spent in recovering some of their lost material and social standing. Taylor reoccupied his property, while Hare did not; but what happened to the other residents affected by the siege? Our excavation and historical study suggest a much broader area for potential analysis. Certainly the material evidence revealed here can be corroborated by documentary evidence detailing similar fates of other residents in the siege area.

**Fig. 2.4.** *Hare House, Petersburg, Virginia. Courtesy of the National Park Service.*

## Case Study Three: The Discovery of the Widow Tapp House Site
### at the Battle of the Wilderness

Archaeological and historical research conducted at the Widow Tapp House, Fredericksburg and Spotsylvania National Military Park, revealed material data of a far more ephemeral nature. Unlike the substantial archaeological evidence uncovered for the Taylor and Hare houses at Petersburg, only the faintest traces of occupation marked this site. Yet it was critical for Civil War scholars to locate the dwelling, since it represented one of the key topographical features for the interpretation of the Battle of the Wilderness. The site also witnessed some of the most celebrated military exploits of the Civil War, which occurred during the morning of May 6, 1864.

Catherine Tapp leased her land from the Lacy family, who owned a large plantation nearby called "Ellwood." The Widow Tapp shared her modest one-and-a-half-story log home with five relatives and a laborer. Comprising a subsistence farm with a small orchard, corn patch, and a few pigs and cows, the property could boast only a small corncrib and a stable as structural improvements. No one can say for sure where the widow was during the battle, but the house was located not too far from the site of the famous "General Lee to the rear incident" which has so electrified southern commentators and Civil War scholars (Foote 1974). Although mythologized and romanticized by subsequent embellishment, this incident nevertheless reflected the desperate nature of the fight and was reported by many an eyewitness, including the following:

> To die in the sight of our grand commander did not seem a hard fate, for he was an idol and an inspiration. Into the affray we started, and he attempted to lead us. A cry of affectionate solicitude sprang to many throats, "Lee to the rear! General Lee to the rear!" There was a rush toward him by several, I can not say how many. Among those who grasped his horse by the bridle I recognized Captain James Harding, of the 1st Texas Regiment. I do not suppose that I would have remembered him but for the fact that a night or two before, one of our company was telling some joke on Harding about his straggling, for which he was noted, but it was remarked then that he was always among the first to "straggle into a fight." (Kelley 1969: 59–60)

The house survived the battle but fell into disrepair shortly thereafter, and the site was abandoned. Locating the house required a combination of historical research and scientific geophysical prospecting, the latter utilizing ground-penetrating radar and magnetometry. An artifact cluster, a dense assemblage of cut nails, and a single questionable architectural feature represented all that remained of the Tapp occupation. Discovery of the site locked in the other areas of the fight and honed our skills in the utilization of magnetometry. Ongoing analysis of the ceramic artifacts and the few organic remnants may shed some light on the hard life of Catherine Tapp and her agrarian world, so violently disrupted during the spring of 1864.

## Case Study Four: The Excavation of General Grant's Headquarters Cabin at City Point, Virginia

For thousands of years, a long succession of peoples has occupied the jut of land called City Point, situated at the confluence of the James and

Appomattox rivers (Orr, Blades, and Campana 1985). With the exception of a brief displacement during the Civil War, City Point remained in the possession of the Eppes family throughout the historical period (1635–1979) until its recent acquisition by the National Park Service. Although City Point bluff holds the archaeological record of people and events from early prehistory to the present, its use as the headquarters for Ulysses S. Grant's Army of the Potomac during the siege of Petersburg commands our immediate attention. The point became an important communications post and the port for one of the modern world's first large-scale military supply operations. The temporary use of the grounds by the Union army needs to be studied, keeping in view the cultural landscapes that archaeological excavation and historical research have revealed at City Point.

Richard Eppes, owner of the large plantation surrounding the bluff, lost possession of his house and grounds when Grant seized them in June 1864. Grant quickly transformed the river front along the base of the bluff into a supply line capable of sustaining his vast command. By November 1864, Grant had erected a small cluster of log buildings directly adjacent to the manor house (fig. 2.5; Orr 1982). The cabins were built mostly of horizontally laid logs and possessed rectangular plans. Excavations confirmed that Grant's cabin and a second one located just west of it differed strikingly from the simple rectangular plans typical of the rest of the complex. The Grants' cabin was T-shaped and consisted of a square front and a rectangular rear room oriented east-west. The vertically positioned logs were toed with large cut spikes into a white pine sill plank, and the gaps between chinked with mortar. One of the foundation trenches contained in its destruction stratum an octagonal mold-blown inkwell, an icon for what "headquarters" means in a military operation!

A detailed description of the cabin's interior was recorded in the *Philadelphia Inquirer* on August 4, 1865: "The front room is warmed by a wood fire, the andirons used to build said fire being constructed of old muskets by a soldier, and presented to General Grant. The tender is made of sheet iron, and is punctured with the letters 'USG,' with a star on either side of the initials. The ceiling is composed of canvas tacked to the rafters."

The fate of Grant's cabin differed dramatically from those of tens of thousands of other such ephemeral structures built to house the com-

*Fig. 2.5.* General Ulysses S. Grant's City Point Headquarters Complex. Grant's cabin is in the near left foreground. Reprinted by permission of the Society for Historical Archaeology.

batants of the Civil War. Unlike the rest, it was carefully dismantled and moved shortly after a photograph of the victorious Union staff, fresh from Appomattox Court House, was taken by Matthew Brady (fig. 2.6; Frassanito 1983). The cabin was sent to Philadelphia's Fairmont Park as a gift to George Hay Stuart, organizer of the United States Christian Commission, which actively assisted the Union soldiers during the war (fig. 2.9). There it remained until the National Park Service acquired it in 1981. It was dismantled once more, and re-erected on its original spot, where it is now open to the public. The cabin was carefully positioned to protect the original *in situ* archaeological data. It exists today as an incredibly significant remnant of the rebellion, the sole survivor of an entire genre of military architecture (Ingle 1988). The sites of several other cabins at City Point also offer important opportunities for future research (Nelson 1982).

Richard Eppes was a large slave owner. Every New Year's Day, on Eppes Island, he gathered together the slave population from his three plantations and gave them instruction for their conduct during the coming year. His speech on one occasion survives, recorded in his diary. It

**Fig. 2.6.** *Headquarters staff of General Ulysses S. Grant, April 1865. This is the last photograph of General Grant at his cabin. Reprinted by permission of the Society for Historical Archaeology.*

begins with this preamble: "We regard you in the light of human beings possessing faculties similar to our own and capable of distinguishing between right and wrong" (Nicholls 1981). Archaeologically, City Point constitutes a rich source of material cultural data illustrative of slavery, one which may provide a significant corollary to the unrivaled historical record exemplified by the above quotation. The Union occupation of the bluff in 1864–65 presents another important primary source for African-American history during the Civil War. In order to fulfill its mission as the principal supplier to the troops besieging Petersburg, the Union army employed a fairly large civilian labor force. Much of this work force consisted of black freedmen. Some of these black workers were shipped to City Point from freedmen's camps in Tidewater Virginia, while others were escapees from the Petersburg area. Some worked on the wharves and railroad loading docks, while others served in the Union hospitals. Many of these black freedmen were organized into labor gangs administered by the Federal Quartermaster Corps. The archaeological evidence for these workers at City Point, such as the site of their quarters, is not known but may exist (Farrar 1991).

## Discussion

At the beginning of this essay I argued that the Civil War was yesterday. Two direct descendants of the two protagonists at City Point, the late Jimmy Eppes and John Griffiths, assisted us in our work. Jimmy represented the direct line of descent from Richard Eppes, the Civil War owner of the property, while John is a direct descendant of Ulysses S. Grant. Both of these men enthusiastically aided our research. The late Elise Eppes Cutchin, another direct descendant of Richard Eppes, provided incalculable assistance to the National Park Service by explaining what it was like to live and work at City Point. She also described the world that preceded her, that of Richard Eppes and his first wife Josephine. Such oral history (and contemporary history) is invaluable in establishing the continuity of the issues raised by the Civil War at City Point, Virginia.

The anthropological significance of the Civil War rests, finally, in an array of sites located, in most instances, far from the battlefield itself. From the industrial sites of Philadelphia's workers—their factories and domiciles—to the industrial sites and workers' housing of Petersburg, Virginia, lies the now latent archaeological data with which someday we may interpret the worlds of workers on both sides of the conflict (Cotter, Roberts, and Parrington 1992: 57–64 and passim; Herman 1984: 277–78). Our scrutiny must include cultural landscapes of life and death as well as individual artifacts. Battlefield sites, such an important and painful legacy for us, must be preserved with a view to instruction, contemplation, and scientific scrutiny. Always they must be linked to the anthropological values of the battles' participants, however diverse and complex. Battlefields are much more than simply chessboards upon which great armies have grappled.

The examples sketched briefly in this chapter suggest how historical archaeology, placed in a well-designed interdisciplinary framework, can make valuable contributions to Civil War scholarship. My colleagues in the National Park Service appear dedicated to the extraction of knowledge from these sites. But we must be vigilant; a hundred threats now face these places. When archaeological evidence is coupled with the rich diversity of our historical sources, the prognosis for a more fruitful examination of the Civil War and its effects on both soldiers and civilians is excellent.

But I want to close with a word of caution. Anthropological and historical analysis probes a past which can be, as David Lowenthal (1985) has told us, "a Foreign Country." All of us need to confront excluded histories, in order to arrive at sound syncretic analyses. Yet, in interpreting war, with its singular power to shatter human perception, we do well to recall the words of Walt Whitman, who worked in Civil War hospitals and, after thinking of writing a book on the subject, finally gave up the idea: "And so good-bye to the war. . . . Future years will never know the seething hell and the black infernal background of countless minor scenes and interiors (not the official surface courteousness of the generals, not a few great battles) of the secession war and it is best they should not. The real war will never get in the books" (qtd. in Edmund Wilson 1962: 481).

## Dedication

This essay is dedicated to the memory of David Lilley, a true colleague and dear friend.

## Acknowledgments

I especially thank all of the National Park Service staff members who assisted my research during the last thirteen years. Among these are Jimmy Blankenship, Chris Calkins, John Davis, Frank Deckert, Wally Elms, and Bill Fluharty at Petersburg National Battlefield; and A. Wilson Greene, Robert Krick, and the late David Lilley at Fredericksburg and Spotsylvania County Battlefields Memorial National Military Park.

I extend special kudos to my staff in the Mid-Atlantic Regional Office of the National Park Service. Nobody could ask for better support or greater dedication. In many ways, this paper reflects the staff's labors in the fields of Petersburg and Fredericksburg.

For all these reasons and more, I thank Brooke S. Blades, Douglas V. Campana, and Allen Cooper. Douglas contributed much to our City Point work, while Allen was field director at the Widow Tapp site. Brooke's recently concluded report on the Taylor House at Petersburg makes clearer the significance of Bruce Bevan's geophysical research. I thank Bruce Bevan also for his personal interest in our research and for his willingness to assist us in any way he could. Bruce will be completing new research on geophysical work he did during 1991 and 1992 at the Taylor House.

Finally, I thank Mike Musick of the National Archives, Washington, D.C., for his assistance.

# Part II.
## Battlefield Analysis and Reconstruction

*In-depth analysis of battles and of the personalities, strate-*
*gies, and tactics involved in them is a well-established part of*
*Civil War research. Growing interest in military reenactment*
*and preservation of battlefield sites, and the need for govern-*
*ment to weigh the rapid growth of communities against the*
*loss of battlefield landscapes—all these factors spur us to try*
*to understand critically and reliably the spatial dimension of*
*battles. The chapters by William Lees, Samuel Smith, and*
*Samuel Margolin illustrate the application of historical ar-*
*chaeology to the definition and interpretation of diverse battle-*
*field settings.*

*Through a systematic metal detector survey, Lees locates*
*and documents the progression of the Mine Creek Battle,*
*which took place in eastern Kansas on August 28, 1864.*
*This could not have been done relying solely on the inad-*
*equate extant historical documentation. During excavations*
*around the Carter House, which served as the Federal com-*
*mand post during the Battle of Franklin on November 30,*
*1864, Smith uncovered the distribution pattern of battle-*
*related artifacts, making possible a clearer understanding of*
*what had transpired. Both studies focused on bullets as their*

primary artifacts, showing the importance of studying them in their spatial context. Lees and Smith also convey an image of the individuals behind (or in front of) these bullets, placing their work within an anthropological frame of reference.

Samuel Margolin directs attention to the study of underwater archaeological sites associated with the Civil War. Military actions occurring on the James River in Virginia between 1861 and 1865 constitute a microcosm of most of the tactics, weapons, defenses, and vessel types that figured prominently in the maritime theaters of the war. In this volume, Margolin reviews the archeological study that identified the remains of the C.S.S. Florida, a prototype for the foreign-built Confederate commerce raiders, and the U.S.S. Cumberland, the first victim of the Confederate ironclad Virginia (alias Merrimack). Additional comments focus on the survey conducted to identify locations of ironclads and other wrecks belonging to the James River Squadron, sunk near Richmond, Virginia, in an effort to deny the Union navy access to that inland port.

*William B. Lees*

# WHEN THE SHOOTING STOPPED, THE WAR BEGAN

T he Civil War is perceived at many different levels. It has importance as a historical event and as part of the fabric of contemporary life. It has national, regional, local, individual, and personal contexts. It is one of the most studied and best documented episodes of the American past. Despite the importance and complexity of this event, the question still arises: Why is it important to study the Civil War through historical archaeology? By searching through numerous contextual strata, this paper addresses this question from the perspective of Kansas and the Mine Creek battlefield.

## Kansas and Civil War

As most Civil War historians know, Kansas Territory was created in 1854 by the Kansas-Nebraska Act. This act repealed the Missouri Compromise of 1820 and established the concept of popular sovereignty in regard to slavery (Randall and Donald 1969). It ushered in the modern era of settlement but led almost immediately to civil war. Seven years before the fateful shot at Fort Sumter, opposing free-state and proslavery interests competed for Kansas, and armed conflict broke out. For good reason, Kansas was known in the late 1850s as "Bleeding Kansas":

— Lawrence, December 1855: The so-called Wakarusa War erupted after an abolitionist was killed by a proslavery sympathizer. An attack on Lawrence was narrowly averted by negotiation between large free-state and proslavery forces (Monaghan 1955: 39–44).

— Lawrence, May 1856: Proslavery sympathizers attacked Lawrence, destroyed the offices of the *Herald of Freedom* and *Kansas Free State* newspapers, and burned the Free-State Hotel and other businesses and homes (Monaghan 1955: 56–58).

— Pottawatomie Creek, May 1856: John Brown and his five sons butchered five proslavery men. Several hundred proslavery men retaliated by attacking Brown's followers at Osawatomie, resulting in casualties on both sides and the burning of the town (Monaghan 1955: 61–63).

— Topeka, July 1856: After an antislavery constitution failed to pass Congress, President Franklin Pierce ordered the free-state legislature dispersed by five companies of U.S. Dragoons (Monaghan 1955: 67–68).

— Marais des Cygnes River, May 1858: Proslavery sympathizers captured eleven unarmed free-state men, drove them into a ravine, and shot them all. Five died from their wounds (Hougen 1985).

In September 1857, a proslavery constitutional convention met at Lecompton and drafted a constitution allowing slavery in Kansas. In December, it was endorsed by a fraudulent popular vote. Although promoted in Washington by President James Buchanan, it failed in Congress. Congress ordered the Lecompton constitution resubmitted for a fair vote, and in August 1858, it was decisively defeated (Perdue 1902).

The debate over the Lecompton constitution was significant in polarizing the nation around the slavery issue. The remanding of the Lecompton constitution to Kansas for a new vote was followed shortly by the Illinois Republican state convention. There, U.S. Senate candidate Abraham Lincoln proclaimed: "A house divided against itself cannot stand. I believe this government cannot endure, permanently half slave and half free" (Randall and Donald 1969: 117).

In October 1859, the free-state Wyandotte Constitution was adopted by a fair popular vote, and the issue of slavery was finally decided in Kansas (Perdue 1902). In April 1860, the U.S. House of Representatives voted to admit Kansas to statehood under this constitution. Because of Southern opposition, Senate approval did not come until January 1861, after several Southern states had seceded. That same month, President Buchanan approved admission of Kansas to the Union as a free state, after South Carolina, Mississippi, Florida, Alabama, Georgia, and Louisiana had seceded (E. B. Long 1971). The shooting had stopped in Kansas, but the Civil War had begun.

Kansas did not escape this national Civil War that had grown from seeds nurtured in its now-free soil. Early in the war, large groups of pro-Union Native Americans from Indian Territory took refuge in the state and remained residents until the war's end (Abel 1919; Danziger 1969). The Office of Indian Affairs never was able to properly provide for these refugees, and their destitute condition and foraging (at times plundering) made them an unwelcome hardship on the resident white and Native American population of the state. In August 1863, the notorious Confederate guerrilla Captain William C. Quantrill sacked and burned Lawrence, and many citizens were killed. This action was in many ways a direct continuation of the border warfare of the 1850s.

In spring 1864, Plains Indians increased their depredations along the western trails in Kansas. In response, U.S. troops were moved to the western part of the state to protect the trails and settlements and to calm the terrified settlers. Later in 1864, a major campaign by Confederate Major General Sterling Price moved through the eastern part of the state, and a series of battles was fought on Kansas soil. Only one month later, war with Plains Indians again broke out, after Colonel J. M. Chivington attacked and massacred as many as five hundred Arapahos and Cheyennes peacefully camped on Sand Creek, Colorado Territory (Josephy 1991; E. B. Long 1971).

For Kansas, therefore, civil war of one sort or another lasted for over ten years, from 1854 to 1865. This nevertheless was the same period during which Kansas was establishing itself in economic, political, and social terms. The Missouri River trade, overland commerce, towns booming and busting, and agricultural settlement of rural Kansas characterized the period. Railroads were being planned, universities were being established, and the future of a new frontier state was being charted.

That this period of armed conflict—first "Bleeding Kansas" and later the Civil War—coincided with the opening of the Kansas frontier was significant in developing a distinctive culture in Kansas. The state's roots lie in this period. Nowhere is this fact better commemorated than in the Kansas state motto: *Ad astra per asperum* ("To the stars through difficulties"). This motto underscores a crucial contextual difference between Kansas and other states: while the Civil War *transformed* the eastern United States, it *formed* Kansas.

In this historical context, then, the battle of Mine Creek was something of an anticlimax to the real civil war that Kansas had known in the 1850s and that still found expression through men like Quantrill during the early 1860s. In a different sense, the battle interrupted the political and economic construction of a new state. Many Kansans remained more concerned by hostilities with the Plains Indians than with the Confederacy.

Kansas clearly was immersed in the events of the Civil War. These events found a form of expression different from that typical in most states so affected. As it came through Kansas, Price's 1864 campaign resulted in the only battles between uniformed U.S. and Confederate troops that occurred in the state. The Battle of Mine Creek thus is recognized as the major battle of the Civil War—and one of very few—to occur in the state.

## The Battle of Mine Creek

On August 28, 1864, Confederate forces under Major General Sterling Price departed from Camden, Arkansas, on a raid into Missouri, with the intended purpose of capturing St. Louis. In issuing orders for this raid, Major General E. Kirby Smith added: "Should you be compelled to withdraw from the State, make your retreat through Kansas and the Indian Territory, sweeping that country of its mules, horses, cattle, and military supplies of all kinds" (qtd. in Langsdorf 1964: 282). This is indeed what happened.

Price entered Missouri on September 19 with a force of twelve thousand, many of whom were unarmed, and fourteen pieces of artillery. Shortly thereafter he decided that St. Louis was too well fortified to attempt capture and moved instead towards Pilot Knob. After a sharp defeat at Pilot Knob on September 27, Price moved on the state capital at Jefferson City. Arriving there on October 7, he determined that it also was too well defended to risk an attack and began a withdrawal towards Kansas. Along the way, he filled an increasingly large wagon train with captured supplies and plunder. At Glascow and Arrow Rock, he was able to capture sizable quantities of much-needed firearms. As he was leaving Marshall, Missouri, twelve thousand Federal troops began to close on his column (Buresh 1977; Langsdorf 1964).

On October 19, Price clashed with the Federals at Lexington, on October 21 at the Little Blue River, on October 22 at the Big Blue River, and on October 23 at Westport—all in the vicinity of modern-day Kansas City, Missouri (fig. 3.1). On October 24, Price moved along the military road between Fort Leavenworth and Fort Scott and entered Kansas. Late that night, Price's troops went into camp along the Marais des Cygnes River at Trading Post. Early on the morning of the 25th, the provisional Army of the Border under Major General Samuel R. Curtis attacked and routed the Confederates at Trading Post. Seven miles down the road and several hours later, the Federal forces engaged the Confederate rear guard at Mine Creek. A short but sharp clash resulted in a decisive Federal victory known as the Battle of Mine Creek (Buresh 1977; Langsdorf 1964).

The Battle of Mine Creek occurred along an unmapped alternate of the road from Fort Leavenworth to Fort Scott. The large Confederate wagon train was completing a difficult fording where this road crossed the rain-swollen creek. The Confederate rear guard at Mine Creek were cavalry divisions under command of Major General John S. Marmaduke and Major General James F. Fagan. A third division of Price's cavalry under Brigadier General Joseph O. Shelby was at the head of the train with General Price when the battle started.

The battle was precipitated when U.S. brigades of Major General Alfred Pleasonton's Second Cavalry Division, commanded by Lieutenant Colonel F. W. Benteen (Fourth Brigade) and Colonel John F. Phillips

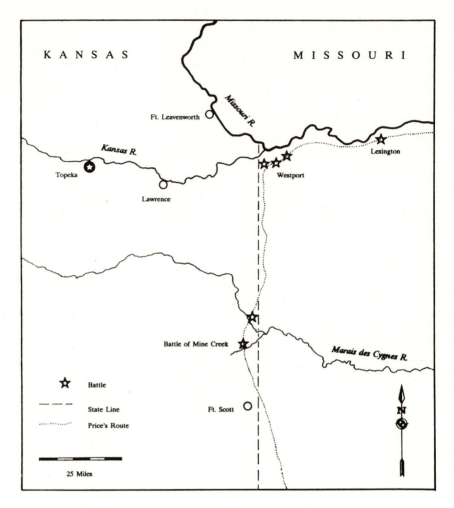

**Fig. 3.1.** *Location of battles of October 19–25, 1864. Courtesy of the Kansas State Historical Society.*

(Second Brigade) approached Mine Creek. Responding to this threat, Marmaduke and Fagan quickly formed ranks on either side of the Fort Scott road in front of Mine Creek. Remaining mounted, they engaged the Federals.

The ensuing battle engaged roughly seven to eight thousand Confederate and twenty-six hundred U.S. cavalry, most of whom remained mounted. It took place on what was then an open grassland sloping gently toward Mine Creek. Confederate artillery was used in the brief engagement, and U.S. cannon arrived when the battle was all but over. Although having an impressive numerical superiority, Marmaduke's and Fagan's troops quickly gave way to the better-armed U.S. cavalry and suffered a substantial loss in killed, wounded, and captured. The fighting lasted less than half an hour but resulted in the deaths of at least three hundred Confederates and the capture of five hundred troops, including Marmaduke, and eight pieces of artillery (Langsdorf 1964; Buresh 1977).

Following the action at Mine Creek, Marmaduke's and Fagan's troops were in disarray. Their retreat, however, was covered by Shelby's division, which had arrived too late to participate in the battle. Skirmishing was almost constant, and a substantial engagement was fought later that day at Shiloh Creek. As his wagon train reached the Marmaton River, Price sealed its fate by ordering it burned and the spare ammunition exploded. On November 28, a final battle in the campaign was fought near Newtonia, Missouri. On November 8, Federal pursuit of what remained of Price's command ceased as it crossed south of the Arkansas River.

The failure of Price's raid was one of a number of significant blows dealt the Confederacy late in 1864. As Price retreated from Kansas, Confederate hopes for the trans-Mississippi West were forever dashed (Langsdorf 1964).

Following the Civil War, the Mine Creek battlefield returned to its rural, agricultural uses. The site was not commemorated by monuments, and, with time, memory of the events of October 25, 1864, was lost. By its centennial, local knowledge of the battle was minimal. A brochure of the Civil War Round Table of Kansas City describes the situation at that time:

The Battle of Mine Creek ... was declared by Congress in 1965 to be of national historic interest. At that time, the exact site of the battlefield had not been identified. Seven years later, in 1972, the precise location of the battlelines and cannon emplacements had been determined by Civil War Round Table members Lumir Buresh and Dan Smith [Civil War Round Table of Kansas City, n.d.].

The late Lumir Buresh is a key figure in the Mine Creek story because of his influence on the interpretation of this event and on efforts to preserve and develop the site. It is his research and conclusions (Buresh 1977) that led the State of Kansas to purchase, in 1974 and 1978, 280 acres of Linn County. While it is unclear how Buresh identified the particular site of the battle, his narrative and maps place all of the key features of this battle (troop positions, artillery, roads, fords, and farmsteads) within this parcel and, therefore, within the state property line.

There was no particular reason to question Buresh's interpretation. The landscape provides no definitive landmarks with which to reconcile the sketchy historical narratives of the battle. The terrain north of Mine Creek rolls gently and is intersected by occasional small ravines that lead down to Mine Creek itself. Most of the land to the north of the creek has been cultivated for years, leaving no signs of former roads or house sites. Along Mine Creek is faint evidence of a ford at the center of the state parcel and distinct evidence of a ford near the state's eastern property line. From this eastern ford, progressively shallower swales of a former road can be followed south-southwest through woods for approximately one-quarter mile. Buresh thought this road postdated the Civil War and therefore interpreted the central ford as the crossing of the Fort Scott Road and the center of battle on October 25, 1864.

## The Archaeological Study

Through the years, the state did little to develop its property at Mine Creek. In 1989, the 125th anniversary of the battle caused renewed interest in this site. At that time, the Kansas State Historical Society came under pressure, both from the state legislature and from private groups interested in developing the site, to conduct archaeological research at Mine Creek to obtain background information for interpretive development. Research conducted in 1989 and 1990 was restricted to the state property.

The immediate archaeological goal of the project was to assess the potential of the site to reveal broad-scale battle patterns of the sort reconstructed for Montana's 1876 Little Bighorn Battlefield (Scott et al.

1989). If sufficient data existed, the project could expand into a comparison of the model of the battle championed locally against that revealed archaeologically. Implicit was an evaluation of the context of the state tract within the battlefield as it might be defined archaeologically.

Research focused on a program of discovering and recording battle-related or potentially battle-related artifacts. Discovery was accomplished with metal detectors operated by volunteers. Instruments were provided by individual volunteers and varied considerably, as did operator ability and experience. Upon discovery and excavation, artifacts were evaluated by an archaeologist. Those that were clearly not battle-related were reburied at their find spot. All other artifacts were assigned a field number, collected, and their locations mapped. Mapping was done with a surveyor's transit and served to tie artifacts to known landmarks. A large-scale map of the project area was later prepared showing the location of each recovered artifact.

Within the 280-acre project area were cultivated fields, tall grass pastures, brushy secondary growth, and relatively mature woods (fig. 3.2). The coil of metal detectors must be operated as close to the ground surface as possible. Conditions that increase the distance between the coil and the ground surface decrease sensitivity and introduce variability. Cultivated fields without furrows and without crops provide the best coverage. Deep furrows, advanced crops, crop stubble, grass, leaves, and other similar conditions result in less than optimal artifact recovery and introduce variability in results. All of these conditions existed at Mine Creek; controlling for these variables was difficult at best.

Under ideal conditions, a line of four to five metal detectors walked side-by-side across fields. When the edge of the field was reached, the line pivoted on one end and recrossed the field in the opposite direction. A field was thus covered by a series of closely spaced (ca. 2–3 m), parallel transects. This approach ensured coverage of the entire area and guarded against operators clustering in "hot spots."

Once again, conditions of coverage affected the ability to achieve consistent coverage. Evenly spaced transects worked well in unfurrowed fields but became increasingly difficult as coverage included tall grasses, steep topography, trees, brush, and vines. To minimize these problems

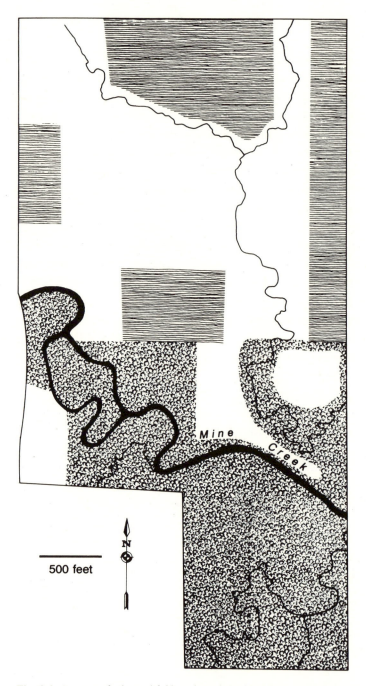

**Fig. 3.2.** *Location of cultivated fields and woods in the 280-acre project area. Areas not coded are currently uncultivated grasslands. Courtesy of the Kansas State Historical Society.*

with ground cover, the project area was broken down into manageable parcels, based on natural features such as streams and ravines and cultural features such as fences and fields. The four weeks of field work, with an average crew size of eight individuals, were undertaken during the winter months to minimize problems posed by vegetation.

Although the entire project area was covered, even in areas having ideal ground cover, total coverage or artifact recovery cannot be assumed (cf. Scott et al. 1989: 27–29). A group of metal detector operators working transects across an area does not achieve total artifact recovery, due to the nature of the equipment. Variables such as depth and size of artifacts and capability of equipment and operators affect recovery. The goal was to achieve consistent coverage, with the recognition that recovery actually may represent less than 10 percent of artifacts present.

Because of variables of ground cover and metal detector capabilities, this study is best defined as a reconnaissance. As will be evident, however, this reconnaissance-level data is sufficient to address the research questions originally posed and to serve as a model capable of informing future research.


## Research Results

Only a very brief summary of the results of the 1989 and 1990 research is possible here. Data consist of 284 definite battle-related artifacts and information on their locations. Artifacts include 275 bullets and cartridge cases, 5 buttons, 2 gun parts, a saddle part, and a canteen. The gun parts, a box of cartridges, canteen, and saddle part were found in the vicinity of a ford across Mine Creek. Except for a trouser button which was found in the northern portion of the project area, the buttons were found to the south of Mine Creek along a road that runs south from this crossing.

The 275 bullets and cartridge cases can be associated with a variety of pistols and breechloading and muzzleloading rifles. Roughly half of all bullets had been fired, although this ratio differed between breechloaders and muzzleloaders (fig. 3.3). Breechloaders identified to date are the Smith and/or Gallagher, Henry, Sharps, Burnside, and Spencer (McKee and Mason 1971; Phillips 1971). The Smith, Gallagher, Sharps, and Burnside were state-of-the-art breechloaders but still were single-shot weapons. The Henry and Spencer were repeaters; the Spencer could fire seven rounds and the Henry fourteen before reloading was necessary. Muzzleloading rifles in .54 and .58 calibers were present, as were pistols in both army (.44) and navy (.36) pattern calibers. A number of round balls in a variety of calibers was also found. These balls may have been ammunition for muzzleloading long arms and pistols, but some may have been used in artillery canister or explosive shells (Ripley 1970).

Based on documentary and some archaeological evidence, muzzleloading bullets are presumed to have been predominantly associated with Confederate use, whereas breechloaders are assumed to have been in Federal hands. Phillips's and Benteen's U.S. troops were armed with a variety of breechloaders (including Burnside, Cosmopolitan, Gallagher, Hall, Henry, Merrill, Sharps, and Spencer), whereas Confederate troops under Marmaduke and Fagan carried muzzleloading carbines and rifles (Langsdorf 1964; Buresh 1977; Coates and Thomas 1990). The Confederates were also equipped with captured arms, which, while probably predominantly muzzleloaders, also included four hundred Sharps rifles.

Bullets for breechloaders are the ones most common on the battlefield, accounting for close to half of all bullet finds. This preponderance is a result of several factors. First is the importance of cavalry in this battle. U.S. cavalry were well equipped by late 1864, and breechloaders were the preferred issue to these troops. Other factors are the ease of reloading and the use of repeaters such as the Spencer and Henry. Although vastly outnumbered, the U.S. soldiers armed with breechloaders certainly fired more rounds per capita than their Confederate counterparts armed with muzzleloaders.

In general, because this was a cavalry engagement, the importance of breechloading bullets at Mine Creek is probably unusually high, as compared to most Civil War battle sites in the East (cf. Legg and Smith 1989). There, most battles were fought between troops similarly equipped with muzzleloading rifles.

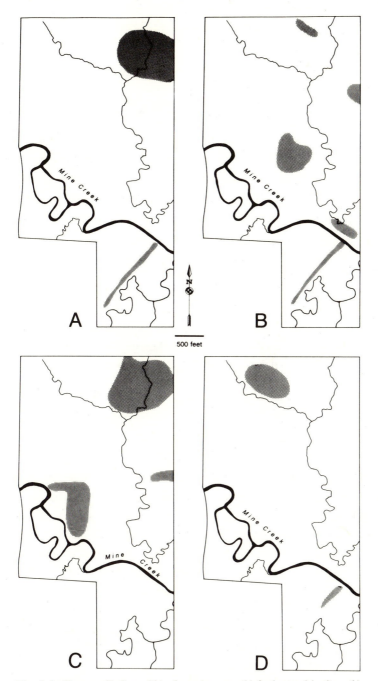

**Fig. 3.3.** *Clusters of bullets within the project area: (a) fired muzzleloading; (b) unfired muzzleloading; (c) fired breechloading; (d) unfired breechloading. Courtesy of the Kansas State Historical Society.*

## Patterns on the Field of Battle

The most useful information comes from a consideration of the distribution of different types of bullets within the study area. Spatial analysis of four categories of conical bullets reveals useful patterns that most certainly relate to battle events. These categories include fired and unfired (dropped/discarded) breechloaders, assumed to be Federal, and fired and unfired (dropped/discarded) muzzleloaders, assumed to be Confederate. Distinct clusters in the categories were observed:

(1)    Fired bullets for muzzleloading guns cluster in the northeastern portion of the project area and along a road trace south of Mine Creek (fig. 3.3a).

(2)    Several small clusters of unfired (dropped/discarded) bullets for muzzleloading guns exist north of Mine Creek. Unfired bullets for muzzleloaders also cluster along the road south of the creek (fig. 3.3b).

(3)    A major cluster of fired breechloading bullets exists in the northeastern portion of the project area, at a location shown earlier as a concentration of bullets fired from muzzleloading guns (fig. 3.3c). Two smaller concentrations are also noted.

(4)    Unfired (dropped/discarded) bullets for breechloading guns clustered in one area along the northern edge of the project area and along the road south of Mine Creek (fig. 3.3d).

These concentrations and the variables on which they are based can be used to reconstruct the movement of troops within the study area (fig. 3.4). It is not difficult to assume that concentrations of dropped or discarded bullets mark troop positions. The distinct patterning in the fired bullets suggests that they also mark troop positions, although certainly with less accuracy than do the patterns of "drops." This is because of the tendency of bullets to travel beyond their targets before eventually hitting the ground. The clusters of fired bullets thus appear to "shadow" troop positions. In one case at Mine Creek, the interpreted troop positions and a "shadow" of fired bullets are so distinctly correlated that the direction of hostile fire can be reconstructed.

Given this, and if it is assumed that breechloading weapons were used primarily by U.S. troops and muzzleloaders primarily by the Confederates, it is possible to postulate the location of U.S. and Confederate posi-

|                        | BREECHLOADING (U.S.)            | MUZZLELOADING (C.S.)            |
| ---------------------- | ------------------------------ | ------------------------------ |
| UNFIRED (DROPPED)      | U.S. POSITION (DIRECT)         | C.S. POSITION (DIRECT)         |
| FIRED                  | C.S. POSITION (INDIRECT)       | U.S. POSITION (INDIRECT)       |

*Fig. 3.4. Matrix showing relationship of variables (fired vs. unfired and breechloading vs. muzzleloading) to interpretation of troop position (US and CS; direct or indirect evidence). Courtesy of the Kansas State Historical Society.*

tions during the battle (fig. 3.5). It is important to note that this and most other Civil War battles were dynamic, rapidly changing events. Positions shown in figure 3.5 are those where troops were stationary for a relatively long period (but still only a few minutes). Troops were present at these locations long enough for a distinct concentration of artifacts to develop. Other, more rapid troop movements may not be identifiable

The data reveal five distinct Confederate positions (appearing as concentrations of dropped cartridges for muzzleloading guns and bullets fired from breechloaders), shown in figure 3.5. Based on historical accounts of the battle, the four Confederate positions north of Mine Creek probably represent two northeast-facing troop lines, while the position south of the creek represents the route of Confederate withdrawal after the battle.

The data reveal just two U.S. positions (concentrations of dropped or discarded breechloading cartridges and bullets fired from muzzleloading guns). One shows as a broad troop line north of and certainly facing Mine Creek (fig. 3.5). The second U.S. position lies south of Mine Creek and certainly marks the line of pursuit of the retreating Confederate forces.

Unlike the Little Bighorn battle study, the construction of an empiri-

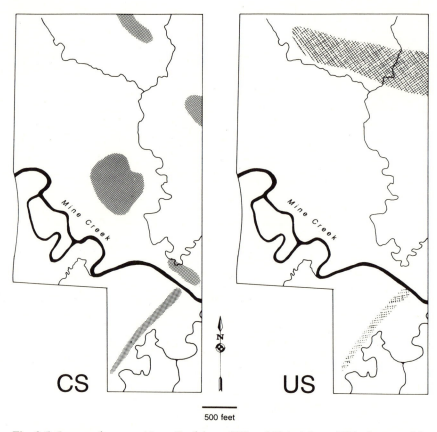

**Fig. 3.5.** *Interpreted troop positions: Confederate (CS) and United States (US). Courtesy of the Kansas State Historical Society.*

cally based sequencing of positions through archaeological survey has not been possible. The Little Bighorn sequence was based largely on cartridge case data. Cartridge cases were rare and in poor condition at Mine Creek and are not common on Civil War sites in general. Given documentary knowledge of the battle, a sequencing of the postulated U.S. and Confederate positions, once again based on clusters of bullets as described in figure 3.4, nevertheless can be proposed for the study area.

Stage 1 (fig. 3.6a): The Confederate positions at the northeast portion of the project area are interpreted as a troop line facing U.S. troops situated to the northeast outside the area of study

Stage 2 (fig. 3.6b): A U.S. troop line replaces the Confederate line

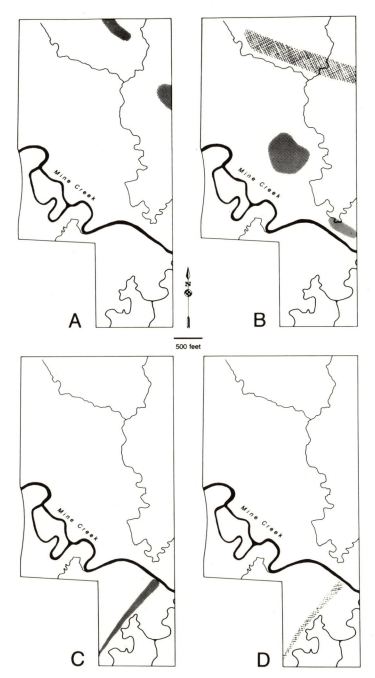

**Fig. 3.6.** *Interpreted battle sequence (a–d) within the project area. Stippled areas represent Confederate positions and cross-hatched areas United State positions. Courtesy of the Kansas State Historical Society.*

identified above, and Confederate positions are now located farther south along Mine Creek. Based on a "shadow" of fired breechloaders, the larger Confederate position is shown to have received fire from the direction of the U.S. positions shown here.

Stage 3 (fig. 3.6c): The Confederates have abandoned the positions north of Mine Creek and are moving in retreat along the Fort Scott Road.

Stage 4 (fig. 3.6d): U.S. troops are moving down the Fort Scott Road in pursuit of the retreating Confederate army.

This sequencing is obviously interpretive. Considering the limitations imposed by the study area, eventual reinterpretation is probably inevitable. Regardless of how they are interpreted in terms of sequencing, the data nevertheless allow confidence in the observed patterns and in their attribution as U.S. and Confederate positions.


## Discussion

A feature of the battlefield that emerges very clearly from the archaeological research is the location of the route of Confederate withdrawal south of Mine Creek. This route is along an abandoned road that now shows as shallow swales and which leads from a rock-bottom ford located along the state's eastern property line. Another ford about half a mile to the west has been interpreted by Buresh (1977) and others as the main ford used during the battle and hence marking the center of battle. Current data shows very little activity in this area and favors the eastern ford as the main ford used during the battle. Thus, the state's eastern property line may bisect the "hottest" portion or core of the battlefield.

If Buresh was incorrect in locating the main ford, it is likely that other interpretations also are in need of reevaluation. The general interpretation that places most significant battle events within the state parcel must be carefully reconsidered. If the main ford and hence the center of battle lies on the state's eastern property line, then the battlefield clearly must also include a substantial area of private property to the east.

The question arises, however, whether the Buresh interpretation is flawed only in terms of placement of the battlefield, or in terms of both placement and scale. If placement is the problem, then the battlefield could still fit within a 280-acre box, but if scale is also a problem, a considerably larger area may be involved.

Expansion of the study area to include private lands lying to the east, north, and west of the state property is crucial to resolving these questions. Examining lands to the east is needed to evaluate whether the state's eastern property line and the battle-period road found there do indeed represent the centerline of the battlefield. Not until these questions of placement and scale are addressed can the relationship of the state parcel to the overall battlefield be resolved.

What is clear from the current research is that the Buresh interpretation and the interpretation from archaeology are in conflict. The archaeological record is in fact providing new information about this battle that probably will substantially revise standing historical interpretations and that will comment directly on the nature and direction of future interpretation of this site.

Overall, however, it is inarguable that these conclusions are very particularistic. Historical data have been retrieved and interpreted in relation to very proscribed questions: Where were the battle lines? Where was the military road? The data seem not to comment on the broader contexts of this battle, such as were referred to in the first part of this paper. By itself, archaeology seems not to comment on the importance of this battle on a regional or national level or help in understanding the social and political milieu within which the battle occurred.

At a very humanistic level, however, archaeology does comment on the importance of the Mine Creek battle and the Civil War. The locations of groups of soldiers who were acting as military units and the path of retreat used by the defeated Confederate forces have been identified. Artifacts used, lost, or discarded by individual soldiers have been used to accomplish this. The dropped bullet is a stark reminder that a soldier stood nearby in October 1864. The lost or discarded canteen, gun parts, bullets, and buttons at the Mine Creek crossing where the retreat began once again announce the presence of individuals. In a different way, the fired bullets testify to the very individual level of conflict; the fired bullets were intended to take an individual's life.

The fact that these data do not seem to comment beyond the battlefield is, in fact, the most profound comment of all. For the individuals involved in this battle, the universe shrank, for a moment, to the fields on either side of Mine Creek. The social and political dynamics that form a context for the battle were no longer a part of the context for the participants. The context became the landscape, the thousands of other individuals who shared the field, and the act of survival. The artifacts and the patterns of battle comment on this.

By looking at the battle in this way, we are able to strip off a contextual shell and perceive the battle as it was probably perceived by those who were participants. A quote from actor Lewis Ayres in the 1930 epic *All Quiet on the Western Front* comes to mind: "We live in the trenches out there. We fight. We try not to be killed. And sometimes we are. That's all" (Universal Pictures 1930). This is probably a contextual level with which many visitors to battlefield parks can and do identify. The battlefield, collectively conceived, is a place where the epics of individuals were staged. Archaeology is a dynamic way to interpret this individual context.

For many, the pragmatic value of battlefield archaeology is particularistic; certainly this realization has been a major value derived from this research. For poorly documented battlefields such as Mine Creek, archaeology offers the unusually attractive potential of being able to anchor details of historical events to a modern landscape. This has begun at Mine Creek through presentation of empirical data and provisional interpretations which blend archaeological and historical information. In the process, a long-standing historically based model of the battle has been questioned. Once again, the battle of Mine Creek is being fought; the opposing armies this time are the proponents of different interpretations of the same past. Fortunately, a rich source of new historical information is available through archaeology. The tug-of-war between theories presents a healthy atmosphere for inquiry and for the advancement of our understanding of the past.

## Acknowledgments

This paper would not have been possible without the many hours volunteered by Jack Ames, Russ Broxterman, Francis Cormode, Dave Cregut, Wayne Donohoe, Mike Duncan, Marylie Faust, Joe Higgins,

Kathy Johnston, Cleta Mulder, Milton Reichart, Henry Roeckers, Dwight Streeter, Dave Tabor, and Daryl Walters. Wayne Donohoe was particularly helpful in pulling together a crew of metal-detector enthusiasts. John Reynolds, assistant state archeologist, was co-director of the 1989 and 1990 field work and has been supportive throughout. Ola May Earnest of the Linn County Historical Society provided invaluable local support and encouragement. Dan Smith served as an essential if unintended devil's advocate, challenging my interpretations; in the process, he provided important support for this project. Ramon Powers, executive director of the Kansas State Historical Society, supported an archaeological approach to this site. Doug Scott of the National Park Service provided the precedent, as well as constant encouragement and technical assistance. Despite the key contributions of all of these individuals and of many others not mentioned, the interpretations and any errors set forth in this paper are my own.

# 4

*Samuel D. Smith*

## EXCAVATION DATA FOR CIVIL WAR ERA MILITARY SITES IN MIDDLE TENNESSEE

An early student of the American Civil War, Frederick Henry Dyer (1908: 595), estimated that Tennessee was the scene of at least 1,462 individual campaigns, battles, skirmishes, and similar actions, with only the state of Virginia having hosted a greater number of such activities. A majority of the Civil War actions that occurred in Tennessee took place in that portion of the state called Middle Tennessee. This is a sociopolitical subdivision that encompasses several physiographic regions, including the Nashville or Central Basin and the Eastern and Western Highland Rims. While during the 1861–65 period Middle Tennessee was part of the much larger war region known as the "Western Theater," it was, nevertheless, a distinct area in terms of the specific military activities carried out here.

The nature of this regional Civil War military activity has been brought into much clearer focus by the completion of a thematic archaeological site survey project designated "A Survey of Civil War Period Military Sites in Middle Tennessee" (Smith, Prouty, and

Nance 1990). This survey is the most recent in a series of major historic site survey projects conducted by the Tennessee Division of Archaeology since the mid-1970s (Samuel D. Smith 1990), and its completion helps to fulfill a long-recognized need. Previously, military sites from the Civil War period were poorly represented in Tennessee's data base of recorded archaeological sites.

The Middle Tennessee survey resulted in the recording of 143 spatial areas defined as "sites" (fig. 4.1). Some of these sites are small remaining portions of what were once large activity areas, such as battlefields, and a majority of them contain more than one "component," a term used to refer to the presence of archaeological remains reflecting a particular type of construction or activity. There are a total of 261 components, arising from 23 definable component types. These component types include such things as large and small battlefields, encampment areas, several specific kinds of earthworks and fortifications, and railroad guardposts supported by structures such as "stockades" (especially common during the early war years) and "blockhouses" (a later innovation). There are also several sites with standing buildings used during the Civil War as military hospitals or headquarters, and a number of single occurrences of components such as a military foundry and a Federal shipyard (Smith, Prouty, and Nance 1990).

The information obtained through recording these 143 Civil War period military sites also makes clear that for such resources there is a serious lack of data collected through archaeological excavation. While Tennessee has long been one of the leading states for Civil War relic collecting (for example, Tennessee locations are mentioned about one hundred times in a recent book devoted to artifacts found by Civil War collectors [Harris 1987: 254–56]), only seven Civil War period military sites (five of them in Middle Tennessee) are known to have had any archaeological excavation. The work on these seven is reported in five archaeological reports that concern the investigation of four forts, or fortlike enclosures, which an organization was interested in reconstructing (Dilliplane 1975; Fox 1978; Mainfort 1980; Gerald Smith 1985, 1987); a preliminary report concerning the excavation of a portion of the battlefield for the Battle of Nashville (Kuttruff 1989); limited discussion of a brief salvage excavation that was conducted on a Federal en-

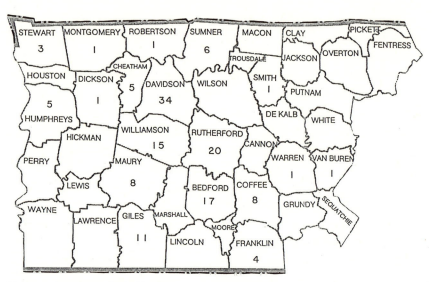

**Fig. 4.1.** *Counties in the Middle Tennessee survey area with Civil War period military sites recorded as of 1990. Courtesy of the Tennessee Department of Environment and Conservation, Division of Archaeology.*

campment site during the Middle Tennessee survey (Smith, Prouty, and Nance 1990: 1, 51); and the results of an archaeological project conducted at the Carter House, a preliminary summary of which is contained in this volume.

In addition to the relative paucity of such reports, it is also obvious that archaeologists in Tennessee almost never have investigated the kinds of Civil War period military sites that would produce large amounts of artifactual information reflecting the day-to-day activities of the soldiers who participated in this event. Contrary to the impression conveyed by the vast body of literature that has been produced by Civil War relic collectors, the limited salvage excavation of a Federal encampment site conducted during the Middle Tennessee survey clearly demonstrates that the major portion of the archaeological record for such sites is not composed of military artifacts made of metal (Smith, Prouty, and Nance 1990: 51). As would be expected in most nineteenth-century sites, those areas where people—in this case soldiers—spent most of their time became major repositories for broken pieces of glass and ceramic containers, common metal items such as nails, and discarded food remains, largely represented in the archaeological record by the bones of domestic animals.

From an archaeological perspective, two major areas of understanding missing from the literature that is based on the results of relic hunting are (1) insights that could be derived from studying mundane items such as faunal remains, and (2) examinations of the distributions of artifacts on sites, including how past activity may be reflected by artifact distribution patterns. This chapter addresses the second of these concerns, by discussing the results of an archaeological interpretation of a portion of a Civil War battlefield, showing how the frequency and distribution of the excavated items can provide a better understanding of what occurred.

The battlefield remains under consideration are from the Middle Tennessee site known as the Carter House. For one brief period on November 30, 1864, the Carter House, which had been appropriated as a Federal command post, became the focal point for the Battle of Franklin, one of the bloodiest battles of the Civil War. To understand how this occurred, some brief historical facts are in order.

## Historical Perspective on the Battle of Franklin

After much wavering on the issue of secession, Tennessee joined the Confederacy on June 8, 1861. The state soon became a principal field of activity for the "Army of Tennessee," which, with an initial strength of about 55,000 troops, was the main Confederate army west of the Appalachian Mountains (Smith, Prouty, and Nance 1990: 6). Confederate control of Tennessee lasted, however, only a few months.

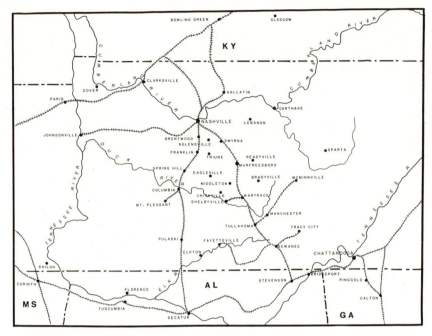

**Fig. 4.2.** *The Middle Tennessee area as it appeared during the Civil War period. Courtesy of the Tennessee Department of Environment and Conservation, Division of Archaeology.*

The first major Confederate loss in Middle Tennessee occurred in February 1862, when Federal troops captured Fort Henry and Fort Donelson on the Tennessee and Cumberland rivers, in the vicinity of Dover, Tennessee (fig. 4.2). The loss of these forts opened the way for the occupation of Nashville, which soon became the principal Federal war-materials depot for the Western Theater and one of the most completely fortified cities in America. Federal control of other strategic locations in Middle Tennessee quickly followed (Wright 1982: 123–27; Hoobler 1986: 19; Horn 1987: 406–407).

Confederate resistance to this Federal occupation was highlighted by the Battle of Murfreesboro, which ended on January 3, 1863, and by a series of smaller battles that forced the Army of Tennessee into the Chattanooga area, where it suffered a major defeat in November 1863 (Smith, Prouty, and Nance 1990: 12). The Army of Tennessee next fought in the Atlanta Campaign, during which period General John Bell Hood became commander (Horn 1977: 7).

After the fall of Atlanta (September 1864), General Hood attempted to carry out a desperate plan. His intent seems to have been to move the Army of Tennessee, now composed of some twenty to thirty thousand men, back across Middle Tennessee, to recapture Nashville, and to drive a wedge into the Federal forces in the Western Theater. The odds against his accomplishing these objectives were tremendous. Almost immediately the Federals began gathering a force at Nashville that soon totaled about seventy thousand soldiers (Horn 1987: 377–84; Ketchum 1960: 545–46).

Hood's army crossed the border into southern Middle Tennessee on November 21, 1864, and headed for the town of Columbia (fig. 4.2). Here he hoped to cut off from Nashville a Federal army of twenty-three thousand men, which was moving northward from the town of Pulaski under the command of General John M. Schofield. Hood twice failed to achieve this objective, at Columbia and at the community of Spring Hill, and Schofield's army reached the town of Franklin at noon on November 30, 1864, several hours ahead of the Confederates (Scofield 1888; Smith, Prouty, and Nance 1990: 14).

At Franklin, eighteen miles south of Nashville, Schofield's progress was halted by the Harpeth River, which was near flood stage. While some of his troops worked to rebuild a partially destroyed railroad bridge so that it could be used to move the Federal supply wagons across the river, the main portion of his army began strengthening and expanding some existing Federal breastworks. These rebuilt works had exterior ditches, earthen walls topped with protective head logs, and sections of fronting abatis and angled palisades. This defensive line formed a large crescent along the south edge of Franklin, with each end anchored on the river (fig. 4.3). A preexisting Federal fort called Fort Granger, located to the rear of this line and north of the Harpeth River, was manned to provided artillery support and became the temporary headquarters for General Schofield (Horn 1987: 393–98; Wright 1982: 164).

Schofield had left Major General Jacob D. Cox in charge of the main line, and Cox had taken over the Carter House, located near the center of the line, as his headquarters. The Carter House had been built about 1830 by Fountain Branch Carter, who still lived there with his family. As it was considered unlikely that Hood would attempt a direct attack,

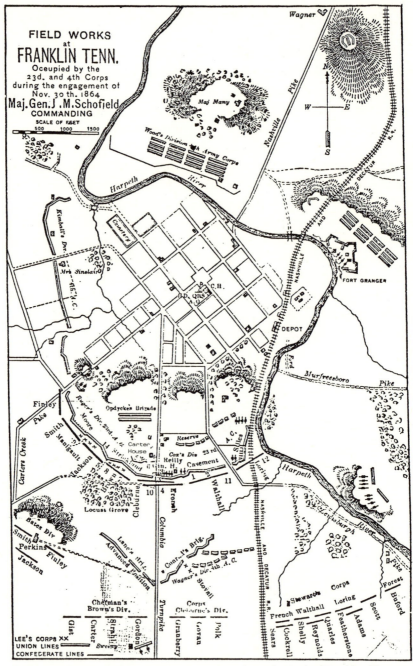

**Fig. 4.3.** Plan of entrenchments and troop positions during the Battle of Franklin, Tennessee. From Scofield 1888: 130–31.

the Carters were allowed to remain in the upper story of their home—
they eventually sought refuge in the basement (Carter 1972).

On the morning of November 30, General Hood was in a rage. The
day before, at Spring Hill, his forces actually had intercepted Schofield's
army, but some confusion in Confederate orders had allowed the
Federals to pass the Confederates during the night. Hood, who at this
point in the war was suffering from several kinds of physical and mental
anguish, reacted to this mistake by marching his army to Franklin and
ordering an immediate frontal assault across an open plain. Since his adversaries by now were well entrenched, the results were disastrous
(Smith, Prouty, and Nance 1990: 14).

The Battle of Franklin began at 3 p.m. on November 30 and lasted
about five hours (McDonough and Connelly 1983). In the initial charge,
the Confederate forces overran an advanced Federal position, driving
the defenders back into the main line. This resulted in a breaching of the
main line at its center, with Confederate troops pouring into the area
between the front line and a secondary line, called a "retrenchment,"
and into the yard area around the Carter House (fig. 4.4). What could
have been a major disaster for the Federals was recouped by the action
of reserve forces, who were able to push back the attackers who had
made the initial breakthrough. While this occurred, there was a period
of fierce hand-to-hand combat in the Carter House yard. After this first
phase of the battle, the retrenchment, located sixty feet south of the
Carter House, became part of the Federal main line. During subsequent
fighting, the Confederates regrouped and attempted to assault this line
about thirteen times. As darkness fell, the surviving Confederates clung
to exterior walls of portions of the Federal works, and some fighting
continued at close quarters until about 8 p.m. Around midnight,
Schofield's troops pulled out of Franklin and continued on to Nashville
(Cox 1897: 56; Smith, Prouty, and Nance 1990: 14–15; Sword 1992:
201–205).

Hood's attack on the Federal works at Franklin was condemned by
his fellow officers at the time and by historians subsequently. Not only
was his opponent well entrenched and supported by artillery, but some
of the Federal troops were armed with the relatively new Spencer and
Henry repeating rifles, which gave them a tremendous fire-power ad-

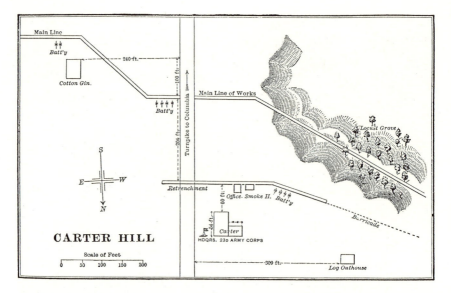

***Fig. 4.4.*** *Plan of Federal defenses in the Carter House area. From Cox 1897: 42–43.*

vantage over the attackers. The best estimate of Hood's Franklin losses is about 6,300 men killed or wounded and about 700 taken prisoner. Five Confederate generals were killed outright, and another died of wounds a few days later. The Federals lost 2,326 men, only 189 of whom were actually killed in battle. In terms of casualty ratios, it was one of the most costly battles fought during the Civil War, with most of the losses sustained by the Army of Tennessee (Smith, Prouty, and Nance 1990: 15–16). While initially it did not appear to be a decisive victory for either side, it clearly was a preamble to the final defeat of the Army of Tennessee two weeks later (December 15 and 16, 1864) at the Battle of Nashville (Horn 1957: v–xiii).

## Results of the Carter House Excavation

One hundred and twenty-four years after the battle, at the Carter House State Historic Site, plans by the Tennessee Department of Conservation to expose the exterior wall of the main house foundation to correct a moisture problem in the basement necessitated an archaeological salvage

***Fig. 4.5.*** *View of the Carter House (facing southwest) during the 1988 excavation (before removal of the intervening excavation units). Courtesy of the Tennessee Department of Environment and Conservation, Division of Archaeology.*

project that was conducted by the department's Division of Archaeology. A main objective of this project was to clear a ten-foot-wide zone around the front and sides of the building, accomplished by digging a series of five-by-ten-foot excavation units in checkerboard fashion (fig. 4.5), then removing the intervening units.

Some general site exploration was also carried out in areas such as the back or south side of the smokehouse, which during the Battle of Franklin was part of the secondary main battle line. The south sides of the smokehouse and an adjacent farm office building (fig. 4.4), as well as the south side of the Carter House, were heavily damaged by incoming Confederate fire on the day of the Battle of Franklin. While much of the damage to the main house was later repaired, the outbuildings still bear dramatic evidence of the many bullet strikes.

The 1988 excavation at the Carter House was conducted using traditional archaeological techniques, including hand excavation, screening of the soil removed to facilitate the recovery of all artifacts, and careful recording of all soil levels and features. The field work was followed by laboratory analysis of the artifacts. While a final project report remains to be completed, the artifact tabulations are complete, and it is possible to make some reasonably conclusive statements concerning the results, which are summarized below.

The archaeological retrieval of artifacts at the Carter House has provided the first glimpse of how materials related to what was once a much larger site, the Battle of Franklin battlefield, are distributed, and in particular how they are distributed around the building that served as the Federal command post and the center of some of the heaviest fighting. This distribution has been examined in several ways, including plotting artifact counts on maps that show the numerical distribution of various groups in terms of the original excavation units. Space does not permit the inclusion of these distribution maps in this summary, but the information they convey is briefly described.

The Carter House excavation produced 2,939 pieces of faunal material (almost all of which can be assumed to relate to the more than one hundred years of domestic occupation of the site), 33,021 domestic artifacts (items probably not related to the Civil War military activity), and 786 items that were tabulated as part of a "Civil War Military Artifact Group." The last, items assumed to have been discarded or lost during the Battle of Franklin, were divided into four major subgroups: (1) Arms and Ammunition (dropped bullets, impacted bullets, mutilated bullets, fired cartridge casings, unfired cartridge casings, dropped percussion caps, fired percussion caps, artillery shot, and gun parts); (2) Military Equipage (percussion cap tins, cartridge box tins, scabbard parts, knapsack buckles, knapsack hooks, and a canteen spout); (3) Uniform Items (three categories of uniform buttons); and (4) Additional Items (a brass token of probable military origin).

An examination of the distribution by excavation unit for the entire collection of 786 Civil War Group artifacts suggests a more or less random distribution, with comparable numbers of Civil War items coming from different sides of the house. Presumably this pattern reflects the general actions that occurred on November 30, 1864, with fighting and other activities taking place at different times on all sides of the house. When certain categories of artifacts are compared, however, some distinct patterns emerge. A specific example is the distribution of impacted versus dropped bullets. Impacted specimens were found concentrated on the south and front sides of the house (the sides facing the numerous volleys of incoming Confederate fire), while dropped bullets were heavily distributed along the north edge of the house (the side that must have provided a sheltered location for Federal soldiers engaged in regrouping and reloading activities).

The most dramatic distribution observed for the Carter House Civil War artifacts, however, is for a particular bullet type. A total of 415 Civil War period bullets (including dropped and fired) was recovered from the site, and these account for over half (52.8 percent) of the Civil War artifacts. While at least fourteen bullet types are represented, over half of the bullet collection is composed of whole or partial examples of what are known as "Williams Cleaner (Type III)" bullets (fig. 4.6a). A total of 227 of these was found, accounting for 54.7 percent of all the bullets recovered.

The .58 caliber cylindro-ogival-shaped cleaner bullet was designed by Elijah D. Williams of Philadelphia, and the earliest type, Type I, was introduced to the Federal military in early 1862. Type II was introduced in December 1862, and Type III came into use sometime in 1863. Type III Williams Cleaner bullets are very similar to Type II, but shorter. Type III bullets are not commonly found on Civil War sites dating earlier than 1864 (Thomas 1981: 16, 27).

The intended purpose of these cleaner bullets was to improve the accuracy of rifles by removing powder residue from the bores. This was accomplished by the use of a zinc disc that was placed between the base of the bullet's nose cast and a headed pin, made of hardened lead, that was inserted into a cavity in the base of the nose. When the gun was fired, the powder gases drove the pin forward, forcing the zinc washer to expand. As the bullet traveled outward, the washer scraped the interior of the gun barrel, supposedly removing powder residue (Thomas 1981: 16; McKee and Mason 1980: 64).

Paper cartridges issued to Federal troops from 1862 to 1863 were packed ten to a bundle. In each bundle, one cartridge, often identified

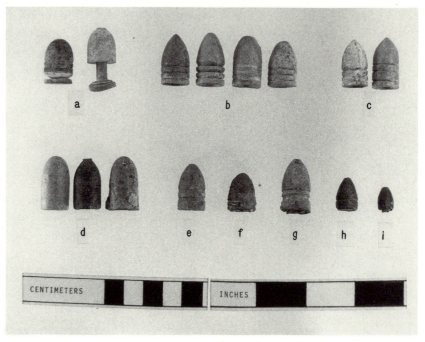

**Fig. 4.6.** *Conical bullet types from the Carter House excavation: (a) Williams Cleaner (Type III); (b) 3-ring Minié (.58 cal.); (c) 3-ring Minié (.54 cal.); (d) Enfield-Pritchett; (e) Sharps; (f) Burnside; (g) Gardner; (h) .44 caliber; (i) .31 caliber. Courtesy of the Tennessee Department of Environment and Conservation, Division of Archaeology.*

by the color of paper (such as blue or red) contained a Williams Cleaner bullet. By April 1863, the ratio was ordered increased to three Williams and seven regulation cartridges (Todd 1980: 187; Thomas 1981: 16, 18, 27). Apparently based in part on the frequency with which unfired cleaner bullets are found by Civil War relic collectors, a few writers have commented that these bullets were unpopular with the enlisted men and that their use was discontinued late in the war (Todd 1980: 187; McKee and Mason 1980: 64). The most accurate information relating to the unpopularity of these cleaner bullets comes from a 1960 study by Berkely Lewis:

> Apparently the bore-cleaning load was discontinued because the troops were prejudiced against it. They said it damaged the bore, though exten-

sive firing tests did not so indicate. A study of reports of the official tests of the Williams bullets and manuscript notes on them by Master Armorer Allin of Springfield Armory shows that the bullets were highly effective in accomplishing their purpose and were also at least as accurate as the standard type. (Berkely Lewis 1960: 125)

Lewis also quotes a September 19, 1864, War Department Ordinance Office Circular (No. 47) directing that:

No more Williams' bullets will be made up into cartridges after the receipt of this circular. Such bullets of that kind as may be on hand will be retained until further orders, but will not be used except in cases of emergency. The cartridges of this kind on hand will be issued, but where they have not been packed, only three will be put in each bundle until those on hand are used up. (Berkely Lewis 1960: 200)

This document also indicates that during the previous month the War Department again had increased the prescribed ratio of use of cleaner bullets. For some reason, these same officials were now reversing themselves by abandoning the use of cleaner bullets entirely, or where they needed to be used up, going back to the former three-to-seven ratio. As this 1864 directive was written only a few weeks before the Battle of Franklin, it is a matter of speculation as to whether or not it would have been in effect at the time of the battle.

Either way, it would appear that the Federal troops deployed around the Carter House still were required by military regulations to use whatever number of Williams Cleaner cartridges were issued to them. If so, then the Carter House excavation has provided what may be the first quantified example in support of the assumption that many Federal soldiers disliked and in some cases refused to use them. Only 12 fired examples of Williams Cleaner bullets were found at the Carter House, and these account for only 13.8 percent of the "Impacted Bullets" that were recovered. In striking contrast, there are 215 unfired Williams Cleaner bullets or parts, composing 68.9 percent of the "Dropped Bullet" category.

There seem to be several possible ways to interpret these data. Assuming that the troops involved thought that they were still required to use Williams Cleaner bullets, it would appear that, at least during battle conditions, large numbers of individual Federal soldiers were choosing not to follow military regulations pertaining to the use of this device. If they were not using the cleaner bullets, it was apparently due to a belief that the cleaning action was ineffective or that the bullets were not accurate when fired at a target. (It also seems possible that the three-part structure of these bullets would have made them prone to lodging in the gun barrel—a frightful predicament during battle—but no documented reference to this has been found.) Second, it may be that the greater number of cleaner bullets (three instead of one) included in cartridge bundles after April 1863 resulted in the discard of substantial numbers of unfired ones; soldiers simply may not have used what they perceived to be "extra" cleaner bullets. A third possibility is that, if the September 19, 1864, War Department circular had become common knowledge by the time of the Battle of Franklin, the high incidence of discard indicated for these bullets may reflect a belief that it was no longer necessary to use them (although the circular clearly states that Williams Cleaner cartridges still on hand were to be used).

It would require a considerable amount of similarly quantified data to understand how the Carter House information concerning Williams Cleaner bullets compares to that found on other sites and during other periods of Civil War activity. The main point of this discussion is that it is the absence of information retrieved in a systematic, archaeological manner that presently hinders what could be a much clearer understanding of numerous questions that can still be asked about what, at some levels, has been the most thoroughly studied episode of American history.

## Acknowledgments

The Carter House is owned by the State of Tennessee and administered by the Carter House Chapter of the Association for the Preservation of Tennessee Antiquities (a private organization), under supervision of the Tennessee Historical Commission. Funding for the 1988 excavation was provided by the Tennessee Department of Conservation, and the work was carried out as a project of that department's Division of Archaeology. Division employees who assisted the author in directing the field work and/or in conducting the artifact analysis include David R. Anderson, Fred M. Prouty, and Mary Beth D. Trubitt.

# 5

*Samuel G. Margolin*

# ENDANGERED LEGACY
*Virginia's Civil War Naval Heritage*

Throughout the Civil War—from the weeks preceding the actual outbreak of hostilities to the final surrender at Appomattox—Virginia's James River was a central focus of strategic maneuvering by both the Union and the Confederacy. Northern General George B. McClellan considered control of the river, as gateway to Richmond, critical to the success of his Peninsular Campaign in 1862. Southern strategists knew that failure to block the enemy's navy on the James at any point in the war would mean the loss of the Confederate capital and, most likely, defeat of the Southern cause. The James was the scene not only of the legendary "Battle of the Ironclads," the most famous naval confrontation of its era, but also of numerous other, less widely known actions of comparable drama and consequence.

Examination of military actions on the river between 1861 and 1865 offers a microcosm of most of the tactics, weapons, defenses, and vessel types that figured prominently in all of the national and international maritime theaters of the conflict, changing the face of naval warfare forever. Until recently, the study of these events and technological developments remained, for the most part, the exclusive province of historians, military professionals, and a small cadre of interested laypeople. Within the last decade, however, archaeologists, with the support of private philanthropists, have become actively involved in the effort to locate, identify, and bring to the attention of the general public the material remains of a series of Civil War episodes crucial to American, maritime, and naval history.

The 1980s witnessed the discovery of a number of historically and archaeologically significant Civil War vessels in the James. The first of these occurred when archaeologists in 1981 succeeded in locating and identifying the remains of both the C.S.S. *Florida,* prototype of the foreign-built Confederate commerce raiders and one of the two most successful ships of that class during the war, and the U.S.S. *Cumberland,* valiant foe and first victim of the ironclad *Virginia* (alias *Merrimack*), in the lower James River off Newport News (Margolin 1987). A survey of sections of the upper James near Richmond the following year revealed the probable locations of ironclads and other wrecks belonging to the sunken Confederate James River Squadron (Underwater Archaeological Joint Ventures [UAJV] 1982). Additional work conducted in 1985 supported conclusions drawn from the previous survey and offered evidence of another noteworthy Civil War wreck site.

The excitement that these discoveries engendered in the first half of the decade was diminished considerably by developments in the final years of the 1980s. A proposed widening and deepening of the channel threatened to destroy many of the suspected Confederate James River Squadron sites. Looting by profit-motivated relic hunters compromised the archaeological integrity of the *Cumberland* and *Florida* and, if left unchecked, likely would have resulted in the destruction of the sites. Fortunately, the danger to all these significant cultural resources was averted, for the present at least, through the timely intervention of private maritime heritage preservationists.

Not everyone, of course, is convinced of the need to protect these shipwrecks. Does it really matter, they ask, whether the sites are destroyed? Why should we be concerned about their survival? By now most archaeologists and interested laypeople are familiar with some of the ways that ancient and historic shipwrecks contribute uniquely to our knowledge and understanding of the past. Most widely recognized is the "time capsule" aspect of wreck sites, that is, their ability to provide unimpeachable dating contexts for artifacts and to preserve materials, especially organic ones, which generally do not survive well in terrestrial environments. Scholars also have theorized about the potential for shipwreck investigations to yield insights about human behavior. By examining the physical evidence of living arrangements on both merchant vessels and warships, researchers hope to learn more about social dynamics within the tightly circumscribed boundaries of the "closed community" that shipboard life exemplifies (Muckelroy 1978: 221–25; Gould 1983: passim).

Less well appreciated is the capacity of wreck sites to reflect—through cargoes, personal possessions, and even hull construction—the values of the civilizations that built or used the vessels and the influences to which these societies were subjected. Since ships commonly represent the pinnacle of technological achievement for the maritime cultures that produced them, they typically reflect the highest scientific and organizational capabilities of those societies (Muckelroy 1978: 3, 230; Bass 1983: 92). Evidence of shortcuts in construction, the use of inferior materials, or timesaving design modifications may be indicative of significant social, economic, political, or ecological changes on a local, regional, or even hemispheric level.

The archaeological investigation of Civil War shipwrecks in Virginia's James River, if the sites are preserved, promises to provide valuable insights regarding these and other important considerations. Collectively, the sunken vessels embrace all the major technological and tactical advances that revolutionized naval warfare in the nineteenth century. The *Cumberland,* the last wind-powered United States warship to sail into battle, symbolizes the majesty and obsolescence of the great wooden men-of-war armed with their smooth-bore cannons.[1] At the other end of the spectrum, the Confederate ironclads *Richmond, Virginia II,* and *Fredericksburg* epitomize the less aesthetically pleasing but more devastating and invincible wave of the future: armorclad, steam-powered, propeller-driven vessels outfitted with batteries of more accurate and destructive rifled guns. The commerce raider *Florida* represents a transitional phase along the evolutionary path, an unarmored cruiser outfitted with rifled armament and designed to operate under both sail and steam.

From sociological and anthropological points of view, the wrecks also offer fascinating and contrasting studies. Engaged until her demise primarily in the blockade of Southern ports, the *Cumberland* hosted a largely homogeneous company of men from the Boston area. The Confederate *Florida,* in contrast, roamed the high seas for months at a stretch, and her crew, by the time of her capture, consisted largely of foreigners. In addition, dangerous or tedious assignments and difficult living conditions created distinct problems of psychological adjustment aboard the various ships. Blockade duty, for example, often was agonizingly monotonous, and commerce raiding could be perilous, but the sailors aboard the ironclads of the James River squadrons faced another challenge: living in a particularly dark and confining environment with even less access to fresh air and sunlight than usual on blockade and raiding ships. The James River shipwrecks very likely contain tangible evidence of how sailors adapted to life under these trying or unusual circumstances.

Investigating the history and remains of these vessels also may help us recapture a sense of national identity—ironic as such a claim may seem when discussing the Civil War. Americans no longer think of themselves as a nautical people, but historically the United States, from its inception at least through the Civil War, was a maritime nation, many of whose citizens took pride in their seafaring skills and traditions. American contributions to, and adaptations of, nineteenth-century advances in marine propulsion, naval gunnery, and (primarily during the war itself) naval armor established the nation as a premier world power. By studying these ships we can reconstruct and to some extent experience the ethos of America's maritime past, as well as gain insight into the nature of shipboard life in that era under a variety of living and operational situations.

## Naval Engagements along the James River

In a profound sense, the epic clash between the *Cumberland* and the *Merrimack* symbolizes both the splendor of America's maritime tradition and the tragedy of a nation divided against itself. For, though the two vessels shared a common origin and purpose, eventually they became locked in mortal combat that destroyed one ship and significantly damaged the other.

By the time of their encounter in 1862, the *Cumberland* was one of the more venerable ships in the Federal fleet. Launched twenty years earlier from the Boston Navy Yard, the three-masted, 175-foot-long warship had served as flagship of the Home, Mediterranean, and African Squadrons during the course of her distinguished career. Also a product of the Boston Navy Yard, the *Merrimack* had been launched in 1855 as part of a new class of steam frigates widely regarded as "the superiors of any war vessel then possessed by any nation in the world" (Bennett 1896: 141).

Before the outbreak of hostilities, both ships were stationed at the Gosport Navy Yard opposite Norfolk in Virginia's Elizabeth River near the entrance to the Chesapeake Bay. It was there, in April 1861, that a series of events transpired which contemporary journalist and politician Horace Greeley characterized as "the most shameful, cowardly, disastrous performance that stains the annals of the American Navy" (John Long 1957: 155). Acting on unsubstantiated rumors of an imminent attack by Southern secessionists, the commander of the Federal forces at Gosport, Charles S. McCauley, ordered the abandonment and demolition of the yard as well as the scuttling of the *Merrimack*. Ironically, it was the officers of the *Cumberland* who sought to remove the *Merrimack* to safety and who pleaded with McCauley to postpone the steam frigate's destruction until help could arrive (Franklin Young 1897: 276; Selfridge 1893: 178). By his refusal, the commander insured that the next meeting between the two vessels would be one between deadly adversaries.

When that time came, the *Merrimack,* rechristened the *Virginia* by the Southerners who had resurrected her, was no longer recognizable as the ship that the Northern mariners had known. Confederate salvors had raised the *Merrimack's* hull with little difficulty and removed the superstructure, replacing it with a heavily armored iron casemate. The conversion process, which included outfitting the *Merrimack* with a battery of new rifled guns, took almost a year. When it was completed, the contest between the *Cumberland* and the *Virginia* on March 8, 1862, marked the dawn of a new age in naval warfare.

No one, least of all the Union sailors, knew what to expect of the former *Merrimack* when she set out that morning on her maiden voyage with the avowed purpose, according to *Virginia* Captain Franklin Buchanan, of destroying the Federal blockading squadron in the James River and especially the flagship of that fleet, the U.S.S. *Cumberland* (Worden, Greene, and Ramsay 1912: 31; Buchanan n.d.: 2). "Hampton Roads, with its fine sheet of water, was indeed beautiful, not a ripple on its surface" when the Confederate ironclad emerged. It was, a *Virginia* gunner later recalled, "a day too beautiful to be bathed in the blood of our fellow man, but thus it was so" (Curtis 1957: 7).

The ensuing battle was distinguished not only by an epochal demonstration of the superiority of armor-plated, steam-driven vessels over traditional wooden-hulled sailing warships, but also by the ferocity of the fighting and the bravery of the outmatched Union sailors. Despite devastating casualties and the certainty of impending doom after the *Virginia*'s ram smashed a gaping hole in the wooden vessel's hull, participants reported that "no one flinched, but everyone went on loading and firing" until the Northern captain issued the order to abandon ship only moments before the *Cumberland* pitched forward and descended to the bottom of the James River with 121 members of her gallant crew (O'Neil 1922: 867, 879; Selfridge 1924: 48; fig. 5.1).

The following day's encounter between the Southern ironclad and her Northern counterpart, the *Monitor,* has commanded far more attention over the years, but that legendary battle, according to high-ranking naval officers, "upon which depended the whole course of the Civil War," might have ended very differently had it not been for the "epic valor of the *Cumberland*" in damaging the *Virginia* to a greater extent than any other vessel, including the *Monitor,* had managed to do (Dudley P. Knox, in Selfridge 1924: iv, v; Selfridge 1924: 55–56; O'Neil 1922: 878–79). The courage of the Northern crew inspired expressions of admiration even from her adversaries on the *Virginia,* one of whom later wrote, "No ship was ever fought more gallantly" (Lieutenant John Taylor Wood, in Johnson and Buel 1884–87: I:696; also see Parker 1985: 275; Curtis 1957: 8; and Buchanan n.d.: 2).

As the *Cumberland* disappeared beneath the waters of Hampton Roads, Confederate agents in Liverpool were preparing for the secret launching of a disguised commerce raider soon to be known as the C.S.S.

**Fig. 5.1.** *Sinking of the U.S.S.* Cumberland *by the C.S.S.* Virginia *on March 8, 1862. Lithograph by F. Newman, issued by Currier and Ives. Courtesy of the Chrysler Museum, Norfolk, Virginia.*

*Florida,* a vessel that stirred international controversy from the early stages of her construction until long after her sinking (fig. 5.2). During two cruises in 1863 and 1864, she and her satellites (prizes converted into commerce raiders) accounted for fifty-eight seizures (Owsley 1987: 187–89). Confounding Union navy efforts to capture the raider on the high seas, the *Florida,* along with her sister ship, the *Alabama,* succeeded in dealing a blow to the American merchant marine from which it has never recovered (Owsley 1987: 12, 162–64; Dalzell 1940: 245–47). The cruiser's career ended abruptly when she was rammed and hijacked by the U.S.S. *Wachusett,* in defiance of international law, from the Brazilian port of Bahia in October 1864. Towed back to the United States, she sank mysteriously less than a month later at an anchorage not far from the final resting place of the *Cumberland* off Newport News, Virginia. The reportedly accidental sinking apparently was the result of a decision by the Union high command to quash the international uproar that the *Florida's* abduction from a neutral port had incited (Owsley 1987: 147–50).

The sinking of the Confederate raider not only precipitated outrage

*Fig. 5.2. The C.S.S.* Florida *in pursuit of a prize on the high seas. Oil on canvas painting by Samuel Walters. Courtesy of the Board of Trustees of the National Museums and Galleries on the Merseyside, Merseyside, England.*

and consternation, but also, some years after the war, elicited the first direct association of the *Florida* with the *Cumberland,* as members of an exalted fraternity of valiant, though vanquished, American fighting ships. Remarking on the demise of the *Florida,* former Confederate States Navy Captain William Parker suggested that "the spot for her sinking was ill-chosen. Could the noble men who lay coffined in that gallant craft (the Cumberland) have risen from the dead and spoken they would have protested against the act as a shameful violation of the laws of honorable warfare" (Parker 1985: 365).

Although the *Cumberland* and *Florida* descended to the river bottom in close physical proximity, momentous changes in the war and naval strategy on the James occurred during the time between the two sinkings. With the arrival of the *Monitor,* Union forces managed to avert disaster at the hands of the *Virginia.* Nevertheless, the power of the Southern ironclad was sufficient to induce apprehensive Union naval authorities to declare the James River off-limits to Northern vessels and to discourage General McClellan from executing his bold plan for a lightning strike against Richmond in spring 1862. Citing the presence of the

*Virginia* as the principal deterrent, the general explained his decision to adopt the more cautious and less expedient approach of proceeding up the York River "as probably safer, though less brilliant" (Daly 1957: 159; Bern Anderson 1962: 79).

But the psychological advantage that the Confederates enjoyed in Hampton Roads was short-lived. By May 1862, Southern forces at Norfolk, believing that their position had grown precarious, decided to abandon the navy yard and redeploy the *Virginia* farther upstream to protect Richmond. However, because the ironclad's deep draft prevented her from ascending the river, the Southerners destroyed the vessel to preclude her falling into enemy hands. With the *Virginia* no longer a threat, Union forces were free to operate in the James, and the Northern high command dispatched an assault force toward Richmond.

The scene of action now shifted to Drewry's Bluff, a fortified precipice about seven miles below Richmond, where the Confederates rapidly concentrated forces and bolstered defenses to protect the Southern capital (Robinson 1961: 167–72). Beneath their gun battery on the bluff (Fort Darling), the Confederates placed a series of obstructions in the river to prevent the Union's James River fleet from advancing on Richmond. The barrier consisted of wooden pilings or "cages loaded with stone," supplemented by sunken wooden vessels, including the steamers *Beaufort, Northampton,* and *Jamestown* (Parker 1985: 307; Robinson 1961: 172; Pat Jones 1939: 8; fig. 5.3).

The obstacle proved to be a mixed blessing for the Southerners. It protected Richmond from a Union naval assault but at the same time prevented the Confederates from launching their own campaign to retake the James-York Peninsula. The situation became particularly frustrating in May 1864, when, having completed the construction of three ironclad warships at Richmond (the C.S.S. *Richmond, Virginia II,* and *Fredericksburg*), the Southerners missed an opportunity to destroy the enemy's fleet of wooden gunboats. By the time Confederate army engineers finally blasted a passage through the obstructions, the opposing squadron had repositioned its wooden steamers downriver, behind the safety of the Union ironclad monitors (Still 1971: 168–74; Parker 1985: 356).

The Northern fleet was not entirely secure below the obstructions,

*Fig. 5.3. "Drewry's Bluff." Oil on canvas painting by John Ross Key, showing sunken vessels and other obstructions in the river below Fort Darling at Drewry's Bluff. Courtesy of the Museum of the Confederacy, Richmond, Virginia.*

however. Capitalizing on their advantage in underwater explosive technology, the Confederates in May 1864 detonated a two-thousand-pound "torpedo," or submerged mine, from a shore-based battery, utterly destroying the Union gunboat *Commodore Jones* (United States Naval History Division [USNHD] 1961–65: 4:56, 4:57; John S. Barnes 1896: 97–100; Parker 1985: 353; Perry 1965: 111–12). Following the disaster, the *Jones's* acting commander reported from the Norfolk Naval Hospital that the torpedo had "exploded directly under the ship with terrible effect, causing her destruction instantly, absolutely blowing the vessel to splinters" (Lieutenant Thomas Wade in USNHD 1961–65: 4:1, 4:56). Observers indicated that the force of the blast, which caused the death of forty Union sailors, lifted the paddle-wheel steamer completely out of the water, so that with "her wheels rapidly revolving in mid-air . . . they could see the green sedge of the banks beneath her keel" (John S. Barnes 1896: 99).[2]

Apart from isolated incidents such as the *Jones* disaster and an abortive Confederate attempt in January 1865 to pass through the obstruction opening and attack the City Point base of Ulysses S. Grant, Union commanding general, a tense stalemate existed between the opposing forces on either side of the barrier. Meanwhile, however, the Confederate predicament began to deteriorate rapidly. Captain William Parker of the *Richmond* reported that "affairs were looking very badly for us about this time. . . . Men were deserting in large numbers from General Lee's army and from the James River squadron" (Parker 1985: 369). When Raphael Semmes, former captain of the raider *Alabama,* assumed command of the Confederate James River fleet in February 1865, he lamented that "great discontent prevails" and that "boat loads" had defected (Semmes 1893: 803–804; Still 1971: 222).

Conditions aboard the ironclads of both squadrons were especially difficult. The previous summer, Union Commander Edward T. Nichols of the U.S.S. *Mendota* had written: "My cabin is about as uncomfortable as it can be. It leaks all over, deck, skylight, combings and stairway. I am sorry I did not bring an umbrella with me" (USNHD 1961–65: 4:69). By winter, for the Confederates at least, the situation had grown too desperate for humor. "In the squadron, where very few of the men were 'to the manner born,'" Captain Parker observed, "the scanty ration was the principal cause of their leaving. A man shut up in an iron-clad with nothing to do after the morning drill, broods over his hunger—it is not like being on shore, where a man can move about and forage a little" (Parker 1985: 369). Besides hunger and inactivity, dimly lit, poorly ventilated living quarters and working areas further contributed to the declining morale (Still 1971: 98, 100).

On April 2, 1865, the breaching of Confederate General Robert E. Lee's Petersburg Line by Grant's forces abruptly altered the tactical status quo, however, and sealed the fate of the South's James River Squadron. With Richmond open to attack by land, the Confederate high command made the critical decision to abandon the capital. To prevent the ships (and especially the ironclads) from falling into enemy hands, Navy Secretary Stephen Mallory ordered Squadron Commander Semmes to destroy the South's James River fleet on the night of April 3 (United States Office of Naval War Records 1901: 191; Semmes 1893: 809–10).

In compliance with Mallory's orders, Semmes dutifully put the three ironclads to the torch and evacuated their crews to the wooden gunboats. Before they had steamed very far, the Confederate mariners experienced "an explosion, like the shock of an earthquake" and, the captain reported, "the air was filled with missiles." Perhaps because he had survived the sinking of his last command in a famous battle with the

U.S.S. *Kearsarge* off the coast of France the previous year, Semmes described the destruction of his flagship, the *Virginia II,* with the peculiar emotional detachment of a battle-hardened veteran. "The spectacle," he recounted with an incongruous aesthetic relish, "was grand beyond description. Her shell rooms had been full . . . and as the shells exploded by twos and threes, and by the dozens, the pyrotechnic effect was very fine" (Semmes 1893: 812).

In contrast, Captain Parker offered a far more poignant and chilling account of the event from his vantage point in Richmond itself. Amid the alarm and confusion of the evacuation, widespread looting had broken out. "To add to the horror of the moment," Parker later recalled, "we now heard the explosions of the vessels and magazines, and this, with the screams and yells of the drunken demons in the streets, and the fires which were now breaking out in every direction, made it seem as though hell itself had broken loose" (Parker 1985: 376).

## Archaeological Investigations of the James River Shipwrecks

Except for several private and government-sponsored salvage efforts conducted intermittently in the decades following the war, the remains of all the sunken vessels in the James lay largely forgotten on the river bottom for well over a century. But in 1980, Clive Cussler, a popular novelist (author of *Raise the Titanic, Deep Six, Sahara,* and other adventure thrillers) and maritime history enthusiast, acted on a long-standing personal interest in the *Cumberland* and the *Florida.* Under the aegis of the National Underwater and Marine Agency (NUMA)—a private, nonprofit organization devoted to the preservation of maritime heritage, over which he presides as chairman—Cussler undertook to locate the wrecks that summer in a cooperative venture with Virginia state archaeologists.

Failing to uncover evidence of either ship, NUMA contracted the following year with Underwater Archaeological Joint Ventures (UAJV, since reorganized as Virginia Archaeological Services) to pursue the search once again. Through a combination of historical research, assistance from local watermen, and systematic remote sensing, UAJV suc-

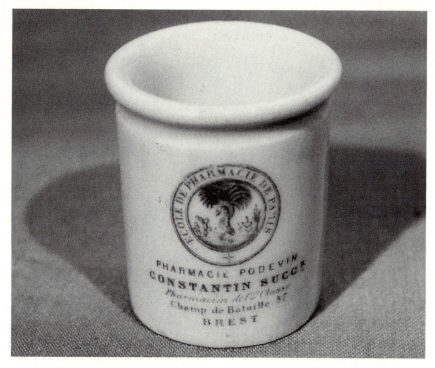

**Fig. 5.4.** *Pharmaceutical jar from Brest, France, recovered from the wreck site of the C.S.S.* Florida. *Courtesy of Virginia Archaeological Services.*

ceeded in locating two promising wreck sites, both approximately sixty-five feet deep, in the main shipping channel of the James River off lower Newport News (Margolin 1987: 54–56).[3]

Subsequent examination produced convincing evidence—in the form of site dimensions, construction features, and diagnostic artifacts—that the wrecks in question did indeed represent the remains of the *Cumberland* and the *Florida.* Preliminary mapping of the suspected *Florida* site produced measurements that closely conformed to the known dimensions of the commerce raider. Recorded site features included boilers and a water intake valve indicative of steam propulsion, and the artifact assemblage contained evidence of rigging, suggesting a vessel that could operate, as the *Florida* did, under both sail and steam. Perhaps the single most compelling piece of evidence was a small ceramic jar bearing a French pharmaceutical seal and the address of a druggist in Brest,

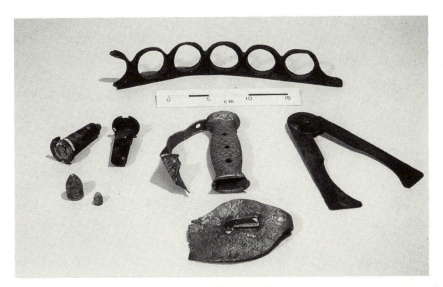

*Fig. 5.5.* *Assortment of armament-related artifacts from the* Cumberland *site (clockwise from right): gunner's calipers, brass sword hilt and handle, bullets, cannon fuses, and part of a rifle rack. Courtesy of Virginia Archaeological Services.*

the European port where the *Florida* spent nearly half a year undergoing repair in 1863 and early 1864 (Margolin 1987: 57, 84; Owsley 1987: 92–97; fig. 5.4).[4]

The recovery of armament-related artifacts contributed substantially to the conclusive identification of the second wreck site. Foremost among these objects was a pair of gunner's calipers practically identical to the standard type catalogued in the U.S. Army ordnance manual of 1862 (U.S. Army 1862); a wooden sabot (a device used to seat cannon-balls properly in cannon bores before firing) the same diameter as that of the *Cumberland's* broadside battery in March 1862; and a touch-hole cover bearing a "U.S.N.Y." (United States Navy Yard) inscription and the year (1856) in which the *Cumberland* was refitted at such a facility in New York (figs. 5.45 and 5.6). In addition, heavy and unusual sedimen-tary deposits on the site corresponded to a nineteenth-century account of a postwar dredging operation in which tons of spoil were dumped on the wreck of the warship, leading an eyewitness to conclude that "no doubt now the boat is entirely covered over" (West 1977: 155; Margolin 1987: 84).

***Fig. 5.6.*** *Touch hole covers recovered from the wreck of the* Cumberland. *Courtesy of Virginia Archaeological Services.*

Following the discovery of the two wrecks off Newport News in 1981, a fortuitous archival find prompted a search for sunken Civil War vessels in the upper James River the following year. While conducting research at the Corps of Engineers Library in Norfolk, Cussler discovered an 1881 map indicating the locations of ships from the South's James River Squadron that had been scuttled adjacent to Drewry's Bluff during the war (fig. 5.7). Assigned the task of removing sunken vessels and other obstacles from the main shipping channel where they constituted hazards to navigation after the Confederate surrender, Federal Engineer James Maillefert had documented his efforts in written dispatches to his superiors and in the form of the chart entitled "Position of Wrecks Drury's [*sic*] Bluff Jas. R."

The discovery of the map was exciting for several reasons. First, it indicated not only the locations of the Confederate steamers sunk as channel obstructions early in the conflict, but also those of the famous Southern ironclads *Fredericksburg* and *Virginia II,* which the Confederates had destroyed during the evacuation of Richmond. Also, since the map appeared to have been executed with some precision, there was reason to believe that the depictions of the wreck sites accurately represented

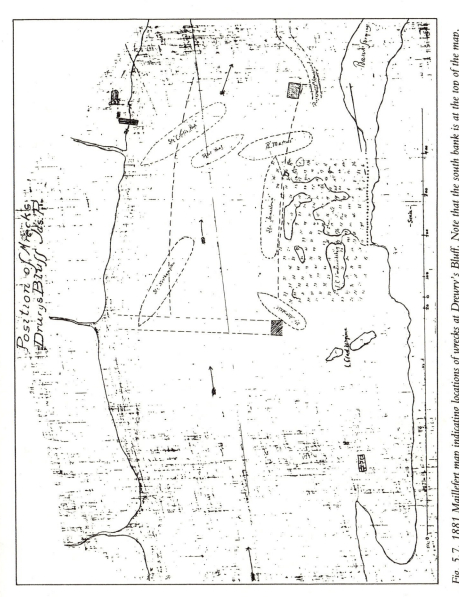

Fig. 5.7. 1881 Maillefert map indicating locations of wrecks at Drewry's Bluff. Note that the south bank is at the top of the map, the north bank at the bottom. Courtesy of the U.S. Army Corps of Engineers, Norfolk, Virginia.

their true locations. Finally, the relatively narrow width of the James River at Drewry's Bluff, less than 250 yards, promised greatly to facilitate efforts to project and record site locations from fixed points on shore.

Field operations began with a remote sensing survey focused primarily on a short section of the river which, according to the Maillefert map, contained all the shipwreck sites in the Drewry's Bluff area. A baseline for recording transit measurements was established in the vicinity of two creeks on the south bank which were readily discernible on both the Maillefert map and modern marine charts. The remote sensing instrument utilized was an underwater gradiometer which was attached to the bow of the survey vessel in a vertical fashion while the boat ran survey lanes parallel to shore at approximate ten-foot intervals.

The gradiometer produced three distinct sets of potentially significant magnetic readings, two along the northern shoreline and one close to the southern bank. Each of these anomalies then was subjected to an intensive remote sensing examination intended to establish the approximate dimensions of the targets. The locations of buoys marking the perimeters of the anomalies were recorded by triangulation from the shore-based transit stations (fig. 5.8). By plotting the buoy positions to the same scale as the Maillefert map, the results of the survey could be compared directly to the 1881 chart by superimposing an overlay. This overlay indicated, in rather dramatic fashion, a close conformance between the gradiometer targets and the locations of the ironclads *Fredericksburg* and *Virginia II* and, to a lesser degree, the steamer *Northampton* as recorded by Maillefert in the nineteenth century (fig. 5.9).

Diving examinations of the two targets near the northern bank revealed no visible shipwreck remains, but investigators probing the bottom with stainless steel rods, extendible up to twenty-one feet, encountered what they believed to be metal at depths ranging from six to fifteen feet along the longitudinal axis of the "Fredericksburg" target. Two sets of factors, one historical and the other geological, are believed to account for the elusiveness of the physical remains of these vessels.

First, the sites have suffered considerable disruption and disintegration as a result of various channel clearing and alteration efforts over the years. Maillefert himself reported having used substantial quantities of explosives to remove channel obstructions (United States Office of Na-

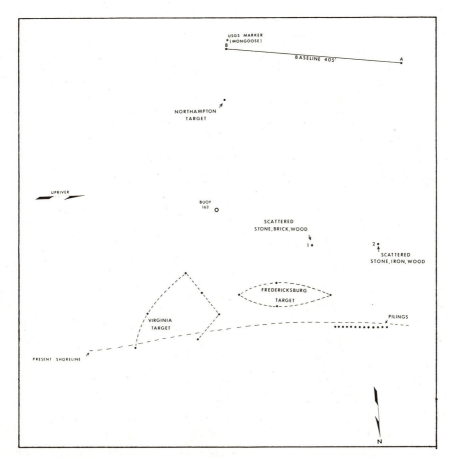

*Fig. 5.8.* Triangulation baseline and gradiometer targets from the 1982 UAJV survey of Drewry's Bluff area of the James River. Courtesy of Virginia Archaeological Services, Inc.

val War Records 1901: 138). Another source indicates that, prior to the detonation of charges along one side of the *Virginia II*'s sunken hull, a trench thirty feet deep was dug into the river bottom on the opposite side to accommodate the ironclad's exploded remains (Perry 1965: 181). Some seven decades later the *Richmond Times-Dispatch* reported that "tons of dynamite" were used in a federally-funded dredging project in 1939 to "blast those buried ships into a million splinters" (Pat Jones 1939: 8).

Second, by comparing Maillefert's map with one drawn ten years earlier, it is apparent that, in the short space of a decade, a considerable

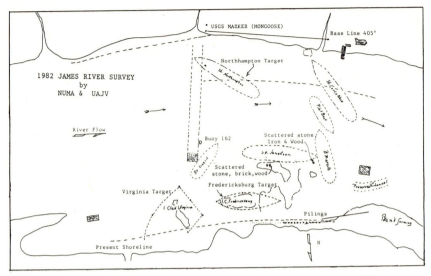

**Fig. 5.9.** *Results of 1982 UAJV gradiometer survey superimposed on 1881 Maillefert map. Courtesy of Virginia Archaeological Services, Inc.*

degree of sediment deposition already had taken place on the northern bank (Mariners Museum Library 1871). The 1881 map indicates the formation of a bank, not indicated on the earlier chart, just upriver of a set of pilings lying offshore of the northern beach and extending eastward over the wreck of the *Virginia II* (see fig. 5.6). A century later, UAJV investigators noted that this sedimentation had proceeded to the point where the set of pilings clearly depicted offshore in 1881 now lay well within the present shoreline (see fig. 5.9). As the river channel migrated southward, the north bank had extended out to the recorded site of the *Virginia II,* which explains why the gradiometer produced high readings right up to, and beyond (i.e., inshore of), the low water mark.

UAJV's underwater examination of the suspected site of the *Northampton* also failed to produce visible evidence of a ship's hull, but did result in the recovery of a number of potentially significant artifacts, including a small section of copper sheathing, part of an iron infantry spade, and two large fragments of cast iron with brass fasteners (probably pieces of steam machinery)—an assemblage not unlike that observed in the wreckage of the 1939 dredging operation, which reportedly contained a marine boiler, brass spikes, bayonets, artillery shells, boots, and "copper-sheeted wood" (Pat Jones 1939: 10). Additional searches of the river bottom in the Drewry's Bluff area revealed concentrations of large rocks, bricks, and wood, almost certainly the scattered remains of the wooden cribs filled with stone and other debris constructed by the Confederates from the ruins of Richmond buildings and subsequently destroyed by Maillefert to clear the channel (United States Office of Naval War Records 1901: 101; Parker 1985: 307; Pat Jones 1939: 8).

The investigation next moved downstream to Chaffin's Bluff, the site where the third ironclad of the Confederate James River Squadron, the *Richmond*, was recorded as having been scuttled (United States Office of Naval War Records 1901: 124). A gradiometer survey of the area revealed the presence of an anomaly of considerable magnetic intensity with gross dimensions of about two hundred feet by eighty feet. During a brief diving examination of the site, archaeologists observed sections of exposed wreckage consisting of wooden timbers with iron fastenings and a series of three rectangular iron boxes, measuring approximately six feet long by three feet wide and at least one foot deep. Constructed of quarter-inch iron plate fastened by rivets extending completely around the top edge, the containers bore a notable resemblance to similar objects observed on the wreck site of the U.S.S. *Cumberland*.

In 1985 NUMA and UAJV returned to the upper James to conduct further investigations. Additional diving on the Chaffin's Bluff site resulted in the discovery of a large, conical artillery shell and a small cannonball lying at the end of a series of square-cut timbers. Tentatively identified as a Parrott shell, the conical projectile would not have matched the C.S.S. *Richmond*'s battery, but may have been loaded on board the vessel the night of April 3, 1865, to help accomplish her destruction. Alternatively, the shell might have been fired from enemy shore batteries, which are known to have included large Parrott guns (United States Office of Naval War Records 1901: 190).

Another component of the 1985 project involved a search for the wreck of the *Commodore Jones*, the Union gunboat destroyed in 1864 by a Confederate torpedo on the western side of Jones Neck, a bend further downriver. UAJV's magnetometer survey of the area produced evidence of a large magnetic anomaly close to the eastern shore of the neck, in the immediate vicinity where a contemporary map indicated that the vessel had been destroyed (USNHD 1961–65: 4:57). Deep probing with metal rods produced no positive results. As was the case at Drewry's Bluff, it appeared that, as the river channel migrated (westward in this case), heavy sedimentation had accrued on the eastern bank, deeply submerging the shipwreck.

## Discussion

In the century and a quarter since the Civil War, the James River has cut through Jones Neck completely, removing the *Commodore Jones* from the main channel of the James River and effectively safeguarding the site from the ravages of any channel alteration projects. The Confederate ironclads, steamers, and cribworks at Drewry's and Chaffin's Bluffs are not so fortunate, however. Situated in or close to the river channel, they lie precariously in harm's way, potential victims of plans to deepen and widen the James for commercial purposes. The *Commodore Jones* also has the benefit of a deep protective layer of sediment to insulate it from possible damage by natural and human agents. Further downriver, though, the *Cumberland* and *Florida* sites have proven all too vulnerable to the destructive effects of a different form of profit-motivated enterprise, the looting of artifacts for sale on the Civil War relic market.

The intentional disturbance of these sites in years past, when the value of historic preservation was much less a part of the national consciousness, seems considerably less reprehensible than it does today. Even as early as 1939, though, enlightened individuals realized that "the tiny bits of historic old ships left by mighty dynamite charges have no story to tell when they rise to the surface" (Pat Jones 1939: 9). In our own time, those who seek to enrich themselves by robbing the graves of Civil War sailors demonstrate an insensitivity as condemnable as that exhibited by the *Norfolk Virginian* in 1875. Obviously captivated by the discovery of "the petrified body of a man, supposed to be . . . an officer" during one of the postwar salvage operations on the *Cumberland,* the newspaper ghoulishly suggested that the corpse "would be a great curiosity" and, if properly promoted and displayed, "would realize a fortune to an enterprising exhibitor" (*Norfolk Virginian* 1875).

Callous disregard for the sanctity of war graves and the pressures of commercial development represent only the most obvious dangers to the survival of these irreplaceable historic relics. Bureaucratic indifference or neglect may prove equally harmful. How the threats to both sets of James River shipwreck sites have been ignored or mismanaged by public officials in recent years should give all citizens committed to the protection of our Civil War naval heritage cause for serious concern. Fortunately, the intercession of dedicated private preservationists successfully met the challenge on this occasion. The next time we may not be so lucky. Archaeologists and historians have demonstrated how careful research and systematic survey techniques can be successfully employed to locate and identify these invaluable vestiges of our national past. Now it is up to all of us, as concerned citizens, to see that they are preserved for future generations.

## Notes

Sections of this chapter originated as parts of "Preserving Virginia's Civil War Naval Heritage," a paper abstracted in *Underwater Archaeology Proceedings from the Society for Historical Archaeology Conference* (Uniontown, Pa.: Society for Historical Archaeology, 1991), 108–10. These sections have been adapted for this chapter with permission of the Society for Historical Archaeology.

1. When the *Virginia* engaged the *Cumberland* in March 1862, the Union ship's battery consisted entirely of smoothbore cannons except for the stern pivot gun, a 70-pounder rifle that the Northern sailors could not bring to bear against their adversaries during the ensuing battle (Selfridge 1893:177; Selfridge 1924: 43, 47).

2. Largely due to the efforts of Virginia hydrographer Matthew F. Maury, the South had developed the science of submarine mine technology to such an advanced degree that Union Admiral David D. Porter, who was aboard the U.S.S. *Greyhound* when it was sunk by a "coal torpedo" in 1864, declared that "in devices for blowing up vessels the Confederates were far ahead of us, putting Yankee ingenuity to shame" (USNHD 1961–65: 4:136). The calamity that befell the *Jones* is especially noteworthy, since by the end of the nineteenth cen-

tury it represented, according to John S. Barnes, "the only instance where the large electric torpedoes were successfully employed" in the history of mine warfare up to that time (John S. Barnes 1896: 98).

3. Remote sensing in underwater archaeology involves the use of electronic instrumentation on the surface to locate potentially significant sites on the bottom. The equipment generally consists of two types, sonar and ferrous metal detectors. By emitting sound waves and recording the resultant echo, various sonar devices can produce graphic images of above-bottom contours over a given distance on either side of the survey vessel (side-scan sonar); profiles of the bottom directly below the survey craft (recording fathometer); or profiles of below-bottom sediments directly beneath the path of the survey vessel (sub-bottom profiler). To detect concentrations of ferrous metal, archaeologists use either a magnetometer or a gradiometer to discover aberrations in the earth's magnetic field. Measured in gammas, the magnitude of these anomalies varies depending upon the mass of the objects being recorded and their distance from the underwater sensing mechanism.

4. Extremely solicitous of the Confederate mariners during their stay in Brest, "the French government," according to one of the *Florida's* officers, "extended us every courtesy." When U.S. government officials protested this treatment, Napoleon III himself intervened. Responding to the specific charge that repairs to the *Florida's* engines were not "necessary" (since she could cruise on wind power alone) and therefore justifiable repairs in a neutral facility, the monarch sarcastically retorted, "Because a duck can swim is no reason why his wings should be cut" (Sinclair 1898: 423).

## Acknowledgments

The author wishes to recognize the following for their respective contributions to the discovery, documentation, and preservation of Virginia's Civil War naval heritage: Michael E. Warner, James L. Knickerbocker, and Richard W. Swete, nautical archaeologists; Clive Cussler, chairman of NUMA; Wilbur Riley, waterman; and John Townley, president of the Confederate Naval Historical Society.

# Part III.

*Fortifications, Encampments, and Camp Life*

*Spurred by continuing interest in reenactment, growing schol-
arly interest in the quality of life available to soldiers of both
the Union and Confederacy, and concern for the preservation
of important Civil War sites, archaeological and historic data
have been increasingly used to document and study military
facilities such as fortifications and encampments. Not only the
structures and layout of such facilities have been of interest,
but the focus of study has expanded to include the human
aspects of their construction and occupation. These aspects include the circumstances confronted by the personnel who
manned them, as well as the quality of life of soldiers who commonly had to contend with poor weather conditions, inadequate
food and medical supplies, and the boredom presented by long
periods of inactivity. Three chapters in this section illustrate
the application of archaeology to investigate such topics.*

*Susan Winter introduces the massive Union fortifications
and campgrounds upon Maryland Heights, which dominated
the strategic transportation crossroads of Harpers Ferry, Virginia. This project—a product of National Park Service interest in protecting, interpreting, and managing this important site—uses historical archaeology as a tool in documenting*

*the development of the fortress. The physical remains encountered serve as the basis for an insightful discussion of the circumstances encountered by the troops who occupied and maintained this extensive defensive system.*

*Chapters prepared by Stephen McBride and by Hunter Lesser, Kim McBride, and Janet Brashler further explore encampment layout and lifeways. Through archaeological excavation at the site of a large Union quartermaster depot and hospital at Fort Nelson, Kentucky, McBride reveals artifact distribution patterns associated with the daily lives of the site's inhabitants. Lesser, McBride, and Brashler illustrate how historical archaeology has contributed to the interpretation of the Confederate Camp Allegheny and the Federal Cheat Summit Fort in mountainous eastern West Virginia. These studies, which consider both structures and artifacts, also stress the importance of placing the material world of the Civil War soldier within its spatial and cultural framework.*

# 6 *Susan E. Winter*

## CIVIL WAR FORTIFICATIONS AND CAMPGROUNDS ON MARYLAND HEIGHTS, THE CITADEL OF HARPERS FERRY

During the course of the Civil War, temporary field fortifications and campgrounds were constructed and occupied in all areas under contention. Most above-ground remains of these sites have disappeared, victims of the plow, subsequent development, or intentional obliteration. Those sites which remain tend to be located on marginal land such as hillsides and mountain slopes. Today, some of the best preserved Civil War era fortifications and campgrounds are found on the mountains surrounding Harpers Ferry, West Virginia, and are protected as part of Harpers Ferry National Historical Park.

This chapter focuses on the results of an extensive archaeological survey of Civil War era sites conducted on one of the mountains, Maryland Heights. The Heights rises steeply from the Potomac River, its southern extremity forming an impressive cliff that soars several hundred feet above Harpers Ferry, at the confluence of the Shenandoah and Potomac rivers. Maryland Heights forms the southern end of Elk Ridge, an outlier of the Blue Ridge Mountains. Elk

Ridge dominates the surrounding area, including Loudoun Heights on the south side of the two rivers and low-lying Bolivar Heights to the west (fig. 6.1). From 1862 to 1865, Maryland Heights witnessed extensive military occupation, as Federal forces sought to defend their hold on strategic Harpers Ferry, gateway to the Shenandoah Valley of Virginia.

The archaeological survey, conducted by the National Park Service through a cooperative agreement with the University of Maryland, systematically sought to record all significant above-ground cultural resources on Maryland Heights (encompassing 765 acres), due to their deterioration as a result of natural forces and vandalism. This survey, conducted over a two-year period, focused in large part upon Civil War era ruins, documenting seven major fortifications and thirteen campground areas (Frye and Frye 1989). Detailed topographic maps completed for each site showed all visible features; no below-ground excavations were conducted. The recorded features ranged from stone hut foundations and platforms cut into the slope to deep pits for powder magazines. Due to heavy ground cover—principally poison ivy—most field work was conducted in the winter, leading to a heightened appreciation of the strenuous conditions confronting the soldiers who had occupied the mountain.

Historical documentation provides the context for the construction and development of the fortifications and campgrounds on Maryland Heights, but archaeological data recorded during the survey places them within their physical and cultural surroundings. Beyond a simple survey of the Civil War fortifications and campgrounds, the Maryland Heights archaeological survey made possible a greater understanding of spatial relationships within and between the Civil War era sites, and of how these sites were integrated into their physical surroundings. Such specific information generally was absent in the historical documentation. In addition, the archeological evidence reflects how the soldiers attempted to adjust to their inhospitable environment and creatively used materials at hand to enhance their occupation of the mountain. These data reveal how the defensive works and campgrounds were molded into the existing landscape, using topography, geology, and cultural features to create, if only temporarily, a new landscape—an impressive earthen fortress with many hundreds of soldiers living in it.

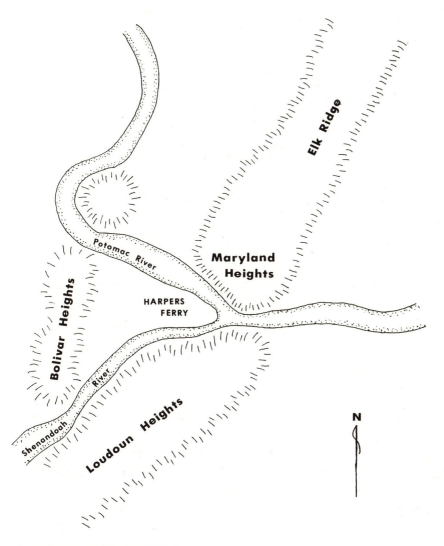

**Fig. 6.1.** *Location of Maryland Heights.*

The intent here is to describe, first, the fortification and campground system created by the occupying Union forces, and, second, how it meshed with its surroundings and with prescribed military regulations. While this study concentrates on the physical remains located on Maryland Heights, hopefully it represents a beginning point for investigating field fortifications and associated campgrounds as components of a definable community born of military necessity and not merely as parts of a strategic defensive system.

## Harpers Ferry during the Civil War

Prior to the Civil War, Harpers Ferry was best known for its Federal armory—one of two national gun-making establishments in the United States. It also served as a center for private industrial development along the Shenandoah River. Two railroads, the Baltimore and Ohio and the Winchester and Potomac, connected this bustling town to other industrial centers during the second quarter of the nineteenth century. In 1859, at the zenith of its development, Harpers Ferry gained notoriety due to abolitionist John Brown's raid, a failed attempt to capture arms and incite a slave insurrection. This event helped precipitate the outbreak of Civil War and the destruction of the Federal armory and arsenal in spring 1861.

Shortly after Virginia seceded from the Union in April 1861, a Confederate force under the command of Colonel Thomas J. Jackson occupied Harpers Ferry. From the beginning, Jackson, a master strategist, realized the importance of Maryland Heights. He discerned that whoever held this dominating bluff—the highest point overlooking the town— also controlled Harpers Ferry (Frye and Frye 1989: 53). Even though Maryland Heights, as its name implies, lay within Union territory, Jackson occupied it with about five hundred soldiers on May 9 and began constructing a large wooden stockade on its crest (Maryland 1861: 145, 178; also see Frye and Frye 1989: 55–56). Jackson's stockade never received the test of fire, however, as shortly after it was erected, Brigadier General Joseph E. Johnston assumed command of Harpers Ferry. Believing Harpers Ferry to be "untenable," Johnston ordered its evacuation in mid-June 1861 (Robert Scott 1880: 471).

When Union Captain John Newton reconnoitered Maryland Heights shortly after Jackson's withdrawal, he reported the steep and inaccessible mountain to be covered with "a small growth of timber and brushwood, and . . . difficult of penetration" (Robert Scott 1880: 711). For over eighty years, the Heights had belonged, in succession, to two iron-making companies—Keep Triste Furnace from 1763 to 1810, and the Antietam Iron Works from 1810 to 1848 (Frye and Frye 1989: 17). The thick undergrowth which impeded Captain Newton was the result of extensive timber cutting, particularly by the Antietam Iron Works, for charcoal production. The last clear-cutting on Maryland Heights occurred around 1840, about twenty years before the onset of the Civil War (Frye and Frye 1989: 48).

In addition to dense underbrush, Newton encountered rough, steep terrain traversed by crude charcoaling roads; he found no reliable water supplies along the crest and slopes (Robert Scott 1880: 732–33). Due in part to Newton's discouraging assessment of Maryland Heights, small units of Federal artillery and infantry only sporadically occupied the mountain throughout the remainder of 1861 and into spring 1862.

The lack of Union defensive preparedness caused great consternation in May 1862, when Thomas J. Jackson—now the feared Confederate General "Stonewall" Jackson—threatened Harpers Ferry from the west after soundly defeating Major General Nathaniel Banks' forces at Winchester, Virginia, on May 25. In great haste, a detachment of artillery from the Washington, D.C., Navy Yard was dispatched to the beleaguered garrison and positioned on the southwest slope of Maryland Heights, its guns aimed toward Bolivar Heights. After this naval battery opened fire on the Confederates, Jackson's forces retreated. This led the Federals to believe, quite wrongly, that the new artillery position on the slope of Maryland Heights had driven Jackson away. In actuality, the Confederate movement toward Bolivar Heights had been simply a diversionary feint to cover a general retreat up the Shenandoah Valley (Frye and Frye 1989: 59–60).

Union complacency following the Confederate withdrawal led to disaster four short months later, when "Stonewall" Jackson returned in earnest, as part of Robert E. Lee's first offensive campaign in the North. As a major part of his plan, Lee expected Federal authorities to order the evacuation of the large garrison at Harpers Ferry, thereby opening supply and communication lines for his forces into the Shenandoah Valley. Federal authorities had other plans, however, ordering commander Colonel Dixon Miles to hold Harpers Ferry "to the last extremity" (Frye

and Frye 1989: 61). In response, on September 10, Lee divided his army
at Frederick, Maryland, sending three separate Confederate columns
under Jackson's command to converge upon the town (Lazelle 1887:
603–4). One of these columns traveled down the crest of Elk Ridge
toward Maryland Heights. The Confederates met stiff resistance on top
of the Heights, but prevailed when the Federal soldiers were inexplica-
bly ordered to retreat off the mountain. Once Southern forces secured
Maryland Heights, the fate of the town was sealed, and on September
15 the Union garrison surrendered.

Following Lee's retreat after the Battle of Antietam (Sept. 17, 1862),
Federal forces reoccupied Harpers Ferry and the surrounding mountains.
The lessons learned from the costly siege and capture prompted the
Union commander, General George B. McClellan, to begin construction of substantial fortifications on Maryland Heights (Snell 1959: 4;
Lazelle 1887: 360–61, 387). The original plans called for construction of
a series of stone blockhouses or redoubts along the crests of both Maryland and Loudoun heights, but the high command in Washington subsequently downgraded those on Maryland Heights to field batteries and
temporary blockhouses (Snell 1959: 11; Lazelle 1887: 441–43, 451, 470).

In October 1862, construction began on three fortifications located
at key strategic points on the north side of the Potomac (fig. 6.2). These
defensive works consisted of Fort Duncan on a high knoll overlooking a
bend in the Potomac River, the Stone Fort on the highest point of the
crest, and the 30-Pounder Battery at the southern edge of the crest overlooking Harpers Ferry and Loudoun Heights (Frye and Frye 1989: 68).
Fort Duncan and the 30-Pounder Battery were designed to protect
Harpers Ferry from attack from the west. The Stone Fort was intended
to ward off Confederate attack via the crest of Elk Ridge, as had occurred during Jackson's attack in September (Frye and Frye 1989: 78).

The three defensive works lay widely separated, with little to protect
areas in between. Engineers' recommendations in spring 1863, along
with threatening Confederate forces in the Shenandoah Valley, led to the
construction of additional defensive works on Maryland Heights from
mid- to late June (Frye and Frye 1989: 68–69). These consisted of several artillery batteries in the narrow valley between the Stone Fort and
Fort Duncan, as well as an emplacement for a 100-pounder gun on the

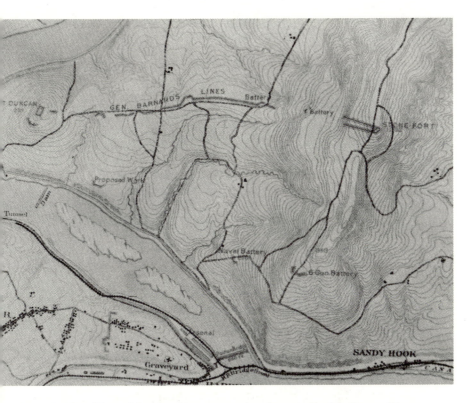

*Fig. 6.2. Plan of Union defensive positions constructed on the north side of the Potomac River at Harpers Ferry. Adapted from* The Official Military Atlas of the Civil War *1983: plate 42.1.*

second highest point on the mountain, between the Stone Fort and the 30-Pounder Battery (fig. 6.2; Frye and Frye 1989: 69, 91). The 100-Pounder Battery had the capability of firing upon or beyond any point along the extended defensive line. In addition, continuous breastworks were constructed along the east edge of the crest, from the Stone Fort south to the 30-Pounder Battery, and between the Stone Fort and Fort Duncan (Frye and Frye 1989: 69, 91).

In mid-June 1863, Robert E. Lee's forces again advanced upon the North. The Union garrison in Harpers Ferry was evacuated to the Maryland side of the Potomac to await the anticipated attack. Over ten thousand troops were positioned behind the newly strengthened defensive works, supported by approximately forty siege guns and light artillery pieces. The Confederates simply bypassed Maryland Heights, however, moving directly northward into Pennsylvania toward the fields of Gettysburg (Frye and Frye 1989: 69).

A year passed before Confederates, this time under the command of Lieutenant General Jubal A. Early, again threatened Harpers Ferry. Early advanced upon the town on July 4, 1864, but quickly withdrew under fire from the big guns on Maryland Heights (Early 1960: 384). Two days later, the Confederates deployed against the Federal entrenchments in the valley between the Stone Fort and Fort Duncan, but again withdrew under fire from the fortifications. General Early eventually sidestepped the Maryland Heights defenses and proceeded as far as the outskirts of Washington, D.C. (Early 1960: 385).

Union troops remained on Maryland Heights until the end of the war, but never again did Confederate forces threaten what became known as the "Citadel of Harpers Ferry."

## Fortifications on Maryland Heights

At the time of the Civil War, three main types of field fortifications were in use, all of which are represented, albeit in modified form, on Maryland Heights. The first type consisted of works open to the rear. The simplest of these was the *redan*, which consisted of two sides pointed to form a salient, or projecting, angle. Often the point of the angle was cut off to form a third side, which increased the range of fire. Another open fortification, the *lunette,* had two faces with two flanks that provided more protection from flanking attacks (Mahan 1862: 12). "Since this type of entrenchment was open at the gorge or rear, that side had to have protection, either from the nature of the ground or else be guarded by supporting works" (Hinds and Fitzgerald 1981: 26).

The second type of fortification was enclosed on all sides. An example of this type is the *redoubt,* which generally was square or pentagonal in form. On hilly terrain, however, its outline sometimes followed natural contours (Hinds and Fitzgerald 1981: 26).

Linear defenses comprised the third type of works. These generally consisted of chains of field fortifications, often linked together by continuous entrenchments such as breastworks, and were designed to cover extended positions (Hinds and Fitzgerald 1981: 25–26; Mahan 1862: 69).

All fortifications, of whatever type, were constructed to take full advantage of natural terrain, as well as to minimize its disadvantages. Not surprisingly, on mountainous sites, the most important military features were the crest and access points to it, and it was to these points that engineers directed their attention (Mahan 1862: 76). Tenets such as these were conveyed through manuals such as D. H. Mahan's *A Treatise on Field Fortifications* (1862), used to train engineers at West Point and carried by them into the field.

The Naval Battery represented the first permanent occupation on Maryland Heights, its construction having been prompted, as noted earlier, by General "Stonewall" Jackson's threatening forces in late May 1862. When the detachment of naval guns arrived from the Washington Navy Yard, a sandbag battery—significantly described as resembling "a broad platform like a ship deck"—was hastily erected on the side of the mountain. This battery sat approximately four hundred feet above the Potomac River and faced Harpers Ferry and Bolivar Heights (Wingate 1896: 58). It was manned by a detachment of about three hundred sailors, who witnessed little action due to Jackson's withdrawal.

The unorthodox open-platform shape of the Naval Battery is evident in a January 1863 plan which delineates seven gun emplacements, along with four powder magazines constructed following Jackson's siege and capture of Harpers Ferry (fig. 6.3). Although only partially shown on the map, this defensive work straddled a major, early nineteenth-century charcoaling and quarry road which extended up the west slope of the Heights. This road certainly provided the quick access needed to carry the heavy Dahlgren guns into position at the battery.

The Naval Battery sat about one-third of the way up the southwestern slope of Maryland Heights. Although this battery commanded Harpers Ferry and its western approaches, the absence of supporting defenses made it vulnerable to attack from the higher slopes to the north. Following construction of the other fortifications on Maryland Heights in late 1862 through early 1863, the Naval Battery was relegated to secondary importance, although never entirely abandoned as a defensive position (Frye and Frye 1989: 104).

Sometime in 1863, probably during the preparations resulting from Lee's Gettysburg campaign, the Naval Battery was rebuilt into a three-sided earthwork open toward the northeast, or upslope, and measuring

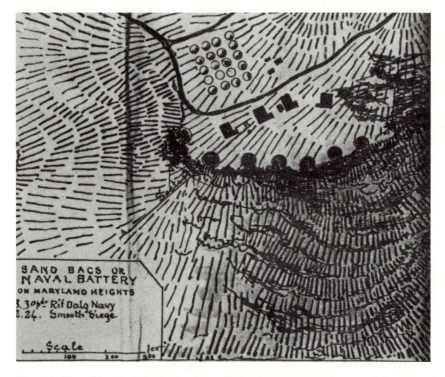

**Fig. 6.3.** *Plan of the Naval Battery by George Kaiser, January 1863. Courtesy of the National Archives.*

approximately ninety feet by fifty feet. As revealed in a topographic map of the existing ruins (fig. 6.4), footprints of two of the seven earlier plat-forms remain (labeled Platforms 2 and 3), and remnants of two of the four magazines are plainly visible (labeled Magazines 1 and 2). Three embrasures were cut through the center rampart facing downslope and an earthen gun platform (labeled Platform 1) erected in the work's southwestern corner.

Forethought was much more evident in the placement of the three additional fortifications begun in October 1862. Fort Duncan occupied a commanding knoll overlooking the Potomac River and effectively pro-tected approaches from both north and west. This position consisted of a rectangular redoubt cut at three corners for greater flexibility in gun emplacement. Below the main earthwork sat a small, open battery de-signed to flank Bolivar Heights across the river. Although an integral

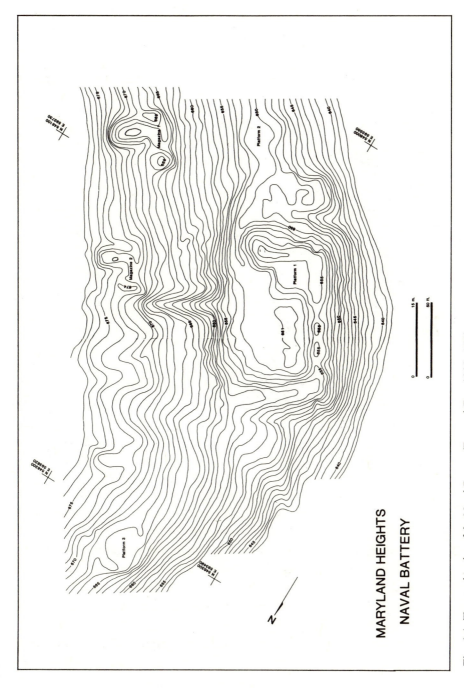

**Fig. 6.4.** *Topographic plan of the Naval Battery (Frye and Frye 1989: 151).*

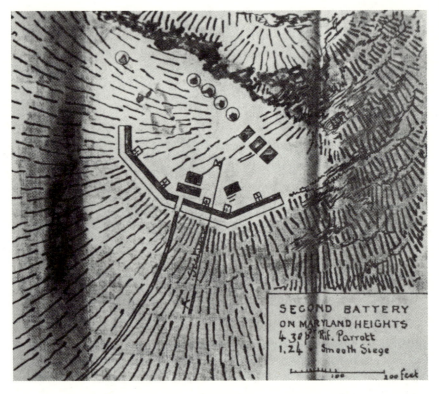

**Fig. 6.5.** *Plan of the 30-Pounder Battery by George Kaiser, January 1863. Courtesy of the National Archives.*

part of the Maryland Heights defensive system, Fort Duncan was not recorded as part of the Maryland Heights survey, as it lay outside the bounds of Harpers Ferry Historical National Park.

The 30-Pounder Battery sat at the southern edge of the mountain crest, just above a steep drop. As an inspecting engineer delightedly noted in June 1863, this earthwork was "well-constructed" and "commanded perfectly the summit of Loudoun Heights as well as Bolivar Heights" (Robert Scott 1889: 14–15).

A January 1863 plan shows that the 30-Pounder Battery consisted of a lunette of four uneven sides and open to the north (fig. 6.5). The east side anchored to the end of the narrow, spiny crest, while the west side extended to the edge of a steep drop. A narrow entrance cut through the center, with some kind of obstruction—most likely a wooden stockade—guarding it. Little or no alterations were made to this well-conceived earthen fortification during the remainder of the war, as evidenced by impressive remains of the steep rampart and ditch that are visible to the present day.

The Stone Fort, situated at the highest point on Maryland Heights, is the most intriguing and unusual Civil War ruin on the mountain. Union engineers designed this fortification as an infantry blockhouse to ward off Confederate attack via the mountain crest. It was the only one of George B. McClellan's proposed grandiose permanent works to be placed under construction—perhaps as a monument for or by the defensively minded McClellan.

In plan, the main structure consists of a rectangle measuring approximately one hundred feet by forty feet, with two bastions at opposing angles (fig. 6.6). The relative importance of the northern approach is revealed in the larger bastion and thicker walls—up to eight feet across—erected at that end. Although the stone foundation of the fortification apparently was completed, a blockhouse superstructure never was constructed. In fact, by fall 1863 the Stone Fort had been transformed into a storage area for commissary supplies; it probably remained as such until the end of the War (Frye and Frye 1989: 156).

As noted earlier, many changes were made to the fortification system in June 1863. One of these was the construction of a substantial earthen parapet a short distance north of the Stone Fort, across a narrow, level section of crest. This parapet formed the north side of a large enclosed rectangle known today as the Interior Fort; the Stone Fort sat in the southeast corner of this earthwork. The Interior Fort strengthened the defensive capabilities of a double line of breastworks that extended down the steep west slope of the mountain to an even steeper cliff.

The basically parallel stone breastworks, defined in historical documentation as rifle pits and known today as the Exterior Fort, extended approximately 550 feet downhill from the northwest and southwest corners of the Interior Fort. It remains unclear when the breastworks were constructed, whether in fall 1862 or June 1863. The core of each breastwork consisted of a dry-laid stone wall varying from four to five feet in width and two to three feet in height. A mounded earthen embankment

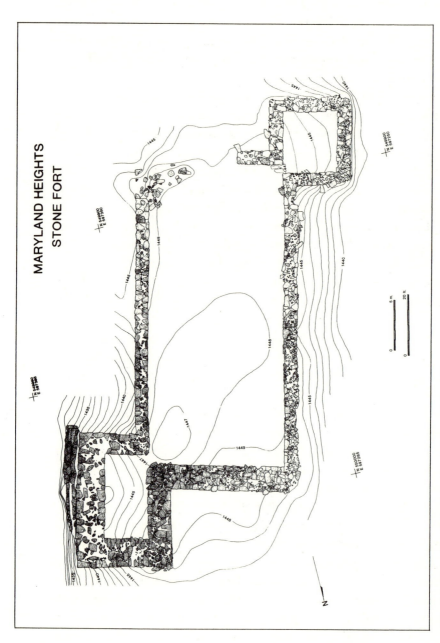

MARYLAND HEIGHTS
STONE FORT

*Fig. 6.6. Plan of the Stone Fort. Frye and Frye 1989: 117.*

covered the north side of the breastworks, which would have protected soldiers firing toward the north.

The final fortification under consideration here is the 100–Pounder Battery, constructed in June 1863 on the crest between the Stone Fort and the 30–Pounder Battery (fig. 6.2). This prominent works, erected on the second highest point on Maryland Heights, could, as one engineer assessed, "be used with effect against an enemy ascending either slope of the mountain, . . . on Loudoun or Bolivar Heights, or on Fort Duncan, and a single shot from it would render the stone fort untenable" (Robert Scott 1889: 15). The 100–pounder thus became the key to the entire position. An artificial earthen platform constructed for the massive gun and measuring roughly twenty feet in diameter remains clearly evident today. It was constructed of earth and stone fill supported by dry–laid stone retaining walls and bedrock ledges.

## Campgrounds on Maryland Heights

Along with the construction of field fortifications on Maryland Heights came a new emphasis on garrisoning the mountain, particularly around the newly erected defenses. As noted previously, steep and rocky Maryland Heights was ill–suited for large–scale human occupation, as it lacked water and other amenities. These drawbacks, however, did not deter commanders from ordering troops up its precipitous roads to rock–strewn and steeply pitched campground areas. At these uninviting locations, soldiers did their best to erect suitable quarters and establish a semblance of military order.

Following the reoccupation of Maryland Heights in late September 1862, Miles Clayton Huyette of the 125th Pennsylvania Volunteer Infantry remembered the steep mountain slope upon which he slept near the Naval Battery: "We drove stakes in the ground and placed logs above them so that we would not slide down hill when sleeping." Huyette and his fellow campmates, however, "would wake nights sitting against the up–hill side of the logs with legs hanging over" (Huyette 1915: 4).

For those who bivouacked on the mountain longer than Huyette, tents became the standard quarters (Frye and Frye 1989: 179). The military issued several types, the most common being the shelter tent conveyed to enlisted men. This tent consisted of two halves measuring about 5.5 feet square, "with buttons and holes on the sides [which] on the sides join six together and two on the back" to form a tent six feet long, one body-length wide, and about three feet high in the center (Ball 1863). On Maryland Heights in 1863, one common tent was issued for every four enlisted men (6th New York Heavy Artillery Regimental Letter and Order Book, Special Order 41).

Circular Sibley tents, eighteen feet in diameter and held up by an interior center pole, also were issued to enlisted men. These tents accommodated twelve to twenty individuals, resulting in, as one soldier noted, "more or less confusion" (Wild 1912: 29). The versatile Sibleys also functioned as storehouses and laundries (6th New York Heavy Artillery Regimental Letter and Order Book Special Order 41).

Larger wedge tents (6 ft. 10 in. by 8 ft. 4 in.) and wall tents (9 ft. square) were reserved principally for officers. The wedge and wall tents could hold up to six men, but on Maryland Heights they generally sheltered four (General Tyler to General Morris, June 23, 1863, 6th New York Heavy Artillery Regimental Letter and Order Book). Finally, hospital tents (approximately 14 ft. square) also stood on the mountain.

Troops improved their standard-issue tents into comfortable habitations (Frye and Frye 1989: 179). Lewis Holt (1862) of the 14th Massachusetts Heavy Artillery noted that his Sibley tent had just been "fixed up to suit us." In addition, "we had it stockaded and a floor in it and a set of bunks built all round it. . . . [W]e have got it stockaded with logs we dug a trench as large round as the tent and set logs up on end planted them solid in the earth and filled the cracks with mud and then set the tent upon it." As Holt concluded, "It makes a great deal more room and is warmer and healthier than a tent set on the ground." The following year, Holt (1863) lived in a wedge tent "set up on stakes and canvas put round it we also have a room in the rear large enough for us all to sleep in (it is made out of some old canvas that we picked up) so we have all the tent for a siting [sic] and dining room."

The tents proved little competition, however, to the log structures that began appearing on Maryland Heights during the late fall and early winter of 1862 (Frye and Frye 1989: 179). Frederick Wild (1912: 29–

30) of Alexander's Baltimore Battery of Light Artillery describes one of these cabins, located near the west base of the mountain:

> Our little group of five built our cabin on the brow of a hill, we dug down about three feet and leveled a space of about eight by ten feet, the sides were built of logs and the chinks filled in with clay; the roof was laid with saplings covered with the earth which we dug while leveling the space. We made a stove out of a piece of heavy sheet iron picked up in the ruins of the old arsenal at Harpers Ferry and enjoyed many delicious meals cooked upon it.

Two years later, Wild (1912: 166) constructed another shelter on the mountain, noting:

> There was no regular plan for the tents, and the various squads grouped together, and used their own ideas, as to what was warm and comfortable. The only shelter the Government furnished, were the pieces of twill muslin, about four by five feet, with buttons and buttonholes on three sides.
>
> My chum and I built a log cabin, about four feet high, and used the muslin for a roof, closing the gable ends, with jute bagging, which had been used for oats bags. The muslin was too short, so we had to build an extension, or a sort of an alcove, for our feet to rest in, this was also lined with bagging and tufted with straw, which made it quite snug and comfortable, next we built a fire place, out of stone and clay, and in it we hung a crane.

Another soldier documented a wide variety of styles in quarters construction:

> If you should stand on the small hill we cross to fetch water and take a view of our camp it almost looks like a village with the chimneys smoking: there are many different kinds of quarters, some built for 2, 4 & 6 and cover with the shelters, others cover with logs and ground on top, some of the boys who were lucky enough to get boards have them covered with boards. Many of the officers have sleeping apartments built on behind to their marquees about the size of the latter others have log huts and the Marquees stretched over it: our officers have one of the neatest quarters in the reg. they have the bedroom on behind.

***Fig. 6.7.*** *Charcoal drawing of Signal Corps campground on Maryland Heights, summer 1864. Artist unknown. Courtesy of Harpers Ferry National Historical Park.*

A detailed charcoal drawing of a Signal Corps campground near the west base of Maryland Heights provides the only known illustration of an encampment upon the mountain (fig. 6.7). Twelve log cabins or huts, aligned in two closely spaced rows of six and separated by what appears to be a company street, dominate the center of the drawing. All of the cabins open toward the street. At the left end of the two rows stands a substantial log structure which may have served as officers' quarters, with a small wedge tent to its right. To the far right of the picture is an open-stalled stable.

Cast-iron stoves appear outside several shelters and, together with the heavy foliage, portray a camp in the summertime. This camp, obviously first constructed for winter use, may have been erected by Alexander's Baltimore Battery of Light Artillery during fall 1862 (Frye and Frye 1989: 201). It was described earlier in this chapter as the first camp-ground occupied by Frederick Wild.

Whatever the style, the primary purpose of all quarters on Maryland Heights, whether tent or log cabin, was to protect the soldiers from the elements (Frye and Frye 1989: 181). This sometimes proved nearly impossible, for, as the 7th Maryland's Joseph Kirkley (n.d.: 34) reminisced: "After a varied experience of wind, snow, sleet, hail, rain, and mud, the men came to the conclusion that it was nowhere else than up here among these mountains that the weather was made and tried on."

## Archaeological Evidence of Campground Areas

As noted initially, the extensive archeological survey on Maryland Heights defined thirteen separate campground areas. Most of these were spatially discrete and probably followed historical boundaries, although some of the archaeologically defined campground areas may have overlapped historically. Almost all of the campground areas were situated in direct association with one or more of the fortifications, generally immediately behind them. Numerous above-ground features associated with the campgrounds were identified and mapped. These features included leveled tent platforms, stone hut foundations, stone walls, earthen terraces, and variously shaped depressions. Two of these campground areas are discussed here as examples of military settlement on the Heights, and are examined both from the perspective of individual shelter types and from that of general camp layout.

## 30–Pounder Battery Campground

The 30-Pounder Battery Campground occupies the end of a gradually sloping plateau on the north, or back, side of the fortification. An abrupt, rocky cliff delineates the western boundary, while the east side is bounded by a steep, short slope leading up to the narrow, spiny mountain crest that defines the east flank of the 30-Pounder Battery. Only the cessation of visible cultural features and an increase in the rockiness of the ground surface define the northern extent of the campground.

Historical records indicate that Company I, 1st Massachusetts Heavy Artillery (formerly 14th Massachusetts Infantry) occupied the 30-Pounder Battery in October 1862 with 150 to 200 men. With the exception of a few short periods, Company I remained at this position for slightly more than a year, leaving at the end of November 1863. Company F of the 5th New York Heavy Artillery shared this bivouac for a short period in June and July 1863. Following the transfer of Company I, 1st Massachusetts, another unit of the 5th New York Heavy Artillery, Company K, occupied the battery. Company K remained in position here until the end of the war (Frye and Frye 1989: 277).

A sketch map dated January 1863 depicts the 30-Pounder Battery and its campground (fig. 6.5). This stylized view shows a row of structures, the eastern half consisting of rectangular tents or cabins, the western half of Sibley tents. Remains of the campground area mapped as part of the archaeological survey (fig. 6.8), on the other hand, consist of scattered, relatively isolated features with no apparent patterning and bearing little resemblance to the historical sketch.

The most striking feature within the 30-Pounder Battery Campground is an exceptionally well-preserved stone foundation (Feature 8) situated along the western edge of the plateau (fig. 6.9). This foundation appears to have been constructed into the east side of a charcoal hearth, as the leveled ground surface to the west and south has the characteristic shape and black soil of a hearth. The well-defined interior faces of all four walls are constructed of dry-laid, medium-sized fieldstone with some small chinking stones. The walls are a uniform 2.5 feet in width and stand a minimum of 2.5 feet high, enclosing an interior which measures 9.7 feet by 7 feet. In the southeastern corner is a south-facing entryway 2 feet wide. A rubble embankment mounds against the exterior sides of the walls.

Other well-defined stone hut foundations of varying dimensions lie scattered throughout the campground area. Narrow terraces define the campground's southern end, separating it from the 30-Pounder Battery. These terraces are flanked by large, oddly configured features of unknown purpose. An example of these is Feature 9, a rectangular, leveled platform measuring about twenty feet by fifteen feet. Massive dry-laid stone retaining walls, some standing three feet high, surround this feature on three sides.

Compared with other campground areas on Maryland Heights, relatively few sections of the 30-Pounder Battery Campground were cleared

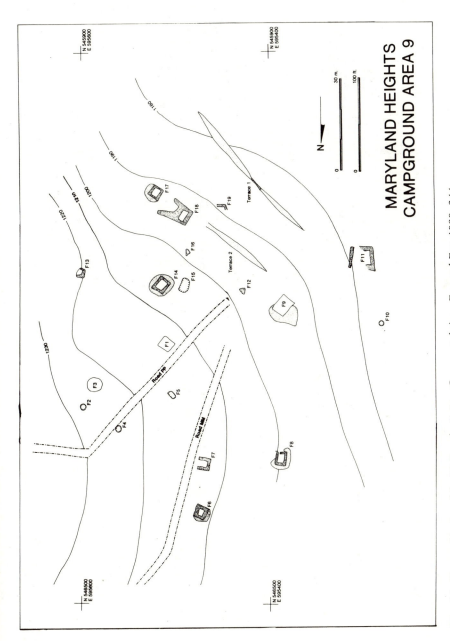

**Fig. 6.8.** Topographic plan of the 30-Pounder Battery Campground Area. Frye and Frye 1989: 244.

*Fig. 6.9. Stone hut foundation (Feature 8), 30-Pounder Battery Campground Area. Courtesy of Harpers Ferry National Historical Park.*

of surface stone, and few ephemeral anomalies were noted. Instead, the majority of the features are substantial in size and exhibit fairly good construction techniques. As a result, it is suggested that the recorded features primarily represent special activity areas—a cookhouse is documented for this campground, for example—and officers' quarters (Frye and Frye 1989: 188). Possible bivouac areas for enlisted men include the terraces constructed along the southern end of the campground, and the ground to the north of the recorded features, but few surface indications of such habitation are evident.

## Campground Area on the South Side of the Exterior Fort

A large campground area extends along a narrow plateau on the south side of the Exterior Fort, just below the western edge of the crest. A historical sketch (Porter 1863) identifies this plateau as the campground of the 9th Maryland Infantry (eight hundred to one thousand men) during summer 1863. Physical remains of this campground area, however, indicate that its occupation extended well beyond the short summer visit of the 9th Maryland. Archaeological survey at this location recorded seventy-two features, many of them substantial stone foundations, implying a long-term sojourn by one or more groups.

Features in this campground area divide into three distinct clusters (figs. 6.10 and 6.11). The northernmost group (fig. 6.10) lies in an extremely rocky area and consists primarily of platforms that probably were associated with habitations. Dimensions ranging from six feet square to eight feet square suggest that the platforms in this area provided a base for shelter and wedge tents. Some of these platforms have crude stone retaining walls about one foot in height constructed along one edge, while the other sides cut into the slope. Several circular platforms were recorded that averaged sixteen feet across and most certainly represent bases for Sibley tents. Several dry-laid stone foundations supported shelter tents or small log structures.

Although faint east-west alignments of features can be discerned in the northern section of the campground, the overall effect is of random arrangements and individual resourcefulness in quarters construction. Separate from the main group of features, at the extreme northern edge of the campground, sits a large, dry-laid stone foundation (Feature 1, fig. 6.10). This structure probably functioned as a stockaded blockhouse to protect the only entrance into the Exterior Fort.

The middle group of features (fig. 6.10) contrasts greatly with the northern group. The features recorded in the former are much larger, and each is unique in configuration. This diversity, together with the fact that they are relatively dispersed, suggests that the middle group represents a special activity area rather than a habitation site. As an example, the large, roughly circular hole at the western edge of this group (Feature 34, fig. 6.10) may have served as a magazine for small arms munitions or as some other type of storage facility. Its five-foot depth and rectangular base are typical of other magazines on Maryland Heights.

A winding rubble wall (Feature 2, fig. 6.10) follows the edge of the plateau and defines the western boundary of the northern half of the campground area (fig. 6.10). In the open space between this wall and the north group of features, and between the northern and the middle

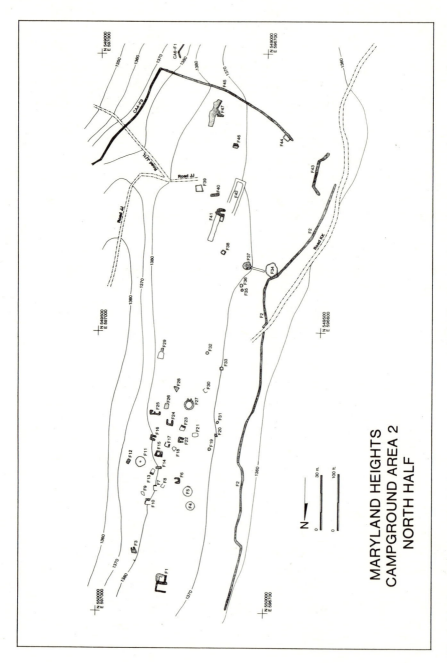

**Fig. 6.10.** *Topographic plan of north half of campground area on south side of Exterior Fort. Frye and Frye 1989: 213.*

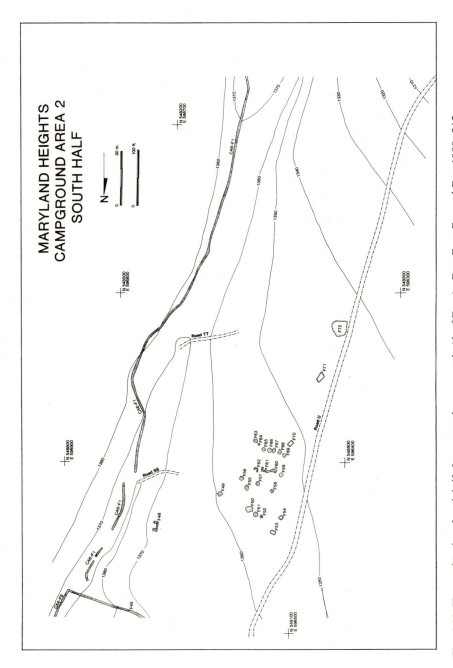

**Fig. 6.11.** *Topographic plan of south half of campground area on south side of Exterior Fort. From Frye and Frye 1989: 215.*

clusters of features, are faintly perceptible anomalies suggestive of rows of tent platforms cut into the slope. Although too indistinct to define accurately and map, the cleared area along the western edge appears to have contained shelter tents, while the second area possibly housed the larger wedge tents. Stone cleared from the latter area apparently was thrown onto the short, steep slope leading to the crest along the eastern edge of the campground.

A second rubble wall (Feature 45, figs. 6.10 and 6.11) extends across the plateau along the southern edge of the middle group of features. It may form a boundary that historically separated the north and middle groups from the remainder of the campground area. Additional evidence supporting this supposition is the fact that the meandering rubble wall along the west edge (Feature 2, fig. 6.10) does not continue south of the other wall. The gap between the two walls may have served as an entryway into the camp, with a short, oddly configured wall (Feature 43, fig. 6.10) restricting the approach.

The southern half of the campground (fig. 6.11) extends across a narrow, relatively level area cleared of almost all surface stone. This area contains faint, almost imperceptible ground anomalies, suggesting that it contained a tent camp. Along the western edge of the plateau lies the third group of features, closely bunched together. The northern half of this cluster consists of randomly placed stone piles. These piles have no structural integrity and perhaps represent efforts at consolidating surface stone. The southern group of features, on the other hand, is comprised of two well-defined rows which contain a mix of small stone foundations and stone piles.

## Discussion

When the Federals moved onto Maryland Heights and began constructing their extensive line of fortifications and supporting campground areas, a cultural and natural landscape was already in place on the mountain. Engineers used these landscapes to advantage in positioning the new defensive works, and altered them as needed. In the case of the cultural landscape, the military made heavy use of, and extensively improved, an intricate network of pre-existing charcoal roads. While these roads may not have influenced placement of the fortifications to a large degree, they did aid in initial construction efforts and provided a base for the subsequent military road network which serviced the defensive works and their supporting infantry and artillery encampments.

At the time of the Civil War, the mountain slopes were covered with a tangled young forest, also a product of clear-cutting by the early nineteenth-century charcoaling industry about twenty years earlier. When cut, these young trees provided an effective defense against infantry attack as ersatz abatis. In civilian claims filed against the U.S. government after the war, destruction of timber lots was the primary loss recorded, with little other civilian property on Maryland Heights damaged or destroyed.

Through trial and error, the Union command came to understand the significance of the mountain's natural landscape and how to use it effectively. The Naval Battery, while presenting a credible defense against attack from the west, was woefully insufficient in view of the total defensive requirements for Harpers Ferry. The Stone Fort, while impressive in appearance and perhaps filling a psychological need to feel invincible, did not adequately address the defense of the crest. Construction of the earthen north parapet of the Interior Fort, in fact, rendered the Stone Fort ineffective as a defensive position. Other fortifications, specifically Fort Duncan, the 30-Pounder Battery, the 100-Pounder Battery, and the entrenchments linking them, however, reveal a carefully laid-out system which incorporated the existing natural and cultural terrain. This system indeed did render Maryland Heights almost invincible.

When Federal troops occupied Maryland Heights, they carried with them the *United States Army Regulations of 1861* and its revised edition published two years later. This official manual described in detail the camp layout for an infantry regiment of one thousand men (U.S. Government Printing Office 1863: 75–76). A regulation camp measured 400 paces (roughly 1,200 feet) across its front and 431 paces (approximately 1,300 feet) along its flanks. The tents were arranged in ranks and files, the number of ranks varying with the strength of the companies and the size of the tents. Each company pitched its tents in two files perpendicular to the color line and facing a street. Artillery camps were laid out by battery. For example, for a battery of six pieces, the men established tents in three files—one for each section (two guns) (U.S. Government Printing Office 1863: 80).

The two irregularly laid out campground areas described in the preceding section represent only a portion of the Civil War occupation on Maryland Heights. None of the recorded campground areas on the mountain, however, followed the *Regulations*. In fact, no two campgrounds had the same layout, although the range and types of features generally were similar. Given the steep and inaccessible mountain slopes, broken only by narrow plateaus paralleling the crest, it is not surprising that irregularities in camp layout existed. The ephemeral nature of many of the archaeological features, along with difficulties in identifying the functions of the few substantial structures, limit our understanding of how these camps looked and functioned in their heyday. In addition, military groups frequently reused abandoned campground areas, rearranging and sometimes rebuilding them to suit their own needs.

A striking contrast emerges between historical accounts of camp shelters and the archaeological survey results. While contemporary writings almost exclusively emphasize wood construction, the archaeological survey predictably recorded stone features and obvious ground disturbances. As a result, this survey probably recorded only a fraction of what historically stood upon Maryland Heights. For example, while the general location of the Signal Corps camp depicted in the charcoal drawing is known, no above-ground traces of this campground have been discovered.

The soldiers garrisoned on the mountain actively molded their physical surroundings to create hospitable living spaces. Using materials close at hand—wood and stone—they leveled tent platforms, constructed log and stone foundations to raise tents off the ground, and erected comfortable log cabins to fend off the cold winter winds. These soldiers cleared stone from the ground surface and used it to construct a variety of structures, as well as crude, meandering walls which extended across the mountain slope.

During the archaeological survey it became evident that little conformity or consistency existed in construction of quarters and other buildings, even in those located adjacent to each other. Each person or group apparently improvised, some doing a better job than others. This spirit of improvisation is evident within the journals and letters of the men stationed on Maryland Heights as well. Such improvisation probably was the norm rather than the exception, as descriptions of other impermanent Civil War campgrounds reveal similar degrees of irregularity in camp layout and construction (Nelson 1982).

In addition to defining camp layout, the *United States Army Regulations of 1861* (U.S. Government Printing Office 1863: 75–76) provided several criteria for locating suitable campground areas. The manual required officers to consider whether the site (1) provided for the health and comfort of the troops, (2) facilitated good communication, (3) offered convenient supplies of wood and water, and (4) provided adequate resources in provisions and food. Maryland Heights met none of these criteria, yet thousands of men spent long months garrisoned on its narrow plateaus and steep slopes. Military considerations obviously overrode concerns for material comfort, although many examples exist in regimental order books of regulations issued by high command to provide as much as possible for the general health of the soldiers.

In sum, military regulations prescribed order and regularity in the layout and construction of fortifications and campgrounds. These regulations obviously were not followed on Maryland Heights, presumably due to the harsh physical terrain. The archaeological evidence and historical documentation reveal an apparent latitude in shelter placement and construction, however, that was not due entirely to physical constraints. Indeed, the variety of construction techniques and sizes of shelters points to individual problem solving and creativity on the part of those who bivouacked on the Heights.

# 7

*W. Stephen McBride*

## CIVIL WAR MATERIAL CULTURE AND CAMP LIFE IN CENTRAL KENTUCKY

*Archaeological Investigations at Camp Nelson*

In fall 1989, the University of Kentucky's Program for Cultural Resource Assessment conducted archaeological survey and excavation along a portion of an AT&T fiber-optics line easement, twenty feet wide. The easement passed through the Civil War era Union quartermaster's depot known as Camp Nelson, in Jessamine County, Kentucky (McBride and Sharp 1991). This project resulted in the location of two sites, the Camp Nelson Hospital and Convalescent Camp (15Js112) and the Camp Nelson Machine Shop (15Js113).

Further excavation also occurred on two previously recorded sites, the Camp Nelson Headquarters Complex (15Js96) and the Owens' House/Camp Nelson Post Office Complex (15Js97). These four sites and the AT&T easement were located just to the west of the old Lexington and Danville Turnpike (present U.S. Highway 27). This strip of land comprised the western edge of Camp Nelson. The entire camp covered approximately four thousand acres (fig. 7.1).

The excavations at the Headquarters Complex and

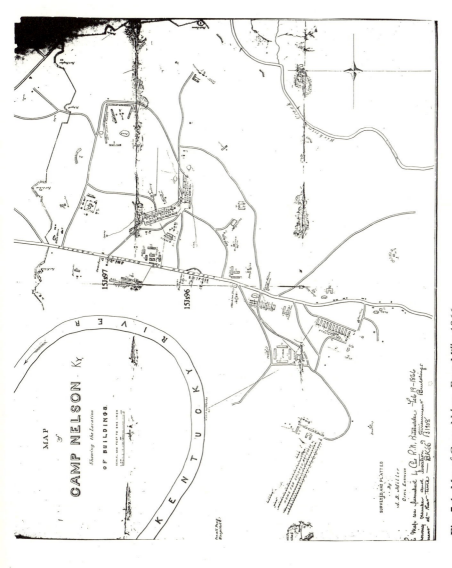

**Fig. 7.1.** *Map of Camp Nelson. From Miller 1866.*

the southern half of the Owens' House/Post Office Complex are the focus of this chapter. These two sites were chosen because archival records and observed archaeological deposits indicated that these locations had been occupied only during the Civil War. Although only a small portion of the Headquarters Complex and the Owens' House/ Post Office Complex were within the AT&T corridor, and therefore excavated, the unmixed Civil War period deposits examined at these sites allow a glimpse into the material aspects of a Civil War garrison in central Kentucky. More specifically, these sites allow an examination of the nature of supplies, arms, provisions, and personal goods at a Kentucky garrison and a comparison with such items from other Civil War sites. This focus, far from common in past Civil War historical research, is ideally suited to illustrate the strengths of historical archaeology.

## History of Camp Nelson

When the Civil War began on April 12, 1861, Kentucky found itself in an awkward position. It was a slave state that did not support secession, and its population was divided on whether to support military action against the seceding states. Initially, Kentucky's political leaders, especially Gov. Beriah Magoffin, attempted to keep Kentucky neutral and both Union and Confederate armies out of the state. This neutrality could only be maintained for a short time, however. By August 1861, it was officially breached when General William Nelson established a Union recruitment and training camp (Camp Dick Robinson) in Garrard County. By September 1861, the neutrality was further eroded as both Confederate and Federal armies began moving into western Kentucky. The final blow came in fall 1861, when a decidedly pro-Union legislature was seated. By the end of 1861, Kentucky found itself split, with Union troops occupying the northern two-thirds of the state and the Confederates occupying the southern one-third.

The Confederate presence in Kentucky was short-lived, however. In February 1862, General Ulysses S. Grant led his Federal troops from the Paducah, Kentucky, area and captured Fort Henry and Fort Donelson in northwestern Tennessee. The fall of these forts and the movement of Federal troops from Louisville under General Don Carlos Buell led to the Confederate abandonment of all positions in western and central Kentucky, and even the abandonment of Nashville (Harrison 1975). The only Confederate forces and fortifications remaining in Kentucky after winter 1862 were in the southeastern part of the state.

The Confederates were not through with Kentucky, however, for between mid-August and early October 1862, General Kirby Smith and twelve thousand Confederates entered central Kentucky from eastern Tennessee, while General Braxton Bragg and twenty-seven thousand men entered southern Kentucky from Chattanooga (Harrison 1975). This campaign resulted in Confederate victories at Richmond and Rogersville and the capture of Frankfort, where Bragg attempted to establish a Confederate government in Kentucky. Bragg hoped that by installing a government, he could increase recruitment and even enact a draft (Harrison 1975; Street 1985). In fact, stimulating pro-Confederate sympathies and recruitment was a major reason for the Kentucky invasion (Harrison 1975).

The Confederate campaign culminated in the Battle of Perryville, where fifteen thousand of Bragg's troops stumbled upon Union General Buell's army of sixty thousand, which had moved down from Louisville. On October 8, 1862, after two days of fighting, Bragg withdrew his troops southward into Tennessee.

Following the invasion of Kentucky by Confederate forces under Generals Bragg and Smith between August and October 1862, the Union command in Kentucky realized that one of its large recruitment centers, Camp Dick Robinson, was vulnerable because of its location on the southern side of the Kentucky River in Garrard County. It was soon decided that the camp should be moved to the northern side of the river (Bartnik 1976).

In June 1863, Major General Ambrose Burnside, commander of the Army of the Ohio, ordered Lieutenant Colonel J. H. Simpson of the Engineering Department to select a site and begin construction of a new camp (Bartnik 1976: 1). The selected site was along the Lexington-Danville Turnpike, about six miles south of Nicholasville (fig. 7.1). The total encampment, which contained approximately four thousand acres, was named Camp Nelson after Major General William Nelson, who had established Camp Dick Robinson. Because of its strategic location on a major transportation route between the Ohio Valley and Tennessee, Camp Nelson soon became a major quartermaster depot, recruitment center, and hospital for the Federal armies operating in Kentucky and East Tennessee.

Bounded on its southern and western sides by the deeply entrenched Kentucky River and on the east by Hickman Creek, Camp Nelson was much more easily defended than Camp Dick Robinson. The only exposed area of the camp was its northern edge. Along this edge a line of eight forts or batteries, rifle entrenchments, and abatis were constructed (fig. 7.1). All trees were cleared to the north of this line to a distance of 1,500 yards, except on the slope to the northwest (Bartnik 1976: 6). Additional fortifications also were placed to the south along Hickman Creek (Battery Studdiford) and the Kentucky River (Fort Bramlette).

Within the camp, numerous structures associated with its functions as quartermaster depot and recruitment center were constructed. These buildings included dozens of warehouses to store rations, clothing, and equipment; stables and sheds to house thousands of horses and mules and their feed; workshops; a saw mill; a machine shop; a prison; a post office; numerous barracks, offices, and mess halls; and the camp headquarters. Most of these buildings, including the headquarters and post office, were identified on 1864 and 1866 maps of Camp Nelson (A. B. Miller 1866; Simpson 1864). A large hospital facility and convalescent camp also were established on the south side of Camp Nelson (fig. 7.1). The hospital received running water from a 500,000-gallon reservoir located on a hill to its rear. Water was pumped up to the reservoir from the Kentucky River four hundred feet below. By the end of the war, as many as three hundred buildings were located within the camp (Bartnik 1976: 3; Hall 1865).

A number of domestic structures already situated within the camp boundaries were commandeered and used by the army. These included the "Owens' House," the "White House," and, undoubtedly, other structures (Bartnik 1976: 3).

Union supplies were shipped to Nicholasville via railroad and then brought to Camp Nelson by wagon. Supplies were stored in the various warehouses and sheds at Camp Nelson until needed by the Union army operating further south, primarily in Tennessee. Some equipment, such as wagons and carriages, actually was constructed or repaired at shops located within Camp Nelson (Hall 1865).

During the initial months of the camp's existence, several regiments were briefly stationed there, including the 6th New Hampshire Infantry, the 3rd Battery of the 1st Ohio Heavy Artillery, Company G of the 14th Kentucky Cavalry, and the 91st Indiana Infantry. During this initial period, the highest ranking of the regimental commanders apparently was in charge of the camp. By 1864, the camp seems to have stabilized, and units were stationed there for longer periods of time. Brigadier General Speed S. Fry was placed in charge of the camp in winter 1863–64. Regiments with longer tours at the camp included the 104th Ohio Infantry, Company F of the 43rd Indiana Infantry, the 22nd Indiana Artillery, the 9th Tennessee Cavalry, and the 47th and 49th Kentucky Mounted Infantry (U.S. National Archives RG 92: E64; U.S. National Archives, Returns U.S. Military Posts M-617, Roll 1527). Two U.S. Veteran Reserve Corps companies (the 61st and 125th) also were stationed for a time at Camp Nelson (Davis, Perry, and Kirkley 1892: 330).

Several regiments were organized and trained at Camp Nelson, including the 47th and 49th Kentucky Mounted Infantry Regiments and Battery E of the Kentucky Light Artillery in 1863 (Dyer 1959). The majority of regiments formed at the camp, however, were U.S. Colored Regiments. The U.S. Colored Regiments also were stationed at the camp for longer periods of time than most others.

After the February 1864 Enrollment Act, which provided specifically for the enrollment of African-American males, a flood of ex-slaves began arriving at Camp Nelson. By August 1864, two thousand black enrollees were at the camp (Lucas 1989: 442). By the end of the war, about ten thousand men, or 40 percent of Kentucky's African-American soldiers, had passed through Camp Nelson, making it the most important recruitment center for African Americans in Kentucky (Lucas 1989: 441). African-American regiments formed at Camp Nelson included the 114th, 116th, 119th, and 124th U.S. Colored Infantry; the 5th and 6th U.S. Colored Cavalry; and the 12th and 13th U.S. Colored Heavy Artillery Regiments (Dyer 1959: 1720–40).

The African-American recruits brought not only themselves to Camp

Nelson, but often their families as well. Families came for many reasons, including fear of retaliation by angry slaveholders and anticipation of better opportunities or even emancipation for the entire family (Lucas 1989; Sears 1986). Later, in winter 1864–65, Assistant Quartermaster Captain Theron E. Hall was appointed superintendent of the refugees and immediately began building barracks to house them (Lucas 1989: 448; Sears 1986: 15). The barracks eventually were found to be inadequate, and in spring 1865, duplex cottages were constructed in the southwestern part of the camp, which was designated the "Home for Colored Refugees" (fig. 7.1) (Lucas 1989: 449). By June 1865, the refugee homes provided housing for 3,060 people, primarily women and children (Sears 1987: 40).

Soon after the war ended in April 1865, military officials began preparing to close Camp Nelson. Inventories of serviceable and unserviceable equipment and supplies were made between spring 1865 and winter 1866. Buildings were also described and inventoried, and decisions were made whether to keep, sell, or dispose of the various items and buildings (Meigs 1865, 1866; Resticaux 1865). After the spring of 1865, the majority of troops occupying Camp Nelson were African Americans and, in fact, African-American troops continued to be enlisted at Camp Nelson as a means of emancipating them until December 1865, when the Thirteenth Amendment was passed. In June 1866, the army finally abandoned Camp Nelson, ending military occupation of the area.

## Archaeological Investigations at the Headquarters Complex and the Owens' House/Post Office Complex

### Field Investigations

The Headquarters Complex (15Js96) and the Owens' House/Post Office Complex (15Js97) initially were identified during investigations associated with anticipated highway construction (Schock 1987). These earlier excavations were located to the west of the AT&T corridor (figs. 7.2 and 7.3) and established the general boundaries of the two site complexes. The University of Kentucky investigations, however, were restricted to the corridor.

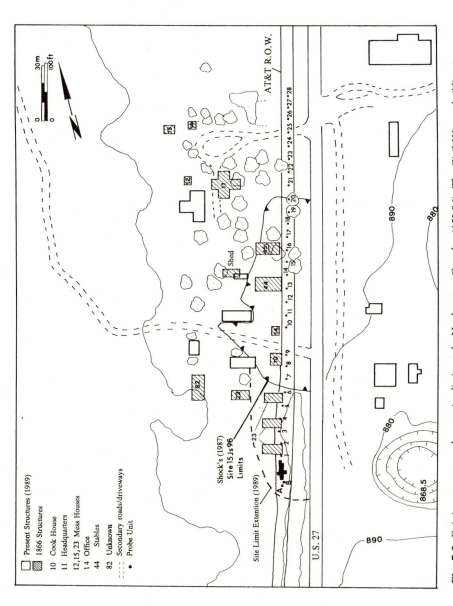

**Fig. 7.2.** *Existing structures and excavation limits at the Headquarters Complex (15Js96). The Civil War era buildings are superimposed. From Miller 1866.*

The University of Kentucky archaeological investigations of the Headquarters Complex and the Owens' House/Post Office Complex began with the excavation of units fifty centimeters square, placed every seven to fourteen meters along the center of the AT&T right-of-way (McBride and Sharp 1991). At the Headquarters Complex, this line of units extended just to the front of the main line of Civil War structures, which included offices, cook houses, stables, mess halls, and the headquarters building (fig. 7.2). Block excavations were conducted across a dense concentration of Civil War period architectural debris and refuse discovered at the south end of the site. This concentration, located approximately ten meters south of a documented mess hall, produced a large quantity of ceramics, bottle glass, clothing and personal items, arms and military accouterments, nails, window glass, and faunal remains. No other concentrations of historic materials were found along the easement portion of the Headquarters Complex.

At the Owens' House/Post Office Complex, excavation resulted in the discovery of the Owens' House foundation and cultural deposits dating from the early to the late nineteenth century (fig. 7.3). The archaeological discovery of the Owens' House foundation in the northern part of the site, and the possible position of Civil War era structures, resulted in a shifting of the AT&T trench to the eastern edge of the right-of-way. Four larger test units (1 by 2 meters) were dug along this new trench line, but since no dense concentrations of artifacts or features were encountered in these units, no further work was recommended.

Excavations conducted in the Owens' House/Post Office Complex, along with documentary data such as maps and deeds, did identify the remains of a discreet Civil War period occupation in the southern half of this test area. Artifacts found here included whiteware, ironstone, modern cut nails, and mid- to late-nineteenth-century bottle glass. The northern half of the site also contained Civil War materials, but pre–Civil War materials, such as creamware, pearlware, and wrought nails, and post–Civil War materials, such as wire nails and machine-made bottle glass, were recovered as well.

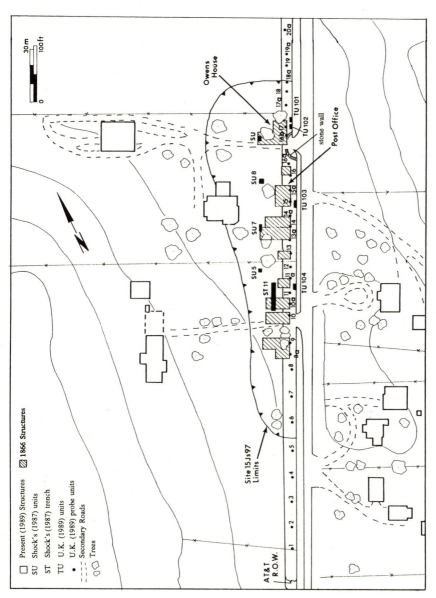

**Fig. 7.3.** *Existing structures and excavation limits at the Owens' House/Post Office Complex (15Js97). The Civil War era buildings are superimposed. From Miller 1866.*

*Artifact Analysis*

While only a small sample of each of the two Camp Nelson sites was excavated during the AT&T project, a number of interesting artifact patterns were noted that, even given the possible biases of a small sample size, appear to reflect the material conditions and supply system of a Civil War camp. These patterns are particularly evident when the Camp Nelson material is compared to other Civil War encampments and to contemporaneous domestic sites. Especially informative artifact groups include refined ceramics, table glassware, bottle glass, clothing items, personal items, nails, arms and ammunition, and faunal remains. In the discussion to follow, these artifact types will be utilized to investigate the furnishing of equipment, provisions, and other goods to camp inhabitants, and also to examine the general material culture conditions of camp life.

Ceramic dishes, such as plates, cups, saucers, and bowls, do not immediately come to mind when one thinks of Civil War equipment, particularly when narratives and photographs usually discuss or illustrate tin cups and plates and split canteens as more typical. Ceramics often were used at encampments, however, and have been found archaeologically on both long- and short-term encampments (Lewis 1963; Mainfort 1980). The types of ceramics used and the variations between different encampment types or locations have been unclear. The ceramics recovered at Camp Nelson will be utilized to examine these questions.

The assemblage of refined ceramics excavated at the Camp Nelson sites includes whiteware, ironstone (white granite), and porcelain. Whiteware and ironstone differ in that the latter has a harder, semi-vitreous, or at least nearly nonporous, paste. In the mid-nineteenth century, ironstone was prized for its durability (George Miller 1980, 1991). The majority of the Camp Nelson Civil War era ceramics came from the Headquarters Complex and included 274 whiteware, 139 ironstone, and 7 porcelain sherds (table 7.1). All but two of these sherds were found in the excavation block located downhill from the site of a mess hall (fig. 7.2). None of the whiteware or porcelain sherds was decorated; only eleven ironstone sherds were color decorated (painted, printed, slipped, or sponged) and three molded. The refined ceramic sherds were inter-

**Table 7.1**. Comparison of Ceramics from Camp Nelson and Other Sites

|  | Ironstone | | Color Decorated | |
| --- | --- | --- | --- | --- |
|  | % of Sherds | % of Vessels | % of Sherds | % of Vessels |
| Headquarters | 33.1 | 60.0 | 2.6 | 8.0 |
| Owens' House | 29.6 | 50.0 | 7.4 | 16.7 |
| Fort Pillow | — | — | 21.9 | 20.9 |
| Barton Sites | 3.0–14.3 | 11.3–22.7 | 21.5–30.5 | 39.8–61.3 |
| Crazy Dog, F.1 | 3.3 | — | 38.4 | — |
| Fall Creek, F.1 ` | 8.3 | — | 24.19 | — |
| Speckhardt, F.1 | 31.8 | — | 4.5 | — |
| Carr, F.25 | 37.3 | — | — | — |

preted to represent a minimum of 1 porcelain, 9 whiteware, and 15 ironstone vessels.

A much lower frequency of refined ceramics was recovered in the southern half of the Owens' House/Post Office Complex. The assemblage from this area includes 19 whiteware sherds (two color decorated) and 8 ironstone sherds (one molded), representing a minimum of three whiteware and three ironstone vessels.

Comparative material on ceramics from other Civil War Union encampments is limited, but at Fort Pillow in western Tennessee, a large sample of ceramics was recovered. Fort Pillow was a Union fortification and encampment occupied by part of seven regiments or batteries from 1862 to 1864 (Mainfort 1980). At Fort Pillow, 20.9 percent of the refined ceramic sherds and vessels are color decorated (Mainfort 1980). This figure is slightly higher but similar to the figures for Camp Nelson sites. Interestingly, 64 percent of the Fort Pillow decorated vessels are only "minimally decorated" (sponged, slipped, or edge decorated; see Miller 1980), suggesting a preference toward plainer wares. Unfortunately, ironstone was not systematically separated from whiteware in the Fort Pillow study.

Another Union encampment to receive extensive excavation was Folly Island, South Carolina (Legg and Smith 1989). This site was occupied for one winter by two infantry regiments and one artillery battery. Only three refined ceramic sherds (one plain, two color decorated) were found at the Folly Island site. This near absence of refined ceramics is likely related both to the short occupation and the extreme isolation of this site on the South Carolina coast.

When compared to domestic sites of the middle to late nineteenth century, the Camp Nelson and Fort Pillow assemblages are notable for their high proportion of ironstone and low proportion of color-decorated wares. Table 7.1 presents the proportion of ironstone and color-decorated refined ceramics at the Civil War sites; four Barton, Mississippi, house sites; and four Illinois farmsteads. Since no archaeological studies of domestic sites occupied only during the Civil War could be found, sites whose occupation bracketed or fell near the Civil War were chosen for comparison. The four Barton house sites dated from around 1850 to 1870 and roughly represent middle- to lower-middle-class merchants, professionals, and craftsmen (W. Stephen McBride and Kim A. McBride 1987; W. Stephen McBride 1991). The Illinois sites include two deposits which dated from about 1855 to 1870 (Crazy Dog, Feature 1; and Fall Creek, Feature 1) and two deposits which dated from around 1870 to 1890 (Speckhart, Feature 1; and Carr, Feature 25) (Mansberger 1986). All of these farmsteads had basically middle-class occupants, except for Speckhart, the residents of which were somewhat less well off (McCorvie 1988).

The only domestic sites similar to the Civil War sites in the proportion of ironstone and color-decorated wares are the two late-nineteenth-century components from the sites in Illinois. These two deposits dated from a period when the price difference between whiteware and ironstone was diminishing and the cost of color-decorated wares was quite high (Esarey 1982; George Miller 1991). The comparisons with domestic sites again illustrate the military's preference, at least at Camp Nelson and probably at Fort Pillow, for plain, durable wares. The long-term nature of both encampments makes it likely that the majority of the ceramics found were furnished by the army. This is particularly true at the Headquarters Complex, where most ceramics were recovered from the vicinity of a mess hall. The comparison with Folly Island suggests that short-term, more isolated encampments can differ greatly in the equipment used for food consumption.

The types of ceramic vessels represented in an assemblage have been shown to reflect food preparation and consumption behavior (Otto 1977). The vessel forms represented in the Headquarters Complex assemblage include five cups (one painted and sponged), six saucers, three bowls, nine plates, and two serving vessels. This assemblage certainly reflects food consumption behavior at the nearby mess hall. The low ratio of bowls to plates (1:3) suggests that soups or stews probably were not the primary meal form served in this mess hall (see Otto 1977). Unfortunately, the vessel count at the Owens' House/Post Office Complex is too small for reliable functional or dietary interpretation. The vessel form proportions at the Headquarters Complex are exactly like those found at Fort Pillow, Tennessee, which suggests a similar diet.

The meat cuts represented in the faunal remains from the Headquarters Complex also suggest that soups or stews were not the primary meal form served in the mess hall. Identifiable faunal elements suggest that the most common pork cuts were hams, feet, and ribs, while the most common beef cuts were short ribs, round steak, and sirloin (Tune 1991). These cuts are primarily of a high to medium quality, which may be related to the likely high proportion of officers at the Headquarters. Again, the faunal sample from the southern half of the Owens' House/ Post Office Complex is too small for this analysis. Like Camp Nelson, the Union encampment at Folly Island, South Carolina, also had fairly high-quality beef and pork cuts at one camp locale (38CH965) (Snyder 1989). At another locale (38CH964), however, the beef cuts were primarily lower-value stew or soup meat cuts, while the pork cuts were of a higher quality (Snyder 1989). The reason for this variability at Folly Island is unclear at present. Unfortunately, no discussion of meat cuts was presented for Fort Pillow (Mainfort 1980).

The most striking aspect of the faunal material from the Headquarters Complex at Camp Nelson, when compared to the Fort Pillow and Folly Island collections, is the difference in species composition (table 7.2). At both Folly Island, South Carolina, and Fort Pillow, Tennessee, cattle bones predominated, accounting for between 65.0 and 87.9 per-

**Table 7.2.** Comparison of Faunal Remains from the Headquarters Complex and Other Sites

| | Camp Nelson Headquarters | | Camp Nelson Owens' Complex | | Folly Island 964 and 965 | | Fort Pillow Fort | | Fort Pillow Barracks | |
|---|---|---|---|---|---|---|---|---|---|---|
| Type | N | % | N | % | N | % | N | % | N | % |
| Cow | 8 | 22.2 | 1 | 50.0 | 516 | 77.0 | 78 | 65.0 | 51 | 87.9 |
| Pig | 12 | 33.3 | 1 | 50.0 | 150 | 22.4 | 42 | 35.0 | 6 | 10.3 |
| Sheep | 5 | 13.9 | 0 | – | 3 | 0.4 | 0 | – | 0 | – |
| Chicken | 4 | 11.1 | 0 | – | 0 | – | 0 | – | 1 | 1.7 |
| Turkey | 2 | 5.6 | 0 | – | 1 | 0.1 | 0 | – | 0 | – |
| Rabbit | 5 | 13.9 | 0 | – | 0 | – | 0 | – | 0 | – |
| Total | 36 | 100.0 | 2 | 100.0 | 670 | 99.9 | 120 | 100.0 | 58 | 99.9 |

cent of the identified food remains (Mainfort 1980; Snyder 1989). The dominance of beef seems to have been the norm in many Union camps, although this is not well documented (Lord 1960: 118). At the Headquarters Complex, cattle skeletal elements accounted for only 22.2 percent of the identified food remains, while pig elements comprised 33.3 percent of the remains. There was also a much greater variety of animal remains at the Headquarters Complex than at Fort Pillow or Folly Island. At the Headquarters Complex, 44.5 percent of the identified remains were species other than cow or pig (table 7.2). Unfortunately, only two identified faunal elements (one cow and one pig) were recovered from the southern half of the Owens' House/Post Office Complex.

The dominance of pork over beef remains at the Headquarters Complex is typical of the Upland South pattern present in domestic sites in Kentucky and bordering states. On four rural nineteenth-century sites from this region (Baldridge and Davis in Illinois, Johnson–Bates in Kentucky, Wynnewood in Tennessee), pig elements accounted for 41.5 to 62.4 percent of the identified faunal food elements, while cow elements ranged from only 1.7 to 28.9 percent (Breitburg 1983; McCorvie 1987; O'Malley 1987). The other identified fauna from these four sites included four to twelve other species, which accounted for 8.7 to 56.8 percent of the identified faunal food elements.

The faunal assemblage found at the Headquarters Complex probably reflects local meat availability and preferences, as well as more autonomous procurement practices at the camp level resulting from Camp Nelson's longevity and its location in Union territory. Fort Pillow and Folly Island were located in more isolated and hostile areas, and Folly Island had a much shorter occupation. The presence of officers and civilians at the Headquarters area also may have influenced the diet selected. Comparisons with other areas of Camp Nelson are needed to understand more fully the causes of the observed faunal pattern.

The table glassware, buttons, and personal items recovered from the Headquarters Complex and the Owens' House/Post Office Complex also exhibit a domestic or civilian pattern. All of these artifact types occur in a greater variety than expected in a military site, especially when compared to artifact assemblages from other Civil War encampments.

Table glassware from the Headquarters Complex and the Owens' House/Post Office Complex includes fragments from at least two fancy fluted tumblers, one stemmed goblet, and two or three other tumblers or stemware. All of these vessels, except one or two tumblers, came from the Headquarters Complex. The glassware vessels are fancier and more fragile than ones found at Folly Island and Fort Pillow. Only one glass tumbler (or mug) fragment each was recovered from Folly Island, South Carolina, which was occupied for one winter, and from Fort Pillow, Tennessee, which was occupied for two years. Both of these sites received more extensive excavation than the Camp Nelson Headquarters Complex or the Owens' House/Post Office Complex (Legg and Smith 1989; Mainfort 1980). The permanence of Camp Nelson and the presence of high-ranking officers at the Headquarters probably contributed to the presence of the table glassware.

The variety of buttons found at the Camp Nelson Headquarters Complex is particularly striking and illustrates the complexity of activities which took place at this site. (No buttons were found in the southern half of the Owens' House/Post Office Complex, although a General Service eagle button was found in the northern half of that site.) The Headquarters Complex assemblage included a U.S. Army General

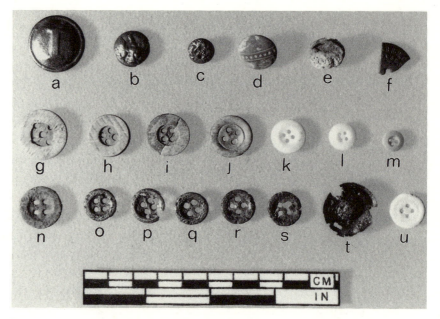

**Fig. 7.4.** *Buttons recovered at the Headquarters Complex: (a) Confederate Army infantry button, (b) U.S. Army eagle button, (c) gilded brass button, (d) enameled brass button, (e) glass and iron button, (f) rubber button, (g–j) bone buttons, (k–m) glass buttons, (n–s) four-hole iron button, (t) riveted iron button, and (u) shell button. Courtesy of the Program for Cultural Resource Assessment and the University of Kentucky.*

Service eagle button, as well as other common military or civilian cloth-ing/underwear buttons, such as four-hole iron buttons, four- and five-hole bone buttons, and four-hole milk-glass buttons (fig. 7.4). The iron buttons were typical trouser-fly and suspender buttons, while the bone and glass buttons probably were from shirts or underwear (Herskovitz 1978: 41, 129; Legg and Smith 1989: 100; Scott and Fox 1987: 92). Iron, bone, and milk-glass buttons commonly have been found on other Union Civil War encampments (see Legg and Smith 1989; Mainfort 1980).

Distinctly nonmilitary buttons from the Headquarters Complex in-clude one stamped and gilded brass button, one stamped and enameled brass button, one iron-backed white glass button, one four-hole shell button, and one four-hole blue glass button (fig. 7.4). The brass buttons and the iron-and-glass button are probably from jackets or dresses, while the shell and blue glass buttons probably are from shirts or underwear.

When compared to the button assemblage from the Union encampments at Folly Island, South Carolina, and Fort Pillow, Tennessee, the Headquarters Complex material is quite distinct. The South Carolina and Tennessee sites have a much higher proportion of eagle buttons (25.3 and 50.2 percent, respectively) than the Headquarters Complex (3.8 percent) (Legg and Smith 1989; Mainfort 1980). Perhaps the most dramatic difference between these two sites and the Headquarters Complex is the lesser variety of buttons at the former two sites, even though their sample sizes are much larger. At the Headquarters Complex are 13 distinctive button types out of 26 buttons. At Fort Pillow and Folly Island, there are only 5 types out of 229, and 9 types out of 79 buttons, respectively. At Folly Island and Fort Pillow, 86.1 and 97.8 percent, respectively, of the buttons are of the three main types: eagle, four-hole iron, and four-hole milk glass. At the Headquarters Complex, only 50 percent of the buttons are of these types.

The variation in button types is interpreted to reflect the complex functional nature of Camp Nelson. Not only did soldiers working and living there have access to more nonmilitary goods than soldiers at the front, but also Camp Nelson employed a large number of civilians to perform various tasks at the camp. Camp Nelson likely was also more accessible to visiting families of the soldiers. The high proportion of officers at the Headquarters Complex may have also been a factor in the button pattern, since officers may have had fancier undergarments and may have worn more civilian clothing than enlisted men.

The personal items recovered from the two Camp Nelson sites afford insights into life at the camp and again underline the diversity of the activities and occupants there. Personal items from the Headquarters Complex include a brass watch key and chain, four rubber comb fragments, a rubber hairpiece fragment, a porcelain doll leg, a porcelain marble, a brass tintype frame, a white glass bead, a graphite pencil, a slate board fragment, a brass thimble, and a white clay pipestem (fig. 7.5). Personal items from the Owens' House/Post Office Complex (southern half) include seventy watch crystal fragments, three iron watch keys, one watch chain tag, one rubber comb tooth, and one brass thimble.

Items such as the comb fragments, the watch parts and accessories, the pencil and slate board fragment, the tintype frame, the thimbles, and

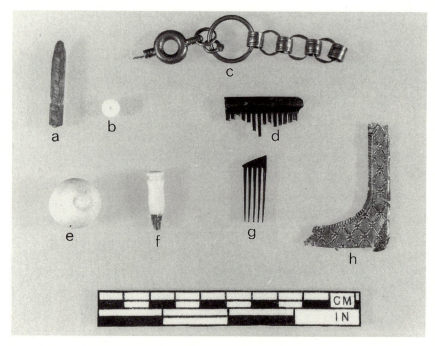

***Fig. 7.5.*** *Personal items recovered at the Headquarters Complex: (a) pencil, (b) glass bead, (c) watch chain and key, (d) rubber comb, (e) marble, (f) porcelain doll leg, (g) rubber comb, and (h) tintype frame. Courtesy of the Program for Cultural Resource Assessment and the University of Kentucky.*

even the marble are items typically possessed by soldiers or officers. The rubber hairpiece, glass bead, and doll's leg, however, point to the probable presence of women and children. Whether the women and children were visiting, living, or working at the Headquarters Complex is unclear, but the presence of these personal items again illustrates the diverse and sometimes nonmilitary character of events taking place in at least this part of Camp Nelson.

Functionally identified bottle fragments from the Headquarters Complex and Owens' House/Post Office Complex provide information on the types of liquids consumed or utilized by soldiers at Camp Nelson. At the Headquarters Complex, medicine or chemical bottles of various types are the most common, followed by alcoholic beverage bottles. One stoneware ale bottle base was found at the Headquarters Complex. In the southern half of the Owens' House/Post Office Complex, only one soda/mineral water bottle lip and one medicine bottle fragment were recovered.

The alcohol bottles from the Headquarters Complex include whiskey, ale, and wine or champagne. These kinds of alcoholic beverages were readily available to officers from sutlers or other sources, including hospitals and nearby towns (James I. Robertson 1984: 60). Although sutlers were generally prohibited from selling alcohol to enlisted men, this regulation often was not strictly enforced (James I. Robertson 1984: 58–60). Soldiers also smuggled whiskey into camp (Legg and Smith 1989: 118; James I. Robertson 1984: 58–60). Alcohol bottles are common artifacts at other Civil War encampments (Legg and Smith 1989: 121; Phelps 1979).

The composition of the bottle assemblage at the Headquarters Complex differs somewhat from those of the other two Union Civil War encampments examined. At both Folly Island, South Carolina, and Fort Pillow, Tennessee, over 75 percent of the identified glass and stoneware bottles were liquor bottles, while only about a third of the bottles at the Headquarters Complex held alcoholic beverages (Legg and Smith 1989; Mainfort 1980). The reason for this difference is unclear, but possible explanations include tighter control of alcohol consumption at the camp headquarters or at Camp Nelson in general, preference for other areas such as barracks for alcohol consumption, fewer feelings of isolation among the Camp Nelson soldiers, or more opportunities to consume alcohol elsewhere. It is also possible that the greater proportion of medicine bottles at the Headquarters Complex is related to the presence of a nearby hospital.

Although only a small number of arms and ammunition–related artifacts was recovered from the Headquarters Complex and the Owens' House/Post Office Complex, those items that were found inform us about arms supply in the western theater in general and at a permanent encampment in particular. At the Headquarters Complex four gun parts were recovered, including two barrel bands from a Model 1816 Springfield, one Enfield Rifle barrel band, and one Model 1858 Remington revolver loading lever (fig. 7.6). The Enfield and Remington were typical Civil War era weapons, but the 1816 Springfield was not typical of a

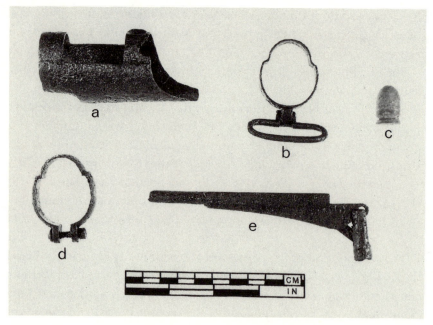

**Fig. 7.6.** *Arms and ammunition recovered at the Headquarters Complex: (a–b) Model 1816 Springfield barrel bands, (c) Williams Type III bullet, (d) Enfield barrel band, and (e) Model 1858 Remington loading lever. Courtesy of the Program for Cultural Resource Assessment and the University of Kentucky.*

1863–66 site (Coates and Thomas 1990: 8; William C. Davis 1989: 171). The 1816 Springfield originally was a smoothbore flintlock musket, although most of these guns had been converted to percussion by the time of the Civil War (Coates and Thomas 1990: 8–9; Lord 1960: 140). The presence of such an antiquated weapon so late in the war is probably related to Camp Nelson's position away from hostile lines. Soldiers at Camp Nelson included some Veteran Reserve Corps and U.S. Colored Regiments, which sometimes received inferior weapons (Berlin 1982: 485; Davis 1989: 171).

Ammunition recovered from the Headquarters Complex and the southern half of the Owens' House/Post Office Complex includes a .58-caliber Williams Type III bullet, a carved .54-caliber bullet, and three .22-caliber short brass cartridges (fig. 7.6). The Williams Type III bullet was first produced in 1863 and was sometimes referred to as a "cleaner," because it removed residue from the rifle barrel when fired. The .22 cartridges, which were from the Owens' House/Post Office Complex, could have been Civil War era, since these were produced by 1857 and had heavy patinas on them. They may have been lost later, however. The carved or whittled bullet is an interesting find and illustrates how some soldiers passed the time. Carved bullets are common on other Civil War sites (Braley 1987; Legg and Smith 1989; Mainfort 1980).

The assemblage of Civil War era ammunition recovered from all Camp Nelson sites receiving archaeological investigation and from two private Camp Nelson collections shows a great diversity. The primary rifle bullet used by Federal troops during the Civil War, the .57- to .58-caliber three-ring Minié type, accounts for only 28.6 percent of the sample at Camp Nelson. This proportion contrasts greatly with the sample from Folly Island, where 98 percent of the ammunition was of the .57 to .58-caliber Minié type, and somewhat with the Fort Pillow sample, where 50 percent of the probable Union ammunition was of that type (Legg and Smith 1989; Mainfort 1980). The differences in the three site samples may be related partly to the number of regiments or even companies represented in the assemblages and the length of occupation. The assemblage at Folly Island probably was associated with only two infantry regiments and one artillery battery for one winter, while the Fort Pillow assemblage was associated with at least parts of seven infantry, cavalry, and artillery regiments or batteries over a two-year period (Legg and Smith 1989; Mainfort 1980). The occurrence of a Confederate attack at Fort Pillow also may have contributed to the variety of ammunition represented, even though Mainfort (1980) carefully separated Union and Confederate ammunition.

At Camp Nelson many more regiments were present, in the form of both long-term garrisoned troops and short-term regiments from different states, than at the other two encampments. Both the larger number of regiments and the fact that Camp Nelson was not at the front line probably contributed to the variety of arms used. Additional excavation in different parts of Camp Nelson, such as regimental camp sites, would assist in understanding weapon variability.

Another artifact group that can provide insights into material procurement and local idiosyncrasies at Camp Nelson is nails. While this

**Table 7.3.** Nail Distribution, by Size, at the Owens' House/Post Office Complex and the Headquarters Complex

| Nail Size | Owens'/Post Office Complex | | Headquarters Complex | |
|---|---|---|---|---|
| | N | % | N | % |
| 2d | 2 | 5.3 | 10 | 1.6 |
| 3d | 1 | 2.6 | 81 | 13.0 |
| 4d | 14 | 36.8 | 206 | 33.0 |
| 5d | 3 | 7.9 | 7 | 1.1 |
| 6d | 7 | 18.4 | 107 | 17.1 |
| 7d | 5 | 13.1 | 24 | 3.8 |
| 8d | 2 | 5.3 | 97 | 15.5 |
| 9d | 3 | 7.9 | 18 | 2.9 |
| 10d | 1 | 2.6 | 50 | 8.0 |
| 12d | 0 | — | 20 | 3.2 |
| >16d | 0 | — | 5 | 0.8 |
| Total | 38 | 99.9 | 625 | 100.0 |

artifact type usually does not receive extensive analysis in archaeological reports, particularly in Civil War site reports, recent examinations of pennyweights and nail conditions (straight, pulled, and clinched) have begun to expand the interpretive potential of nails (Jurney 1987; Young and Carr 1989). A large sample of cut nails was recovered from the excavation block at the Headquarters Complex and in the south-central part of the Owens' House/Post Office Complex (Probe Units 11 and 11A and Test Unit 104). Map analysis suggests that the Headquarters Complex excavation block was located downhill from a mess hall and that the Owens' House/Post Office nail concentration was adjacent to an unidentified Civil War structure (figs. 7.2 and 7.3).

The pennyweights of the whole nails from the two Camp Nelson concentrations are illustrated in table 7.3. The nail-size distributions at the two sites are fairly consistent and contain a wide variety of nail sizes.

**Table 7.4.**  U.S. Army Construction Specifications for Officers' Mess Nail Size, by Function

| Nail Size | Functions/Structural Elements | % in Mess Hall |
|---|---|---|
| 3d | Lathing | 53.7 |
| 6d | Shingles | 18.3 |
| 8d | Furring | 1.9 |
| 10d | Flooring, clapboarding, sheathing | 25.1 |
| 20d | Framing, roof | 1.0 |

SOURCE: U.S. Army 1860.

Interestingly, the variety of nail sizes used at the Camp Nelson sites is much greater than was specified in the 1860 U.S. Army building manual. This manual specifies using only 3d, 6d, 8d, 10d, and 20d nails in all buildings. The most common nail size at the Camp Nelson sites, 4d, is not even specified in the manual. Extensive additions and substitutions of different-sized nails evidently occurred at Camp Nelson.

A possible explanation of how these substitutions and additions were made can be derived by examining the common function of nails by pennyweight. Table 7.4 gives army specifications for Officer's Mess Hall nail size and proportions by function. Table 7.5 compares these proportions with those of nail-size groups from the Camp Nelson Headquarters Complex. Since the structure at the Owens' House/Post Office was unidentified, its nails were not compared in detail to those from any building type in the army manual. The nail-size groups from the Headquarters Complex were based on the common function of different-sized nails (see table 7.6). The Camp Nelson messes closely resembled the Officer's Mess in the building manual in size and exterior construction. The nail proportions from the excavation block presented in table 7.5 fall surprisingly close to the army specifications. These results should be viewed with caution, however, since the appropriateness of the penny-weight combinations are difficult to assess. This is particularly true for classifying 4d nails as lathing nails. Although they may have been used in lathing (Fiegel 1990: 14), 4d nails more commonly were used for fasten-

**Table 7.5.**   Nail Distribution, by Size, at the Headquarters Complex,
Compared with U.S. Army Specifications

| Nail Size | Headquarters, Exc. Block (%) | Army Specifications, Mess Hall (%) |
|:---:|:---:|:---:|
| 2d–4d | 47.6 | 53.7 |
| 6d | 17.1 | 18.3 |
| 8d–10d | 26.4 | 27.0 |
| 12d+ | 4.0 | 1.0 |
| 5d, 7d | 4.8 | .0 |

SOURCE: U.S. Army 1860.

ing wooden shakes and shingles (Fontana and Greenleaf 1962; Jurney 1987; Walker 1971; Young and Carr 1989). The high frequency and proportion of 4d nails may suggest the use of wooden shingles, and the lower frequency and proportion of 2d and 3d nails may suggest a lack of complete lathing in this structure.

Another factor in the size distribution of nails is that some of the smaller nails could have come from boxes or crates, rather than from a structure. The spatial distribution of cut nails from Camp Nelson, however, does not show variation by nail size and therefore makes this suggestion unlikely. For instance, a Chi-square test on the nails from the Headquarters indicates that there is no significant difference (even at the 0.1 level) between the distribution of the 4d nails, which are the most numerous nails found that were not recommended in the U.S. Army specifications, and the larger whole nails from that site. Nails of all sizes from the Headquarters Complex were concentrated at the northern end of the excavation block (McBride and Sharp 1991). Since this pattern of concentration differed from that in the kitchen refuse, which concentrated at the southern end of the block, it may indicate that the nearby mess house fell or was pushed into this area and allowed to rot.

A number of factors could explain why the Camp Nelson buildings varied from specifications. Material access problems, costs, or personal

**Table 7.6.** Common Functions for Nails, by Nail Size

| Nail Size | Functions/Structural Elements |
| --- | --- |
| 2d–3d | Lathing, shingles |
| 4d–5d | Shingles, shakes, tin roof, lathing |
| 6d–7d | Clapboards, wall boards, batten, ceiling |
| 8d–10d | Flooring, furring, boarding, siding |
| 12d+ | Framing, joists, rafters, studs |

SOURCES: Fiegel 1989; Fontana and Greenleaf 1962; Jurney 1987; Walker 1971; Young and Carr 1989.

preference could lead to variance from specifications. Compromises with official army specifications and regulations were common throughout the Civil War in many aspects of army life (Lord 1960: 141; James I. Robertson 1984: 47; Wiley 1987: 127). This was particularly true in the western theater, where supplies were notoriously in short supply (Wiley 1987: 61, 227). Variation from specifications would be particularly likely if nails were bought locally or civilians were contracted to build structures. Although elevation drawings and photographs indicate that the Camp Nelson buildings generally followed army plans, when it came to nails, the builders largely ignored army specifications.

## Discussion

While only a very limited and localized program of excavation was carried out at Camp Nelson in these investigations, a surprisingly rich and diverse collection of artifacts was recovered. This material, although concentrated in only a few areas of the camp, has added to our knowledge of material conditions and behavior at Camp Nelson, particularly in the procurement and use or consumption of certain material goods and in the diversity of personnel who visited or worked at the camp. Given the diversity of sites at Camp Nelson, and their generally good state of preservation, this camp offers great potential for future archaeological research on such topics as arms and supply, provisioning, military status differentiation, regimental differentiation, the conditions of African-American troops and refugees, architectural form, overall camp layout including tent areas, refuse disposal patterns, military industries, and medical conditions and practices. Additional excavations at Camp Nelson are necessary to test the representativeness of the artifact patterns identified in this chapter.

The investigation of these topics would be greatly assisted by an enlargement in the comparative record from Civil War sites. A larger sample of Union and Confederate encampment sites from different contexts, including front-line and rear-line sites and short-term and long-term sites, is needed to understand and interpret artifact and feature patterns on individual sites more fully. This volume is certainly a step toward this goal.

At present, the significance and even the existence of Camp Nelson is not known to most Kentuckians. This obscurity probably is the result of its nonbattlefield status and perhaps of its Union rather than Confederate affiliation. Hopefully, a combination of efforts, including educating the public and preservation community about the significance of Civil War archaeological deposits, will allow sites like Camp Nelson to be better interpreted, protected, and appreciated.

## Acknowledgments

Funding for this project was provided by American Telephone and Telegraph Company (AT&T). In their roles as the local contact persons, Don King and Rodney Strong of Colony Communication Corporation's AT&T Field Office provided much-appreciated assistance.

Thanks are also due to David Pollack of the Kentucky Heritage Council for his advice on field methods, and to Kurt Fiegel and Douglas Lambert of the Kentucky Transportation Cabinet for sharing their knowledge of the documentary sources on Camp Nelson. The assistance and advice of the staff at the National Archives military history section is greatly appreciated. Local Camp Nelson buffs Larry Zwagil and Ron Mobley are thanked for sharing their knowledge of the site and for allowing us to examine their collections. Larry also spent a number of days volunteering in the field; for this he is additionally thanked.

Many personnel of the Program for Cultural Resource Assessment were instrumental in completing the research at Camp Nelson. The field and lab crews consisted of Will Daley, Paul Freeman, Gwynn Henderson, Julie O'Shaughnessy, and Teresa Tune. The efforts of all of these people are greatly appreciated. Administrative support was provided by Barbara Gortman, Richard Jefferies, John Scarry, and Ed Winkle. William E. Sharp supervised significant portions of the field excavation and co-authored the final technical report. Sande Thomas drafted all figures. Tom Sussenbach assisted in spatial and statistical analysis. Kim A. McBride provided clerical and editorial assistance on this paper. Many thanks to all of these persons.

# 8

*W. Hunter Lesser, Kim A. McBride, and Janet G. Brashler*

## CHEAT SUMMIT FORT AND CAMP ALLEGHENY
### *Early Civil War Encampments in West Virginia*

Two Civil War era fortifications were acquired by the Forest Service, United States Department of Agriculture, in 1987. These sites consist of the Federal Cheat Summit Fort and portions of Confederate Camp Allegheny. Both were constructed during summer 1861 along the Staunton-Parkersburg Turnpike in Randolph and Pocahontas counties, West Virginia (fig. 8.1). Cheat Summit Fort is situated within the Appalachian Plateau physiographic province, while Camp Allegheny lies at the crest of the Allegheny Front, which divides the Ridge and Valley physiographic province from the Appalachian Plateau country. Both sites lie in isolated areas at high elevations and have relatively severe weather. These factors led to abandonment by their respective sides in April 1862. This chapter describes historical research and archaeological investigations conducted on the sites, as well as interpretive plans.

Location of Cheat Summit Fort, Randolph County (A) and Camp Allegheny, Pocahontas County (B).

*Fig. 8.1. Location of (A) Cheat Summit Fort, Randolph County, and (B) Camp Allegheny, Pocahontas County, West Virginia.*

## History of Cheat Summit Fort

The remains of Cheat Summit Fort (also referred to as Fort Milroy, White Top, Camp McClellan, and Cheat Pass) are located near U.S. Route 250 south of Huttonsville, West Virginia. The site is situated on the nineteenth-century route of the Staunton-Parkersburg Turnpike, approximately 1.5 miles from its juncture at Cheat Bridge, at an elevation of about four thousand feet above mean sea level.

Federal troops constructed Cheat Summit Fort in July 1861, soon after the withdrawal of Confederate forces to the Greenbrier River following Union victories at Rich Mountain and Corricks Ford. Construction of the fort commenced under orders of Major General George B.

**Fig. 8.2.** *Illustration of Cheat Summit Fort by a member of the 2nd (West) Virginia Infantry. From Reader 1890.*

McClellan just before he was promoted to command of the Army of the Potomac (Beatty 1879: 28).

The fort was built on the farm of an elderly mountaineer named White. One of the Federal soldiers remembered the spot as "a splendid farm of twenty acres on which were about ten rocks to one blade of grass, on an average" (Pool 1862: 18). Six companies of the 14th Indiana Infantry began fortifying the position on July 16, 1861 (Landon 1933: 352). The Federals cleared several acres on each side of the Turnpike at White's. Along the outer boundary they felled tall spruce trees, partially trimmed and debarked, with their tops outward, presenting a mass of sharp points known as abatis to anyone approaching. Large earthen breastworks were erected inside this perimeter of felled timber. Augustus Van Dyke (1903: 24–25) of the 14th Indiana described the construction and appearance of this redoubt: "And then began the building of an immense fort. . . . The walls were fourteen feet high, eight feet through at the base, narrowing to four feet at the top. These walls were built of pine or hemlock or spruce . . . and the space filled in with earth and stone."

The fort originally consisted of a large earthen fortification and block-house on a hillside northeast of the point where the turnpike crosses the gap at "White Top." A second, smaller enclosure was located just across the turnpike to the southwest. A covered, or semi-subterranean, passage connected the two. Southwest of the turnpike, cabins were erected along the hillside and a burial ground established nearby (fig. 8.2). The completed fortress was believed to be impregnable to both artillery or frontal assault (Van Dyke 1903: 24–25).

Elements of the 14th Indiana regiment and the 24th and 25th Ohio regiments under the command of Colonel Nathan Kimball were positioned at Cheat Summit Fort when a Confederate force led by Colonel Albert Rust, under the direct command of General Robert E. Lee, moved against the position on September 12, 1861. Colonel Rust believed the fort to be impregnable and failed to fulfill his part of Lee's strategy in the Cheat Mountain Campaign. As a result, Lee withdrew from the area after several days of skirmishing (Scott 1881: 184–92).

On October 2, 1861, General Joseph J. Reynolds assembled a Union force totaling approximately five thousand men at Cheat Summit Fort and led them on a "reconnaissance in force" of Confederate Camp Bartow. This fortification was situated about twelve miles west of Cheat Summit Fort on the Staunton-Parkersburg Turnpike at present-day Bartow, West Virginia. After a rather indecisive artillery duel lasting over four hours, the Federals retraced their steps on October 3. This action is usually referred to as the Battle of Greenbrier River (Robert N. Scott 1881: 220–21).

Federal troops occupying Cheat Summit Fort over the winter of 1861–62 suffered terribly from the dampness and bitter cold in that exposed position. Snow fell there as early as August 13 (Pool 1862: 33). Upon reflection, a Federal captain believed Cheat Mountain to be "the severest campaign of this company. Its severity consisted of the cold and rain in this dreary and uninhabited country, the lack of sufficient rations and clothing. In the usually mild September, horses chilled to death in that camp" (Baxter 1980: 49).

During this winter habitation, General Robert H. Milroy led an attack from Cheat Summit Fort against Camp Allegheny on December 13, 1861. The Federals were repulsed in a hotly contested fight with a Confederate force under Colonel Edward Johnson (Robert N. Scott 1881: 456). Milroy's troops retreated and settled back into their snow-covered shelters on Cheat Mountain for the long winter.

The Federals abandoned Cheat Summit Fort in April 1862 (Reader 1890: 161). An Indiana volunteer gleefully recalled his departure: "With what a light step all started. Soon on the road turning at the brow of the hill, the Fourteenth took what I fondly hope is their last look at Cheat Mountain" (Baxter 1980: 65).

## Archaeological Investigations of Cheat Summit Fort

Prior to its acquisition by the U.S. Forest Service in 1987, a private cor-poration owned Cheat Summit Fort and its environs. For roughly the past fifty years, surface coal mining and lumbering took place adjacent to the fort. In fact, mining activity destroyed the small enclosure directly southwest of the turnpike, as well as some cabin sites. However, the main fortification northeast of the turnpike was avoided and is well preserved. Surface features such as cabin foundations and chimney falls can be seen plainly when seasonal vegetation is down (Lesser 1982).

State Archaeologist Edward V. McMichael, Clifford M. Lewis, and others partially mapped Cheat Summit Fort as part of a survey of area Civil War sites undertaken by the West Virginia Centennial National Youth Science Camp in 1963. Lewis dismissed the site at that time as "unpromising for archeological development" due to strip mining, lumbering, an impassable road, and danger of forest fire (Clifford M. Lewis 1963: 34).

Limited archaeological survey and testing were conducted at Cheat Summit Fort in 1980 to document the possible existence of intact sub-surface remains at the site. Excavation of a six-foot square in a circular, mounded feature just inside the breastworks revealed the remains of a rock-lined hearth and chimney fall. These probably were associated with one of a series of structures constructed at the fort (Reader 1890: 153).

Artifacts recovered from the test unit included machine-cut nails, me-tallic and porcelain buttons, .58- and .69-caliber conical small arms projectiles, .32- and .69-caliber round ball projectiles likely used in buck and ball loads, fire-melted ordnance, a canteen stop puller, glass spirit and medicine bottle fragments, tin can fragments, and small animal bone fragments (Lesser 1981).

## History of Camp Allegheny

Confederate forces constructed Camp Allegheny, also known as Camp Baldwin or Camp Johnson, astride the Staunton-Parkersburg Turnpike at Top of Allegheny in summer 1861. The camp was designed to bar any Federal advances toward Staunton and the Shenandoah Valley. At approximately 4,400 feet above mean sea level, Camp Allegheny is reported to have been the highest fortification in the eastern theater of the Civil War (Clifford M. Lewis 1963: 33).

Camp Allegheny consisted of an earthen fortification south of the turnpike, with associated cabins and earthworks on a hill to the north. The fort was constructed on the farm of John Yeager. The Confederates reportedly cut down a large sugar maple grove on the property and used the wood for building cabins (Beard 1969: 32). The position was held by about 1,200 Confederates under Colonel Edward Johnson of the 12th Georgia Regiment (Robert N. Scott 1881: 983).

Newly promoted Brigadier General Robert H. Milroy, commander of Federal forces in the Cheat Mountain Division, determined to destroy the Confederate outpost at Camp Allegheny. He assembled a force of about 1,900 men at Cheat Summit Fort and advanced on the morning of December 12, 1861. That night Milroy seized abandoned Camp Bartow and bivouacked. Milroy divided his force here, hoping to strike Camp Allegheny from both the right and the left (north and south flanks) at daybreak. His main force advanced up the Staunton-Parkersburg Turnpike, leaving that road and scrambling up the steep mountainside about two miles from Camp Allegheny.

Milroy's intent was to encircle the right and rear of the Confederate position. Meanwhile, the second Federal column under Colonel Moody was to march up the Green Bank Road and simultaneously attack the left flank. Milroy's force, however, encountered a strong Confederate picket and began the fight prematurely. The Confederates advanced from their earthworks toward Milroy but were driven back by the superior long-range rifles of the Federals (Robert N. Scott 1881: 463). They quickly rallied, however, and returned fire in force from the trenches and log cabins. Fighting occurred at such close quarters that the Confederate cannon could not be used effectively (Robert N. Scott 1881: 458). Finally breaking off the engagement, Milroy gathered his dead and wounded from the open field and retreated toward the turnpike.

At this point, Colonel Moody made his hopelessly late attack on the left flank of Camp Allegheny. Colonel Johnson now was able to commit his entire force against Moody. Worn out by the long march (and rumored to have visited a local cider mill), Moody's troops were driven back after a stubborn fight. They retreated down the mountainside and rejoined Milroy.

The battle at Camp Allegheny opened at 7:15 A.M. on December 13 and was over by 2:00 P.M., with the Confederates still in control and Milroy's Federals in full retreat to Cheat Summit Fort. Casualties, however, were almost even, with each side reporting twenty killed and a little over one hundred wounded and missing (Robert N. Scott 1881: 456–68).

The engagement at Camp Allegheny effectively ended campaigning for the winter. The Confederates suffered even more in their exposed position during the miserable winter of 1861–62 than did the Federals at Cheat Summit. Measles, pneumonia, and other illnesses swept through the camp. Numerous cemeteries in the area bear witness to their effects (Henderson n.d.). George P. Moore (1961: 205) of the 31st Virginia Infantry noted in his diary for August 20, 1861: "Between the measels [*sic*] and the worst climate ever seen I am still dragging out a kind of miserable existence unable to do military duty or anything else. Here on top of the Allegheny Mountain it rains in torrents nearly every day, and when not raining, we are in the midst of clouds through which one can't see fifty yards."

Colonel Johnson's troops abandoned the works at Camp Allegheny in April 1862. Soon after, local partisans apparently set fire to much of the camp (Beard 1969: 33). The site saw sporadic use during various raids later in the war (Davis, Perry, and Kirkley 1881: 448).

*Fig. 8.3. Earthworks and cabin remains at Camp Allegheny. Courtesy of W. Hunter Lesser.*

## Archaeological Investigations of Camp Allegheny

Camp Allegheny has been extremely well preserved. The locale today looks much as it did in 1861, consisting primarily of open pasture. Presently, the Forest Service has acquired only that portion of the site situated north of the Staunton-Parkersburg Turnpike. This acquisition includes three rows of stone piles and surface depressions representing the remains of at least thirty-five cabin sites. The hillside above this point contains a shallow trench. This hillside and the ridge flat above are the locations of General Milroy's morning attack on December 13, 1861 (Robert N. Scott 1881: 461).

On private property south of the turnpike lie extensive earth and stone breastworks on the summit of Buffalo Ridge (fig. 8.3). These breastworks enclose well-defined gun emplacements, a possible powder magazine, stone piles representing additional cabin locations, and a prominent oval earthen enclosure on the hilltop often referred to as a "command post" (Clifford M. Lewis 1963: 41). More stone piles and cabin sites lie to the east, along with remnants of the Yeager homestead and several cemeteries. Poorly marked Confederate burial grounds lie on both the federal and private tracts.

Camp Allegheny was investigated concurrently with Cheat Summit Fort as part of the West Virginia Centennial National Youth Science Camp in 1963. In that same year, the fortifications were mapped by civil engineers from Union Carbide Corporation and Clifford M. Lewis. Dr. Edward V. McMichael conducted an informal surface survey of the site and excavated a test unit at one cabin site located within the main fortification. Numerous artifacts associated with the Civil War occupation were recorded. These included whiteware and stoneware ceramic sherds, pipe fragments, melted bottle glass, pewter spoons, a fork handle, ration can fragments, a frying pan, kettle fragments, a curry comb, knives, axes, horseshoes, hinges, unidentified iron objects, bone fragments, and cut nails (Clifford M. Lewis 1963: 43).

## Site Mapping and Documentation

As part of a program to protect and interpret Cheat Summit Fort and Camp Allegheny, the Forest Service conducted detailed topographic mapping of the sites, historical background research, and preparation of National Register nomination forms. The University of Kentucky Program for Cultural Resource Assessment conducted this work.

### Site Mapping

A manual surveyor's transit was used for mapping the sites. Several data were chosen for both locations. General relief was recorded by shooting a series of overlapping rays from each datum, while cultural features were singled out for additional readings. At Cheat Summit Fort, these features included a large ditch and embankment around the site, numerous chimney falls and depressions defining cabin sites, and small level platforms marking tent locations. At Camp Allegheny, cultural features included trenches, rifle pits, cabin foundation outlines, chimney falls, and circular holes which may represent privies or storage pits (fig. 8.4).

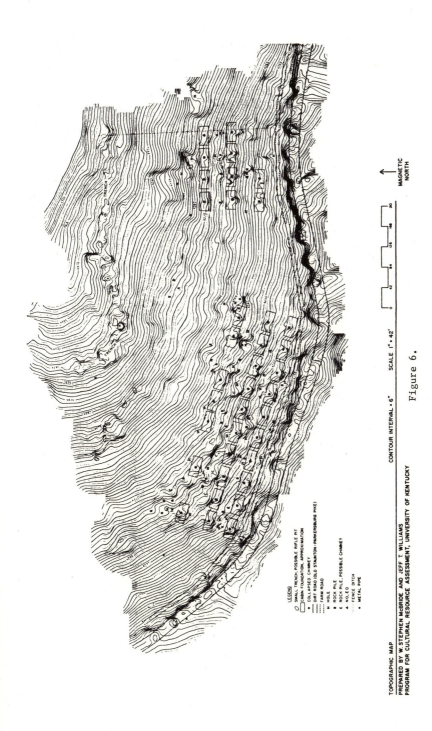

LEGEND

⊘ SMALL TRENCH, POSSIBLE RIFLE PIT
☐ CABIN FOUNDATION, APPROXIMATION
• COLLAPSED CHIMNEY
---- DIRT ROAD (OLD STAUNTON-PARKERSBURG PIKE)
····· FARM ROAD
H HOLE
R ROCK PILE
C ROCK PILE, POSSIBLE CHIMNEY
△ N.O.E.O.
---- FENCE DITCH
• METAL PIPE

TOPOGRAPHIC MAP

PREPARED BY W. STEPHEN McBRIDE AND JEFF T. WILLIAMS
PROGRAM FOR CULTURAL RESOURCE ASSESSMENT, UNIVERSITY OF KENTUCKY

CONTOUR INTERVAL = 6"        SCALE 1" = 42'

Figure 6.

0    42    84    126    168    20

MAGNETIC
NORTH

*Fig. 8.4.* Topographic map of Confederate cabin remains at Camp Allegheny. Courtesy of the Monongahela National Forest.

Between two thousand and three thousand transit readings were recorded for each site. A computer calculated distances and translated the readings into $x$, $y$, and $z$ coordinates. These coordinates were then entered into a computer-mapping program called *Surface*, which interpolated over five times as many additional readings as actually had been entered, then plotted the maps. The program provided options regarding orientation of view, exaggeration of relief, contour interval, etc. It allowed for either topographic or three-dimensional views. The latter, especially with exaggeration, were helpful in pinpointing data errors.

Each site presented a unique set of challenges in mapping and interpretation. Dense vegetation at Cheat Summit Fort necessitated conducting the work during the late fall, when foliage was at a minimum. In turn, this choice created problems with adverse weather conditions at the high-elevation site; both equipment and crew suffered. In contrast, visibility at Camp Allegheny was good, and work therefore was conducted in mid-summer. The major problem encountered at Camp Allegheny was that the steep natural slope on which this part of the camp had been constructed masked the relief of the cultural features. Because of this, a higher number of readings had to be recorded. Even then, all cultural features did not stand out as well as they had at Cheat Summit. Thus the final step in the map construction was manual delineation of those features which did not show up by relief alone.

The end result of this work was accurate and detailed maps that will be used for site interpretation and research. The maps can provide a visual orientation for visitors, guiding identification of cultural features on the ground.

## Historical Documentation

The second aspect of the project involved historical background research and construction of a detailed bibliography of sources relating to the sites for nominations to the National Register of Historic Places. The goal was to assemble relevant site-specific materials, including primary and secondary written sources and oral history information. A separate bibliography was prepared for each of the sites (McBride and McBride 1989; McBride and McBride 1990).

Secondary sources generally were available in most sizable libraries. Some out-of-print volumes, especially those published in the late nineteenth or early twentieth centuries, were located only in the Library of Congress. Most primary sources could only be researched by visiting historical societies, state and county libraries or archives, and major research collections located near the home areas of the units encamped at these sites. For example, twenty-one libraries in eight states were consulted in compiling the bibliographies for these two West Virginia sites.

Few primary war-related records are organized by geographical locales, to which the archaeologist most commonly is oriented. Rather, the records are organized by companies or regiments, often under the name of the author. Therefore it was important to be familiar with the companies and regiments who stayed at the sites and, if possible, the names of the company commanders and their home towns. Familiarity with the structure of the armies from the division down to the regimental level also was valuable, especially when researching official records. Primary among these official records is *War of the Rebellion: A Compilation of the Official Records of the Union and Confederate Armies.*

Diaries and letters provided the best detail on daily life and camp structure. These records were more difficult to locate than published reminiscences, however, since often they are part of unpublished manuscript collections. Period newspapers from the home towns of units involved in a battle or located at a campsite provide an often overlooked source of first-hand information and generally are easier to locate and access than manuscript collections. No one was more interested in information about camp conditions than the folks back home. As a result, these sources provide the kind of mundane detail sought by archaeologists. For example, we were able to locate letters describing life at Cheat Summit Fort and Camp Allegheny in period newspapers from Indiana and Georgia, respectively.

Many Civil War reminiscences were published in the late nineteenth and early twentieth centuries, often by company commanders. These are subject to error, however, as many were not recorded until the authors were some years removed from the events in question. Still, such reminiscences are a good source of information on camp structure and life. As with unpublished materials, they were most easily located in local repositories, listed by author or company and regimental divisions.

## Discussion

The high level of site integrity and the existence of detailed background historical data together suggest that these sites hold great research potential. More than 150 separate reminiscences, diaries, or letters, and a total of over 500 sources were located. These sources, along with the more than 125 archaeological features recorded during the mapping project, may guide further research. As domestic sites, Camp Allegheny and Cheat Summit Fort present opportunities to address a broader range of research topics than do pure battle sites. Additionally, these two fortified camps were scenes of battle.

Camp Allegheny and Cheat Summit Fort exist as sites of nearly equal duration, time period, and setting, from opposite sides of the Civil War struggle. They present an opportunity for controlled comparison of Federal and Confederate domestic and military conditions. Discrete areas of Camp Allegheny also are known to have been occupied by regiments from different parts of the Confederacy, providing opportunities for additional controlled comparisons. The same possibly holds true for Cheat Summit Fort. Future research topics likely will focus on military lifeways and material provisioning. These might have been affected by such factors as length of occupation, Confederate versus Union allegiance, temporal placement, military rank, and ethnicity.

The preliminary archaeological test excavations, intensive site mapping, and detailed bibliographical research for Cheat Summit Fort and Camp Allegheny have provided solid baseline data to guide future research at the sites. Additional archaeological research questions may be addressed effectively from the corpus of historic documentation. Site preservation and stabilization issues have also been identified through this work. Interpretive opportunities revealed by the archaeological and historical data have resulted in brochures, signing, and a plan to foster public appreciation for these superbly preserved Civil War sites.

# Part IV.

## *Other Directions*

*The primary goal of this book is to draw attention to the broad range of topics related to the Civil War, to whose study historical archaeology can contribute significantly. The following four chapters illustrate this diversity of application. Charles Orser offers an exploratory work that looks at broad, regional changes in northern agriculture, specifically that of the Midwest corn belt, during and following the Civil War period. He proposes a strategy for studying this complex subject which encompasses both archaeological field work and extensive research into primary historical documentation. By considering an area of the United States which experienced little military action, Orser illustrates the significant secondary impacts that the war had on the nation as a whole.*

*Following Orser's focus on the agricultural economy of a region, Clarence Geier illustrates the impact of the war on a specific family. The chapter introduces the family of Thomas Cheatham, who lived between Richmond and Petersburg, Virginia, just prior to the onset of the Civil War. In 1864, their farm came to lie in a "no-man's land" between Confederate fortifications protecting the southern perimeter of Richmond, and the advancing Union Army of the James.*

*The chapter documents a Union attack on the Richmond defenses on May 6–16, 1864, and considers the impact the military occupation of the Cheatham home had on the farm, its dwellings, and the family.*

*Joel W. Grossman takes the reader into the realms of espionage and artillery manufacture. His chapter reviews important excavations conducted at the site of the West Point Foundry, in Cold Spring, New York. Not only do the excavations provide important insight into gun testing facilities and the housing of laborers, but also they illustrate how historical interpretation sometimes can create false or misleading perceptions of past reality.*

*Paul Shackel studies the use of landscapes in establishing and reinforcing dominant ideologies. He uses Harpers Ferry, West Virginia, as a case study to show how northern industrialists used industrial ruins created by the Civil War to reinforce an industrial ideology during the latter half of the nineteenth century.*

9

*Charles E. Orser, Jr.*

## CORN-BELT AGRICULTURE DURING THE CIVIL WAR PERIOD, 1850–70
### *A Research Prospectus for Historical Archaeology*

The impact of the American Civil War on the rural South was immediate and significant. Rich, normally productive agricultural fields were burned, huge mansions were ransacked and destroyed, livestock were set free or slaughtered, some four million enslaved African Americans—many of them agricultural laborers—were emancipated, and as many as 62 percent of white farmers served in the Confederate Army (Wiley 1959: 7). In the South's agricultural world, slave plantations gave way to tenant plantations, and small-scale farmers returning from the war—some of whom once owned one or two slaves and some of whom owned none—found themselves competing with a new labor force: the freedman farmer.

Numerous researchers have focused on the social nature of Southern agriculture, both before and after the American Civil War. Historians have explored various aspects of Southern agriculture in both the antebellum and the postbellum periods (see, for example, Fite 1984; Gray 1933; Wayne 1983; Wiener 1978). Rural sociologists have commented on postwar southern farm tenancy and its effects on southern rural development (see, e.g., Raper 1936; Vance 1929). And historical archaeologists have illustrated some ways in which the study of southern farm tenancy can inform the developing archaeological understanding of nineteenth-century life in the rural South (see, for example, Joseph, Reed, and Cantley 1991; Jurney and Moir 1987; Moir and Jurney 1987; Orser 1988a and 1991; Orser and Holland 1984; Raab 1982).

The wholesale changes in the rural South, best symbolized by African-American freedom and by the alterations made in plantation organization, seem not to have been mirrored in the rural North. At first glance, the rural North seems to be a place unaffected by the changes wrought by the Civil War; in 1860, the North had no plantations and no slaves. Nonetheless, in 1864 the superintendent of the federal census felt justified in writing that "American agriculture is in a transition state" (Kennedy 1864a: x).

Many historians have focused on northern agriculture, but the long-standing presence of slavery in the South and a generally widespread fascination with human bondage has allowed some scholars to argue that northern agriculture has not received the same careful treatment as its southern counterpart (Atack and Bateman 1987: 5). The disproportionate interest in the agricultural South, as compared with the North, seems to imply that, for American agriculture, North and South were distinct places. Thus, the North and the South appear to present two models of farming, one northern and one southern. Such a dichotomous view of American agriculture probably has developed from the perception that agriculture in the South—a discrete region containing nineteenth-century slavery (Orser 1990: 1–4)—was more dynamic than agriculture in the North, if for no other reason than the demise of plantation slavery. In archaeology, in any case, studies of the agricultural South generally have had a higher profile than studies of the agricultural North, with the rise of a subfield known as "plantation archaeology" serving to demonstrate the interest in at least one aspect of southern agriculture.

Archaeologists have not exactly ignored northern farmers, but they generally have not focused on the social dynamics of nineteenth-century northern farming with the same intensity as that directed toward southern plantation dynamics. A few archaeologists, however, have explored northern farming in archaeological and anthropological terms, and these works are instructive (see, for example, William Adams 1990; Grantz 1984). To demonstrate some of the important topics that archaeologists can explore at northern farm sites, this chapter focuses on one section of the Midwest, the corn belt, during the period bracketing the Civil War, or from about 1850 to 1870. The corn belt is defined as incorporating Illinois, Indiana, Iowa, and Ohio (Baker 1926).

## Society, Production, and Historical Archaeology

A major premise of this chapter is that the American Civil War can be understood in a social sense as well as in the more prevalent military, political, and economic senses. This paper accepts the view that "the Civil War directly affected the lives of most Americans at that time and left behind a legacy that continued to influence them many years after Appomattox" (Vinovskis 1989: 57). The adoption of this overtly social assertion avoids the hotly debated issue of whether the war accelerated some aspects of American industrialization and economic growth (see, for example, Bruins 1987; Salisbury 1962), retarded growth (Cochran 1961), or had little overall effect (Conzen 1971; Marcus and Segal 1989; North 1974). Rather, the perspective here is that the lasting impacts of the war, beyond African-American emancipation, were largely in the areas of social thought and ideology (Fredrickson 1965: 183–84).

Historical archaeology can help modern scholars to understand "the life course of nineteenth-century Americans" (Vinovskis 1990a: vii) resulting from the Civil War. Historical archaeology can be used to document and explain many aspects of nineteenth-century life because the field is particularly well suited to providing unique information about the "capitalist transformation of rural America," a process with clear relevance to the study of the period of the American Civil War (Hahn and Prude 1985). Whatever one's perspective regarding the effects of the Civil War on industrial life, it cannot be doubted that the war played at least some role in helping to transform the United States from a rural to an industrial nation. The understanding of this transformation, rightly a major topic of research in American historical archaeology, can be ap-

proached by using a class perspective, or one that "assumes that class relations are the basis for understanding cultural and material change"
(Paynter 1988: 409; for a similar comment, see Orser 1988b).

At the root of the class perspective is the concept of social relations
(Orser 1989: 37). This perspective accepts the idea that societies are composed of individuals who are linked by a complex web of social interac-
tions or mutual relations that are dynamic "realities in flux and motion."
These relations constantly change within the context of the society in
which they are formulated (Godelier 1986: 18).

An excellent way to conceptualize a web of social relations is by using the concept of the "network." A "network" can be broadly defined
as an interconnected arrangement of material and immaterial elements
that stand in relation to one another and are tied together in some fashion. Networks can be rooted in a specific kind of relation that links "a
defined set of persons, objects, or events" (Knoke and Kuklinski 1982:
12). Anthropologist Alexander Lesser (1961: 42) uses the term "social
field" to describe the "weblike, netlike connections" between people and
social groups that are multidimensional and stretch across time and space
(after J. A. Barnes 1954: 43n). A central aspect of the network concept is
that social fields are "fields of relationships" (Wolf 1984: 397) that are
defined in culturally relevant ways and that can include power relations,
environmental outlooks, and economic strategies.

Social relations can assume myriad forms, principal among them often being relations of production. Relations of production can be defined in association with socioeconomic class, because (1) such relations
determine access to resources within a society, (2) they control the conditions of production, (3) they organize the labor of individuals in society, and (4) they determine the social characteristics of resource circula-
tion and redistribution.

Some anthropologists have questioned the use of the mode-of-pro-
duction concept in connection with nonindustrial societies because most
of the world's nonindustrial cultures use kinship, hunting and collecting,
cattle rearing, or some other decidedly "nonproductive," or perhaps non–
surplus producing, form of life as the primary organizing principle (see,
for example, Bloch 1985: 135–38; Sahlins 1976). It must be remembered, however, that production occurs in all spheres of life: economic,

political, and even ideological (Nowak 1983). Social relations only become relations of economic production when they serve as one framework for the exploitation of nature (Godelier 1986: 50). In fully capitalist societies, relations of economic production generally predominate. In any case, economic relations of production are exceedingly important in industrialized societies incorporating advanced agriculture, such as that found in the rural North from 1850 to 1870.

In all cultures, forces of production articulate with the complex web of interacting social relations. These forces include the tools of production, the raw materials, and the skills, knowledge, and strength needed for production (Cohen 1978: 32). Forces of production usually are assumed to relate solely to economic production, but the concept easily can be expanded to include the production of ideas, belief systems, political thought, and other nonmaterial aspects of life.

The elements of production, in whatever sphere of life they occur at a particular time, do not exist alone; they are woven together in articulated modes of production (Godelier 1986: 131). These modes of production are not idealized, static entities into which certain conditions fit, but rather are historically created and recreated sets of social relations. In their simplest sense, these relations can be either horizontal—stretching between people of relatively equal social position—or vertical—stretching between people who are socially unequal and hierarchically arranged. Modes of production "exist as discoverable patterns in the events of everyday life," requiring intellectual work and empirical research for their identification (Merrill 1977: 64).

The concept of "mode of production" can be situated within a purely analytical framework by reference to the concept of "scale." As explained by William Marquardt (1985: 69), "scale" refers to a "mode of access that, if applied critically and rigorously, can lead to an understanding of productive forces, social relations, ideologies, and the multiple and contradictory relations among them." While scales, or perhaps "levels of resolution" (Haggett 1990: 23), have obvious importance in geographical and spatial studies (Crumley 1979: 143–44), the significance of "scale" as used here is that it refers to both space and time. Time and space can be subdivided into an infinite number of scales. "Effective scales," scales at which patterns can be discerned, occur within the complex layerings and interweavings of scales that theoretically can exist in space and time (Marquardt and Crumley 1987: 7). For example, for a farmer wishing to plant crops, the effective scales—both temporal and spatial—are determined by the sociohistorical structures (which may include the amount of land available, her or his ownership of the land or personal relations with the landlord, and financial requirements), and by the physical structures (soil quality, climate, weather, topography, and, in some cases, even the position of the moon) (Marquardt 1992: 107). The farmer, seeking to plant crops, leaves upon the land certain landscape signatures that provide evidence for the options he or she accepted. Interpreters—archaeologists, geographers, historians—of the landscape signatures that result from such human-environment and human-human relationships bring to the study their own notions of an effective scale, as they analyze and interpret the patterns they perceive. Ideally, the scales should emerge as the study progresses, in effect letting the region define itself by setting its own spatial and temporal boundaries; but, as a purely practical matter, an initial scale must be defined by the analyst. It would be nice if we could imagine today that our scales match those of the past peoples we study, but no such correlation is required.

An analysis at one scale may suggest findings that contradict those obtained from analysis at another scale. Rather than demonstrating the inadequacy of either analysis, however, these findings merely show the complexity of life within the interwoven networks created by the physical and sociohistorical structures. Even though one scale negates an earlier one by transcending it, the understanding of the entire sociohistorical formation is increased by such negation, because none of the scales is forgotten. As a result, the best analyses are multiscalar (Marquardt 1992: 107; also see Ames 1991; Crumley and Marquardt 1987; Little and Shackel 1989). In the study of modern American history, the various spatial scales that may be used are intercontinental, continental, national, regional, state-level, local, property-specific; and the various temporal scales that may be used are short-term (individual), intermediate (social), and long-term (geographical) time (following Little and Shackel 1989: 496). The spatial focus of archaeology often is limited to regional, local, and site-level scales. The most thorough studies, however, may be those that take into account the larger regional, national, and even international social, economic, political, and ideological trends that affected the inhabitants of specific sites and communities of sites. Attempts to link specific sites to the larger world often entail some attention to multiscalar analysis. The principal task of the archaeologist is to decide on what scales the analysis should proceed and how the various layers of scale should be laid upon one another in interpreting the historical and cultural activities at individual archaeological sites.

The use of concepts such as "scale," "relations of production," and "mode of production" has relevance to archaeological research because of the profession's overriding concern with material production, usually expressed in terms of technology and technological change. A broader view of production, as something that occurs in every aspect of human life, however, has application both for cultural materialist archaeology (Kohl 1981) and for post-processual and critical archaeology (Leone 1986). The focus of this chapter is mainly on the economic relations of production in agriculture, such as farm tenancy, and the interconnecting social relations engendered by these economic relations. The principal spatial scales are the corn belt, the state of Illinois, and Pike County, Illinois, with the main temporal scale being largely from 1850 to 1870.

## Corn-Belt Agriculture, 1850–70

In 1850, the corn belt contained 328,716 farms. This figure grew by 57.0 percent in 1860 to 516,188, and by another 65.1 percent in 1870 to 852,294. Overall, from 1850 to 1870, the number of farms in the corn belt increased by 159.3 percent. The total improved acreage concomitantly expanded from 20,762,263 acres in 1850 to 53,299,831 improved acres in 1870, an increase of 156.7 percent. In 1860, on the eve of the Civil War, 37,756,743 acres of improved farmland existed in the corn belt (table 9.1). The 816,196 farmers in the corn belt comprised 13.4 percent of the total population in the region, and corn-belt farmers contributed 25.4 percent of the nation's total number of 3,219,574 farmers in 1860.

The statistical figures compiled by the federal census bureau could be used to reinforce the commonly held perception that a number of inde-

**Table 9.1.** Number of Farms and Improved Acreage in the Corn Belt, 1850–70

| Year | Number of Farms | % Change | Improved Acres | % Change |
|------|-----------------|----------|----------------|----------|
| 1850 | 328,716 | — | 20,762,263 | — |
| 1860 | 516,188 | +57.0 | 37,756,743 | +81.9 |
| 1870 | 852,294 | +65.1 | 53,299,831 | +41.2 |

SOURCES: Kennedy 1864a: 222; Walker and Seaton 1883: xii.

pendent farmers worked the land of the corn belt in small parcels. Closer examination of the published census data, however, reveals that the situation actually was much less straightforward.

In 1860, the census enumerators classified 191,723 of all farmers in the corn belt (22.5 percent) as "farm laborers" (Kennedy 1864b: 662–63). Even though the exact meaning of this term is open to debate, it seems clear that the census takers were suggesting that not all of the farmers in the corn belt were independent owner-operators. In fact, almost one-quarter of the farmers in the region were farm laborers. The presence of a large number of farm laborers in the corn belt illuminates an important reality of American farming in the nineteenth century, including the Civil War period: farm tenancy was not solely a characteristic of southern agricultural life that developed with the end of American slavery. Rather, the European system of land tenure had been brought to the New World by the earliest colonists (Rutman 1971: 55–58) and ever since had been employed much as it had been in Europe (see Orser 1988a: 37–38). This system of land tenure was based largely on hierarchical social relations.

The hierarchical structure of farm ownership generally has been defined by a model called the "agricultural ladder." The agricultural ladder ranks farmers from unpaid, young laborers still at home, on the bottom, to independent owner-operators, on the top. The middle of the ladder includes farm tenants of various kinds (Spillman 1919).

The concept of the agricultural ladder and its accompanying complexities have been debated by scholars for some time (see the discussion in Winters 1978: 5–7), but the ladder operated because most farmers lacked the capital necessary to buy a farm immediately upon coming of age or when first settling in a region. In fact, many of the farmers who were prosperous in the late nineteenth century had spent some time as tenants working the farms of landlords (Bogue 1963: 56). The agricultural ladder, however, was not always a certain route to happiness and economic security because, while it seemed to be straightforward, it actually was multifaceted and complex. A farmer could descend as well as ascend the ladder as the result of her or his actions or through the actions of people far beyond the farmer's control or even acquaintance. In addition, evidence suggests that, at least in the South, the agricultural ladder was more accessible to European-American farmers than to their African-American counterparts (Orser 1988a: 110). In any case, buying a farm was better than renting one or working on one as a laborer (Atack and Bateman 1987: 145). Unfortunately, contemporary historical sources, such as county histories, generally record the lives and exploits of those farmers who moved up the ladder but not those who moved down.

The corn belt had its share of truly large landowners who typically served as landlords, and who either were at the top of the agricultural ladder as owner-operators or were off the ladder as rich, nonfarming landlords. In fact, much of the public land in the region was purchased by large-scale speculators in the 1830s. In Illinois, for example, twenty-six speculators bought 513,650 acres of land, or well over 19,000 acres each, between 1833 and 1840 (Gates 1941: 68). One of the largest landowners was an Irish landlord, William Scully, who by 1890 owned over 180,000 acres of land in Illinois, Kansas, and Nebraska (Socolofsky 1985: 134; also see Bogue 1963: 57–58; Socolofsky 1979). Scully is said to have operated the "most forlorn-looking estate in Illinois," with "miserable tenants" who lived in unpainted "sheds" (Gates 1941: 76).

The development of large estates in prairie states such as Illinois was encouraged by a number of factors, including the setting aside of more than sixty million acres for veterans, the land policies of the Illinois Central Railroad, and the dumping of wetlands on the market. Wetlands could sell for as little as sixty cents an acre, but extensive drainage systems were needed to make them arable. The Illinois Central Railroad asked between five and twenty dollars per acre for its land, and made it quite clear to all potential small-scale farmers that at least one thousand dollars would be needed to start a farm (Gates 1945: 148–51).

The Civil War generally was good to large landowners. The demand for grain to be used as livestock feed during the war encouraged corn production and made the drainage of wetlands more feasible economically (M. Bogue 1959: 58). One of the problems most prevalent during the war, however, was a chronic shortage of labor. Statistics compiled for two towns in New Hampshire, although well outside the corn belt, indicate that "farmers" accounted for only 3 and 8 percent of the war enlistments for each town, while "unskilled workers," including both farm laborers and factory workers, accounted for 20 and 34 percent of the enlistments (Kemp 1990: 63–64). If these statistics can be viewed as representative of the entire North—and similar figures can be traced as far back as the 1760s (Fred Anderson 1984)—then it can be assumed that the labor shortage, albeit not a lasting problem in all areas (see, for example, Conzen 1971: 161n), did have some effect on farm production. Part of the shortage of labor was ameliorated by the work of women and immigrants (Anderson 1929: 5).

Unfortunately, statistics on tenancy were not collected by census takers until 1880. As a result, analysts have had to devise various ways to calculate the rates of farm tenancy before then (see, for example, Bogue 1963: 63–65; Winters 1978). In their study of northern agriculture, Atack and Bateman (1987: 111) use a small sample of farms to estimate the rates of tenancy in the four corn-belt states in 1860. In Illinois, of 850 farms in their sample, 698 (82.1 percent) were owner-operator farms, 36 (4.2 percent) were worked by part-tenants who owned some property, and 116 (13.6 percent) were farmed by whole-tenants. In Indiana, of 2,910 farms, 2,298 (79.0 percent) were owner-operator farms, 170 (5.8 percent) were part-tenant farms, and 442 (15.2 percent) were whole-tenant farms. In Iowa, of 326 farms, 264 (81.0 percent) were owner-operator farms, 19 (5.8 percent) were part-tenant farms, and 43 (13.2 percent) were whole-tenant farms. And in Ohio, of 422 farms, 364 (86.3 percent) were owner-operator farms, 41 (9.7 percent) were part-tenant farms, and 17 (4.0 percent) were whole-tenant farms.

These statistics suggest that, in the corn belt of 1860, about 82 percent of the farmers were independent owner-operators, while the remaining 18 percent were farming on some kind of tenancy arrangement. This percentage of tenants does not seem large. When the total number of farms in the region is considered, however, the percentage of tenants means that in 1860 around 93,000 farms in the corn belt were farmed by tenants (roughly 26,000 in Illinois; 24,000 in Indiana; 11,000 in Iowa; and 32,000 in Ohio). Such numbers clearly are not insignificant. The numbers of people hired by the owners can be only surmised, but the mere recognition of their presence in the corn belt illustrates the hierarchical nature of agriculture in the North.

A survey of the 1860 manuscript census for Griggsville Township, Pike County, Illinois—a county that has been the focus of considerable activity by historical archaeologists (Blank-Roper 1990a, 1990b; Esarey et al. 1985; Phillippe 1985; Smith and Bonath 1982)—reveals that, of 169 individuals in the sample, fully 42.0 percent of those listed as "farmers" had no real estate. Of the remaining "farmers," 24.9 percent had between $100 and $2,500 in real estate, 17.2 percent had between $2,500 and $5,000 in real estate, 10.7 percent had between $5,000 and $10,000 in real estate, and 5.3 percent had real estate worth over $10,000. Interestingly, many of the farmers having over $2,000 in real estate were followed in the census list by farmers having no property. For example, one farmer with $3,200 in property was followed in the census by six farmers having none. Many of these farmers also were followed by individuals listed as "laborers." The temptation, of course, is to suppose that these unpropertied farmers, and certainly the laborers, worked for the aforementioned propertied farmers.

Comparing the figures for 1860 with those for 1870 is provocative because, after the Civil War, the real estate values associated with farmers in the same township appear to have changed radically (table 9.2). (The same farmers are not necessarily represented in both samples.) Whereas before the war only 16.0 percent of the sampled farmers owned over $5,000 in real estate, after the war this figure jumped to 45.0 percent. Even though the historical reasons for this change undoubtedly are complex, the figures imply that important shifts in the structure of northern farming can be identified between 1860 and 1870, the period bracketing the Civil War. Unfortunately, such hierarchical complexity in the

**Table 9.2.** Real Estate Valuations for 169 Farmers in Griggsville
Township, Pike County, Illinois, 1860 and 1870

| | 1860 | | 1870 | |
| Real Estate Values ($) | N | % | N | % |
|---|---|---|---|---|
| 0 | 71 | 42.0 | 49 | 29.0 |
| 100–2,500 | 42 | 24.9 | 10 | 5.9 |
| 2,500–5,000 | 29 | 17.2 | 34 | 20.1 |
| 5,000–10,000 | 18 | 10.7 | 41 | 24.3 |
| >10,000 | 9 | 5.3 | 35 | 20.7 |
| Total | 169 | 100.1 | 169 | 100.0 |

SOURCES: Population Schedules, Manuscript Census, Pike County, Illinois, 1860 and
1870.

social relations of northern agriculture has been overlooked by the archaeologists who have examined farm sites in Pike County.

## Historical Archaeology and Corn-Belt Agriculture

Even this brief historical sketch shows that northern agriculture was
composed of individual farmers who were arranged in hierarchical social relations of production during the 1850–70 period. In the North, as
in the South before the Civil War but most dramatically after it, landlords and tenants were arranged across the landscape in a shifting set of
interconnected relations. Although social relations in the North were
perhaps not as rigidly hierarchical as those in the South, power and control was accorded to some northern farmers and not to others (Atack
and Bateman 1987: 100; Merrill 1980: 144). The North was not a homogeneous landscape of agrarian equality that stood in stark contrast to
the South; some farmers clearly were better off than others in both regions.

Many avenues of inquiry may be pursued to assist in developing an
archaeological understanding of the social relations of production in corn-
belt agriculture during the mid-nineteenth century. At a minimum,

historical archaeologists excavating northern farmsteads should realize that farm tenancy was not restricted to the postbellum South. The agricultural ladder shows that, even in the generally prosperous corn belt, not all agriculturalists were independent owner-operators.

One fruitful approach for archaeologists seeking to understand the social aspects of the agricultural North during the nineteenth century, and particularly during the "transition" period that occurred from about 1850 to about 1870, might be to focus initially on what has been termed the "household" (Merrill 1977) or "domestic" (Wild 1989) mode of production. The household mode of production, like all relations of production, exists merely as a theoretical construct, not as a universal set of characteristics to be matched at individual archaeological sites. A focus on the household, however, brings the analysis down to a unit of study that has clear archaeological relevance. The basis of the household mode of production rests on the idea that farmers in the corn belt in 1850–70 were not the self-sufficient yeomen of the romanticized American past, but rather continuously created and recreated a complex web of social relations. This web of relations allowed them to articulate with the constantly transforming capitalist mode of production as it appeared between 1850 and 1870 (Merrill 1980: 143). The primary economic and social unit of the household mode of production was the family, and family relationships cannot be divorced from the economics of daily life (Henretta 1978: 21). As such, these relationships constitute a significant part of the anthropological analysis of corn-belt agriculture.

The intertwining of family relationships with the economics of farm life suggests that modes of production are not static. On the contrary, the modes are in a constant state of readjustment and realignment. As times changed in the past, of course, this mode of production was altered along lines that made regional, historical, and cultural sense. Such changes can be seen, for example, in comparing farmhouse designs before and after the Civil War, as the role of the family changed with concomitant changes in commonly held perceptions (see, for example, McMurry 1988: 56–134). In this sense, then, the household mode of production—which incorporates both personal relationships and material objects—would not be the same in 1870 as it was in 1850, even at the same farms.

Changes in social and material relations between 1850 and 1870 should not be viewed as merely extensions the idealized view of northern, self-sufficient agrarian life, expressed in different terms. Instead, the modes of production should be seen as incorporating key vertical relations of production between tenant and landlord. Archaeologists, by their detailed examinations of farm life, can help to illustrate the complexities of the material conditions of the household mode of production and its constituent changes. The rise of nineteenth-century capitalism in the United States, within the rural North as well as elsewhere, incorporated, among many other conditions, "a shift from local self-sufficiency in food and clothing toward increased dependence on outside markets" as well as the movement of control of manufacturing "from independent household producers into the hands of entrepreneurs" (Clark 1979: 169). Archaeologists, by their careful studies of artifact distributions, faunal resource exploitation, house design change, construction and placement of farm-support buildings, among other kinds of material analysis, should be able to discern at least some of the significant changes that occurred during the transition from antebellum to postbellum agriculture in the North. In considering the rural North specifically, the vertical relations of production, the growing dependence on outside material goods, and the rise of entrepreneurial activity all must, in some fashion, be taken into account by archaeologists (see, for example, Orser, in press). Obviously, a multiscalar approach can be extremely beneficial in such a complex study.

The strategy for operationalizing a multiscalar program of archaeological research will be complex to formulate and difficult to conduct. The complexities of the program can be seen as a metaphor for the multilevel nature of the webs of social relations that once operated in the society under study. Space does not permit the presentation of an example of how such an analysis may be conducted, but a few thoughts on the approaches to be used in such a complex relational analysis nonetheless can be offered.

The selection of sites is the initial issue to be resolved in such an analysis. In a multiscalar analysis, the first step should be to select, within a region, a number of distinct sites known to be associated with farmers located on different rungs of the agricultural ladder. Adopting this scheme may require detailed investigation of some sites that at first may appear to be rather unimpressive and possibly even unimportant. Archaeological research in the South has shown that some of the physical evidence of farm tenancy can be extremely ephemeral (Anderson and Muse 1982) and lack focus and visibility (after Deetz 1977:94). As a practical matter, archaeologists may find it difficult to convince funding agencies, who are often unwilling to commit adequate amounts of money to the archaeological study of the recent past, that such sites are potentially significant from a research standpoint (but see Moir and Jurney 1987). To compound the problem, it may be difficult to locate such sites, and upon excavation they may not yield many artifacts. When these obstacles are overcome, however, the excavation of agrarian sites must be conducted in such a manner that their samples are statistically comparable.

The selection of sites should be conducted in conjunction with historical research that has as one purpose the association of particular sites with known individuals at certain points in time. Property records for each site should be searched thoroughly (following Langhorne and Babits 1988) and the names of farmers compared against manuscript census materials. This historiographic process should suggest the tenure status of the sites' past inhabitants and show how these peoples' status may have changed in ten-year intervals, or, in the present case, from 1850 to 1860 to 1870. As most historical archaeologists already know, the important process of correlating specific archaeological sites with particular individuals can be extremely time consuming and frustrating, but only through this formidable process will it be possible to associate certain sites with known members of the vertical hierarchy of American agriculture.

The task of associating distinct individuals with known archaeological sites can be exceedingly difficult because of the way in which farms were inhabited, abandoned, and reinhabited as personal and historical circumstances changed (for the South, see Orser and Holland 1984). Archaeological research at the Bartlett Site in western Illinois, for example, indicates that this one nineteenth-century farmstead had two, and possibly three, distinct occupations. The inhabitants of each occupation functioned "within distinctive economic and social systems" (Blank-Roper 1990b: 182), or within different networks. The first occupation was a habitation, historically undocumented, that occurred in the 1840s and early 1850s; the second occupation occurred from the mid-1860s to about 1915. An intermediate occupation from the 1850s to the 1860s is problematical.

If it can be assumed that the farmers at the Bartlett Site during the two readily identifiable periods actually were members of different networks, then one could expect to observe different artifact distributions within the deposits, a different usage of the landscape, or some complex interaction between landscape and artifact presence and distribution. A complete analysis is beyond the scope of this paper, but even a quick examination of just the glassware collected during the archaeological investigations demonstrates some distinct differences between the two occupations. Whereas the early features excavated at the site yielded no fragments of canning jars, medicine bottles, or beverage bottles, the features from the later occupation yielded 123 pieces of canning jars, 88 fragments of medicine bottles, and 29 sherds of beverage bottles (Blank-Roper 1990b: 172).

The reasons for the differences in artifact presence in the two occupations are clearly complex and may be related to numerous sociohistorical factors, including perhaps consumer preference, artifact availability, and different marketing strategies. The important point, however, is that archaeologists must examine the inhabitants of historic farms along some common social dimension in order to make such comparisons meaningful both to historical archaeology and to wider social science. I advocate a concentration on a dimension that focuses on the vertical relations between landlord and tenant, with the realization that other, equally valid dimensions also could, and should, be analyzed. That the artifacts at the nearby Ferris Site, a property owned by a man clearly near the top of the agricultural ladder (Blank-Roper 1990b: 24), more closely resembles those from the later occupation than those from the earlier one may indicate something about the agricultural positions of the inhabitants of both early and late occupations.

Once sites have been selected, investigated archaeologically, and dated using all possible historical and archaeological information, a second analysis can be conducted in which the perspective is widened from the individual sites to all of the sites studied in the region. At this point, an understanding of the material dynamics of the vertical hierarchies will emerge, as differences and similarities between the material cultures of tenants and of independent owner-operators—who also may have been landlords—are understood in different terms, some temporal, some functional, and some ideological.

As the number of sites that can be associated with both landlords and tenants grows, more numerous and more revealing comparisons can be made using various scales. Such scales could include comparisons made within the Pike County agricultural ladder, between Pike County and other agrarian sites throughout Illinois, with sites throughout the corn belt, and with other tenant and landlord sites outside the corn belt, such as in the antebellum and postbellum South. Fruitful topics of additional analysis may include the contradictions between positions on the agricultural ladder, the role of race in structuring farm ownership, and the place of kinship in rural life.

With this comparative analysis complete, a new scale can be added to the analysis in order to shed light on the larger sectional and even national place of the sites under study. A similar kind of analysis already has been pursued by some historical archaeologists, albeit with a different underlying theory in mind (see, for example, William Adams 1976, Riordan and Adams 1985). This scale of investigation focuses on the market flow of material objects into individual regions and sites at particular points in time. This sort of analysis will provide information about the rise of capitalism in the rural North between 1850 and 1870 and even throughout the nineteenth century, as the temporal scale is further broadened.

## Discussion

This exploratory paper does not attempt to present an example of the research program outlined here. Clearly, the operationalization of this program will be time consuming and difficult, and will require a large amount of space to explore fully. Given the complexities of agricultural life, the significant impact of the Civil War upon it, and the effects of regional, sectional, national, and even international forces on farm production, it cannot be expected that the archaeological understanding of northern agrarian life in 1850–70 should be any easier or more straightforward than has been the study of southern farming. In any case, the kinds of analyses pursued at southern tenant sites certainly can be addressed in the rural North. Many issues can be addressed by historical archaeologists studying agricultural life in the North (for further comments, see Friedlander 1990), especially those involving the nature and extent of the region's social relations of production in all of its historical forms.

Meaningful archaeological analysis is difficult even in the best situations. The complexities of past farm life require a multiscalar approach that can disassemble the past in clear analytical ways. Northern farm dynamics are surely worthy of archaeological study, and the American Civil War provides a focus for such analyses in the same way that it has for studies of the agricultural South. This chapter provides thoughts and possible directions for analysis, in the hope that other historical archaeologists will see value in studying agricultural life in the North.

## Acknowledgments

I thank Janice L. Orser for her insightful comments on and assistance with this paper. I also thank William Marquardt for sending me a copy of his paper before it was published. In addition, the editors of this volume and their anonymous reviewers have assisted me by offering their suggestions and ideas. This essay is better for all the commentary I have received.

*Clarence R. Geier, Jr.*

# TOWARD A SOCIAL HISTORY OF THE CIVIL WAR

## *The Hatcher-Cheatham Site*

F ew events in history have had as dramatic an influence in shaping the character of our nation as the Civil War. Direct and indirect impacts of this event continue to influence the dynamics of our society at local and national levels. Given the war's importance, both scholarly and lay communities have given considerable attention to the Civil War and its associated battles and skirmishes. Recently, attention has focused increasingly on the war's impact on the lives of soldiers and civilians in the United States during and after the war. A growing interest in military reenactment has heightened popular interest in the daily lives of the soldiers. Unfortunately, academic research into these and broader questions of impact on lifeways has been slow to develop.

Though the Civil War has been recognized as an important, often romanticized event of history, many of its students have treated it as if it were a self-contained event. For all the war's epic quality, the conduct and cessation of hostilities were certainly not ends in themselves. Instead, the war must be regarded as the beginning of a progression of major economic, social, political, demographic, and philosophical events that have shaped, and continue to shape, our nation.

While many explanations can be given to account for attitudes prevalent today and for the current state of knowledge, the fact is that, until recently, the majority of historians and social scientists have shown little interest in the human and developmental implications of the war. As historians and social scientists turn to the social history of the second half of the nineteenth century (Vinovskis 1989, 1990b), the necessary role of archaeology as an extension of, and compliment to, the historic record becomes apparent. Except for occasional diaries and personal letters, few comprehensive statements attempt to document the impressions of common soldiers or civilians concerning their lifeways and experiences during and following the war. As we investigate questions concerning the impact of the war on freed blacks and lower-class whites, illiteracy within these groups creates a barrier to understanding their lifeways and the problems and circumstances they confronted. As a result of deliberate action or neglect, pertinent legal records and documents from many parts of the country were lost during and following the war. In those areas, and for those topics where the written record is inadequate, archaeological sites that are the product of those human events contain the only remaining evidence of certain aspects of personal, local, and regional social history. In this situation, the method and technique of archaeology, in conjunction with the remaining historic record, supply a voice and an identity to those people and events which otherwise would be lost to history.

As efforts are made to give priority to the social history of the Civil War and the subsequent Reconstruction era, our perception of what is historically and archaeologically significant needs to be broadened. Looking at and interpreting battlefields and other military sites does not address the effect of the battle and subsequent occupation by victorious forces on the local population and economy. Indeed, many areas seriously impacted by the war may never have been impacted by battle. While battlefields, campsites, communications, and transport facilities will retain their importance, it is essential that we recognize the significance of burned, abandoned, renovated, and improved industries, farms, and residential neighborhoods. Such sites can yield insights into specific impacts on particular families and groups and, when considered together with other sites from across the landscape, provide an essential picture of the effect military activities had on local lifeways during and following the war.

This chapter abstracts the results of excavations and historic document analyses of the Hatcher-Cheatham Site in rural Chesterfield County, Virginia (Geier, McCartney, and Cromwell 1989; McCartney 1988). These results are presented as one illustration of how the interaction of archaeological process and archival research can provide evidence of events not apparent in the historical record. In addition, these two sources of data are used to consider the dynamics of a battle as it impacted the property and lifeways of a specific family living south of Richmond, Virginia, during the Civil War. The field research which was carried out in 1986 was sponsored by the Virginia Department of Highways and Transportation. Excavations centered on the site of a complex of domestic structures (Geier et al. 1989). These structures include those associated with the initial settlement of the property by Archibald Hatcher in the late 1790s, expansion and improvements to the property by his descendants, and the subsequent sale of the property to Dr. Thomas Cheatham in 1858. Discussion here focuses upon the Cheatham period of residence.

## The Cheatham Family and Site: 1857–61

Thomas James Cheatham, at age twenty-seven, married twenty-year-old Mary Frances Gregory on December 19, 1850, only a few months after his graduation from the University of Virginia Medical School. While Thomas had a middle-class background, Mary's father Nelson Gregory was a prominent upper-middle-class Chesterfield County landowner and planter (Geier, McCartney, and Cromwell 1989: 33–35).

In 1857 Nelson Gregory purchased a 252-acre parcel of property (Virginia, Chesterfield County, Deed Book [CCDB] 42: 617) south of Proctors Creek and west of the Richmond-Petersburg Turnpike (figs. 10.1 and 10.2). This tract included a dwelling that had been the home of the Hatcher family, local middle-class farmers. Excavations at the site (fig. 10.3) showed the Hatcher home to have been a simple rectangular hall-and-chamber structure constructed of wood frame on brick piers with opposing end chimneys. Evidence of only one support building was found near it and within the study area. Apparently the Hatcher home had deteriorated structurally, land tax records revealing evidence of its declining value in the decades prior to the sale (Virginia, Chesterfield County, Personal Property Tax Lists 1850–57). In support of this interpretation, site archaeology showed no evidence of any effort to renovate or repair the house from the time of initial construction.

Tax assessments from 1857 and 1858 show that Nelson Gregory made significant improvements to the property in those years, nearly tripling the value of existing structures. Analyses of structures identified archaeologically and of the artifacts attributed to their use indicate that Gregory substantially improved the domestic complex to prepare a modest but modern residence with appropriate support buildings.

The original Hatcher dwelling was substantially renovated and remodeled by constructing additions to the west end and rear of the dwelling (fig. 10.3). The interior floor plan was also revised. An icehouse, multipurpose kitchen/domestic structure, and shed were built to the rear of the house (fig. 10.4). To the west, within a large fenced area, at least one structure, interpreted as a slave quarter, was constructed. A well was excavated just outside the enclosure between the slave quarters and the kitchen. Brick-rubble walkways were placed to allow access to the room on the west of the Cheatham home from a roadway passing along its front. Additional rubble walkways were constructed from the house to the domestic structures to its rear, and from those west to the well. A gate in the fenced enclosure allowed slaves access to the well and icehouse area. No effort was made to construct a brick pathway to the slave quarters.

In 1858 Nelson Gregory sold the renovated house and a parcel of land to his son-in-law Thomas Cheatham (Virginia, CCDB 43: 607). In residence with Cheatham where his wife, Mary Frances, who was pregnant, two children, and five slaves over the age of sixteen. Compared to their neighbors, the Cheathams owned a substantial investment in household and kitchen furnishings, though it is uncertain whether these were

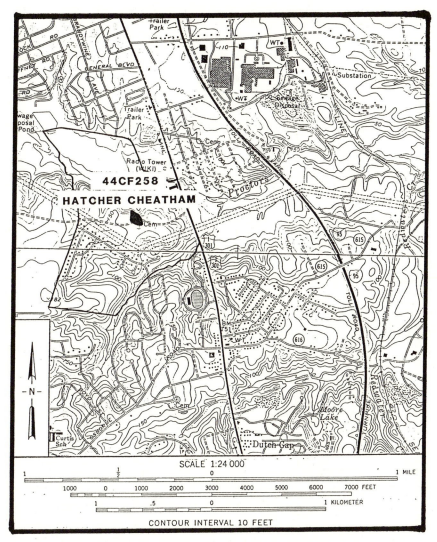

**Fig. 10.1.** *Map of Hatcher-Cheatham farm boundaries. Detail of 1981 U.S. Geological Service quadrangles for Chester and Drewry's Bluff, Virginia. Courtesy of the Department of Sociology and Anthropology, James Madison University.*

inheritances and/or their own purchases (Virginia, Chesterfield County, Personal Property Tax Lists 1858).

Cheatham began practicing medicine as soon as he became established in his new home in 1858. By 1860 he had also established a productive

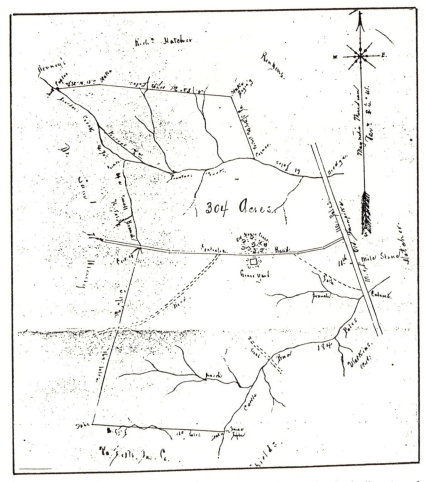

**Fig. 10.2.** *Plat of Dr. Thomas J. Cheatham's farm in 1902. Note that the dwelling site and graveyard are identified. From Chesterfield County Plat Book 1: 176.*

working farm. The number of his slaves had increased to eight, four of whom were older than twelve years of age (Virginia, Chesterfield County, Slave Schedules 1860). The 1860 agricultural census indicates that he had 152 acres in crops, including Indian corn and oats, as well as Irish potatoes and sweet potatoes. He had five milk cows and twenty-seven head of swine. While hardly engaged in plantation agriculture, with the aid of his slaves Cheatham did manage an agricultural operation which appears to have met most of the needs of his family, slaves,

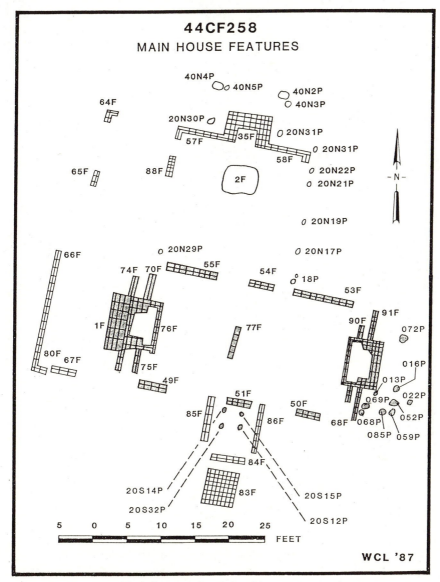

**Fig. 10.3.** *Reconstructed brick features and postholes of the main house at the Hatcher-Cheatham Site. Courtesy of the Department of Sociology and Anthropology, James Madison University.*

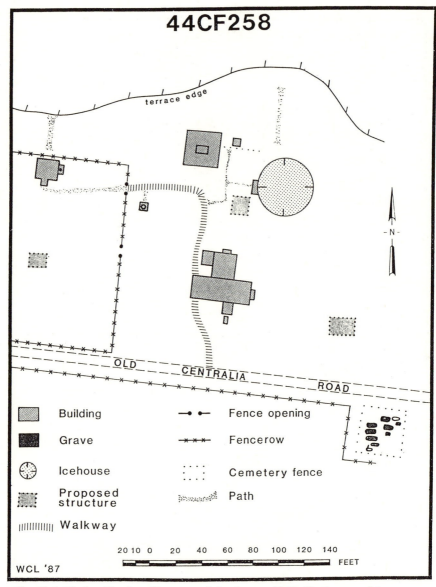

**Fig. 10.4.** *Hatcher-Cheatham Site, proposed site plan, ca. 1857–58. Courtesy of the Department of Sociology and Anthropology, James Madison University.*

and livestock. Analysis of food remains from the site (Geier 1989) indicate that pork and, less frequently, beef played important roles in the diet of the site's occupants. Small numbers of oyster and fish from the coast suggest that occasionally the family purchased food, probably for special occasions.

The proximity of the residence to the turnpike and to Centralia Road, which passed in front of the house, would have been important to Cheatham as a physician (fig. 10.2). These important local roads would have allowed his patients ready access to his office and would have allowed Cheatham to make house calls in a timely manner. The construction of a brick walkway from Centralia Road to the room addition at the west end of the main house (fig. 10.4) suggests that the wing may have doubled as a surgery or office. The walkway would have allowed patients ready access to Dr. Cheatham, without intruding on the normal activities of his family.

## Overview of the War Years: 1861–65

On April 17, 1861, Virginia seceded from the Union. From June 1861, when the capital of the Confederacy was shifted to Richmond, until the close of the war four years later, Virginia was the focus of intense military conflict. Little historical information is available on the war years' effects on the Cheathams. Legal documents for the period are virtually nonexistent, and Thomas and Mary Cheatham chose not to write about the period or pass on their remembrances.

Existing military records indicate that Dr. Cheatham served the Confederacy as a civilian contract physician with the rank of assistant surgeon. While little is known of his activities, most of his duties were probably performed at the nearby medical facility at Fort Darling or Drewry's Bluff. Confederate pay vouchers for 1862 and 1863 indicate that he provided service meeting routine medical needs and dispensing medicines. He also was paid for the services of his slaves, who apparently were employed in the construction of new fortifications at Drewry's Bluff (Confederate States of America, Pay Vouchers 1862, 1863). Indirect evidence suggests that Dr. Cheatham may have been in service at Fort Darling

during the bloody confrontation between Confederates who were manning Drewry's Bluff and Union naval vessels which attempted to approach Richmond via the James River on May 15, 1862. An eyewitness
account of the battle prepared by Judge William I. Clopton (Clopton
1905: 34, 82–98) following the war has Dr. Cheatham's signature affixed
as a verification of the report's authenticity.

Despite its position west of the midpoint of the turnpike between
Richmond and Petersburg, there is no evidence of significant military
activity in the vicinity of the Cheatham home until May 1864. By this
time, the Cheathams would have found themselves in a very vulnerable
position. An elaborate series of entrenchments, batteries, and redoubts
had been constructed half a mile to the north as protection for the southern approaches to Richmond (fig. 10.5). The first line of entrenchments
extended from Fort Darling southwest for 3.5 miles to Wooldridge Hill.
Behind this front line was a second, more extensive defensive perimeter
interlaced with batteries, redans, and redoubts, all connected by lines linking them with the Fort Darling entrenchments. The fact that primary
routes of transport to Richmond lay immediately to the east (Richmond-
Petersburg Turnpike) and 1.75 miles to the west (Richmond-Petersburg
Railroad), and the fact that these two routes were joined by the Centralia
Road which passed to the front of the Cheatham home, increased the
strategic importance of the area and hence its vulnerability.

In March 1864, Lieutenant General Ulysses S. Grant, general-in-chief
of the U.S. Army, developed a complex, multipronged spring offensive.
Concurrent with a major offensive in Tennessee and Georgia, Major
General George A. Meade's Army of the Potomac was to strike General
Robert E. Lee's troops in Virginia. Three smaller concurrent offensives
were to take place in conjunction with these larger actions. One of these
involved the Army of the James, with Major General Benjamin Butler
commanding. Butler's forces were to threaten Richmond from the south,
severing the city's rail lines and hampering Lee's lines of supply. Grant
hoped that the threat posed by this plan would force Lee to retire to the
Richmond entrenchments to meet Butler's army. Grant then would be
able to unite the Army of the Potomac and the Army of the James at
Richmond and crush Lee (Nash 1969: 191–94; J.C. Robertson 1987: 14;
Simon 1982: 245–47; Wise 1865: 230).

On May 5, 1864, General Butler and his army of thirty-five thousand

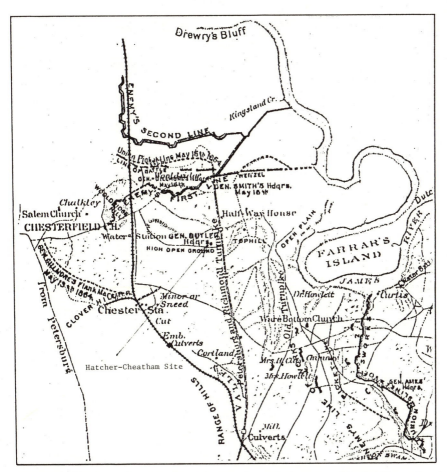

**Fig. 10.5.** *Placement of Hatcher-Cheatham Site within military context of Battle of Drewry's Bluff. Abstracted from map prepared by Engineers Office, Tenth Army Corps in Davis, et al., 1978, plate LXV:1.*

troops landed at City Point, Virginia. From May 6 to May 16, Union and Confederate forces skirmished and fought over the eastern half of Chesterfield County. Between May 12 and May 16, Union troops conducted a major offensive against the Drewry's Bluff defenses. In that engagement, Butler's strategy was to conduct a feint in force against the Confederate positions at Richmond, the intent being to obligate General Pierre G. T. Beauregard, commander of the Confederate forces, to maintain his army south of Richmond. This would prevent Beauregard from sending reinforcements to Lee, who at that time was engaged with

Meade's troops at Spotsylvania Courthouse. The advance also would allow Federal cavalry, virtually uncontested, to cut and destroy rail lines, roads, bridges, and canals in Chesterfield County (Butler 1892: 650–51; Robertson 1987: 143; Robert N. Scott 1891).

The Drewry's Bluff offensive began on May 12, 1864, under Butler's personal command. Heavy rains and dense vegetation made the advance on the 12th and 13th particularly difficult and slow. On May 12, the Federal forces reached a prominence on the heights south of Proctors Creek near the Cheatham home. Believing the heights to the north of the creek to be effectively defended and entrenched by Confederate forces, the troops halted and awaited the arrival of support troops. On May 13, the Union forces crossed Proctors Creek. The forces were arrayed in a line of advance extending from the James River on the east, to the Richmond-Petersburg Railroad on the west, with the Cheatham farm situated near the center of the line. Early on May 14, Federal forces closed on the first line of Confederate fortifications and, finding them abandoned, occupied the entrenchments. Plans to attack the second, more imposing set of earthworks which lay to the north were held up. While the Union forces assumed a defensive posture, General Beauregard took advantage of their slowness and indecision, reinforcing his southern defenses and thus offsetting Butler's numerical superiority. At 4:45 A.M. on May 16, in a very thick fog, the Confederate troops began a counterattack against the Federals, concentrating on the Union right flank. Again, indecision and failures in communication prevented the Union forces from responding to the attack in a timely and appropriate manner. As a result, late in the afternoon, Butler ordered a general withdrawal (Butler 1892; Robertson 1987; Robert Scott 1891; Simon 1982; Trefousse 1957).

The fighting and skirmishing, which took place from May 6 to 16, affected Chesterfield County from the James River west to Chesterfield Courthouse, and from Kingsland Creek on the north to Swift Creek on the south. Fields were littered with troop paraphernalia, while substantial damage had been done to farmland and "several fine homes" that had been in Union hands (Robertson 1987: 218; Lutz 1954; O'Dell 1983).

Strategic position placed the Cheatham home in the heart of the battle. The farm topographically was situated on a high promontory immediately above and south of Proctors Creek. From this vantage point, movements along the Richmond-Petersburg Turnpike, 1,500 feet to the east, and the Confederate first line of defense to the north could be observed. The farm was situated almost at the midpoint of what was to become the Federal offensive on May 12 and 13. The Centralia Road which ran west from the turnpike and south of the Cheatham home, crossed the front of the Wooldridge Hill entrenchments and provided access to the Richmond-Petersburg Railroad. Army forces at this location could command the bottomlands of Proctors Creek, which were an important defensive feature, and could control the movements of troops and materials along Centralia Road between the turnpike and railroad and to the rear of the Union left flank.

Military records provide evidence of the strategic military importance that the Cheatham property assumed and of its use and ultimate destruction. Official military records indicate that the farm was a focus of Union troop movement and encampment throughout the action. On May 12, Brigadier General Burnham, commander of the 2nd Brigade, reported that he made contact with the enemy "near Dr. Cheathams house." He skirmished with the Confederates and slowly pushed them back across Proctors Creek. Colonel Aaron Stephens, of the 13th New Hampshire, writes that his troops were engaged as skirmishers near the Cheatham house on May 12 and that after pushing Confederate forces across Proctors Creek, his regiment withdrew to a line of support and encamped in the vicinity of Cheatham's (Robert Scott 1891: 139–41). Another report from Lieutenant Colonel Horace Saunders, of the 19th Wisconsin Infantry, indicates that his regiment moved north along the turnpike on May 12, forming in line of battle with the 88th Pennsylvania Volunteers. The report suggests that they stopped on the heights above Proctors Creek and encamped on the Cheathams' property between the turnpike and the Cheatham home. On May 13, troops of Major General William F. Smith crossed Cattle Run in the bottomlands of Proctors Creek roughly 1,600 feet southeast of the Cheatham home. One final report placing a large body of troops on the Cheatham property states that, during the Union withdrawal on May 16, Brigadier General Turner and the 2nd Division of X Corps, took position on the south side of

Proctors Creek, protecting the west side of the Turnpike (Robert Scott 1891: 95, 141).

Significant activity is also reported for the Cheatham house proper. General Butler's headquarters was located at the home on May 13 during the Union advance, and then again on May 16 during the withdrawal. A signal station for the purpose of maintaining contact with troops at the front also was in place. General Smith of the 18th Army Corps and commander of forces comprising the east wing of the Federal advance had headquartered at the Cheathams' on May 12 prior to his advance to the north of Proctors Creek (Scott 1891: 23).

## The Battle of Drewry's Bluff: The Archaeological Record

Excavations at the Cheatham house (Cromwell 1989; Andrews and Mullins 1989) provided evidence of marginal involvement in local fighting activity. Canister, shell fragments, and fired bullets were found in the vicinity of the dwelling and in the yards to the north and east. These could be products of the Federal advance to Proctors Creek on May 12 and of the skirmishing that took place to dislodge Confederate advance forces.

Certain types of encampment debris were of the same type and kind that might be found in a domestic site of the same period. Accordingly, it is impossible to determine whether artifacts were of military origin or products of the Cheatham residence. Those artifacts identified as having a high possibility of representing encampment activities were concentrated in the yard area to the north of the Cheatham dwelling and in the vicinity of the kitchen/domestic structure and ice house (fig. 10.6). These include eating utensils, fragments of iron griddles, cauldrons, and tin cans of types common to Civil War camps. Artifacts associated with leisure or sedentary behavior were found and include reed stemmed pipes, jaw harps, harmonica plates, dice, and bullets carved into gaming pieces. Given the encampment of troops in this area from May 12 to 16, the occurrence of these materials is appropriate.

No specific artifacts or features were identified which could be attributed to the presence of General Butler or General Smith and their staffs, nor is there archaeological evidence of the signal station that was in operation May 12–16. It is possible that the artifacts noted above could be attributed to the support of these groups rather than to a general troop encampment. The artifacts, instead of being scattered across the yard areas about the Cheatham dwelling, as might be expected in an area of general encampment, are limited in their placement to the north and east house yards, suggesting a more localized and restricted activity.

Archaeological excavations provided evidence of military activity beyond that indicated by military records alone. Artifacts indicate that the domestic structure to the north of the Cheatham house may have been used as a primary medical aid station during the battle, and that at some time during or following the engagement, the Cheatham house was burned (Cromwell 1989; Buchanon 1989).

Artifacts attributed to the operation of a Federal primary aid station were found in the yard areas about the kitchen/domestic structure and between it and the icehouse. A primary aid station served as a front line first-aid facility. These stations were located close to the front but out of the range of musket fire. Activities there primarily involved preparing wounded for transfer to more capable field or base hospitals. At such facilities, clothing that had been soiled or bloodied commonly was removed to secure access to the wounds. The wounded often received new underwear and were covered with blankets to keep them warm (George Adams 1952: 116). Whiskey often was provided to counter shock, and opiates and morphine, when available, were used for pain. Only in the most extreme instances was surgery carried out. Typically these stations were stocked with pails, basins, sponges, lint, bandages, splints, tourniquets, chloroform, opium, morphine, and a fair amount of whiskey (Brooks 1966: 34).

Artifacts indicative of the aid station are of several categories. These include clothing parts; military hardware; and whiskey, ale, porter, beer, and pharmaceutical bottles (Andrews and Mullins 1989). Significantly, it is not the individual artifacts themselves but their presence as a set within a spatially defined area of the larger site that suggests the presence of the aid station. Another factor contributing to the assignment of certain of the pharmaceutical and other container bottles to the military aid station is their state of preservation. Some of the ale, porter, and beer bottles

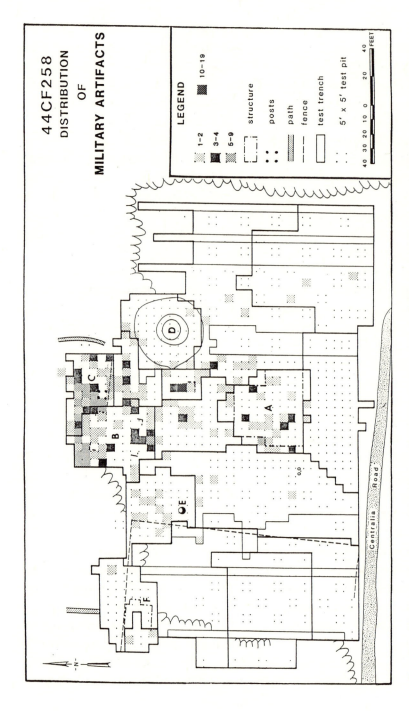

**Fig. 10.6.** *Distribution of military artifacts, Hatcher-Cheatham Site. Courtesy of the Department of Sociology and Anthropology, James Madison University.*

were found complete on the floor of the excavated cellar. In other in-stances, bottles were reconstructed from assemblages of glass, suggesting that the bottles had been broken and then left in place in the yard areas north of the house. This pattern and character of placement was incon-sistent with that of other artifacts more clearly associated with the Cheatham occupation.

Pharmaceutical bottles (n=110) represent the largest assemblage of container glass at the site. Of the total number, 46 could be attributed to a specific pharmacy or medicine. Certain of the bottles (27) come from Richmond or Petersburg sources and are attributed to Dr. Cheatham. Nineteen embossed pharmaceutical bottles are attributed to sources in the northeastern United States. Two of the brands, Hostetter's Bitters and Adolph Wolfe's Schnapps, have been found in Civil War sites else-where. Fragments from these bottles were most common in yard areas which enclose the kitchen structure, with secondary concentrations in the yard areas north of the house. Given Dr. Cheatham's known service as a surgeon and doctor, it is assumed that at least a significant number of these artifacts are a product of his activities.

Whiskey bottles include an array of flasks and case gin bottles of types which postdate 1850. Two of the flasks exhibit pro-Union motifs. A Union eagle was embossed on one, and the other was embossed with hands clasped in support of the Union. Remaining bottle types are simi-lar to those found elsewhere in Civil War sites. Bottle remains, some showing evidence of having been broken in place, are numerous in the area around the kitchen structure. Lesser concentrations were identified in the yards north of the main house. The greater number of bottles was found in fill at the surface of the icehouse floor.

Twenty-five unfired bullets/casings had been dropped or discarded in the yards immediately north and northeast of the kitchen, and in a lin-ear pattern to the north of the fence between the kitchen and icehouse (Cromwell 1989; fig. 10.7). An additional 25 bullets, showing evidence of having been fired, were also identified. Eleven of these were found in the vicinity of the main house, the remainder with the previously de-scribed concentration of unfired bullets. Eight bullets (seven from the yard east of the kitchen) exhibited human teeth marks. Such bullets are common to Civil War hospital sites and reflect use in the treatment of the wounded (Lord 1979). Percussion caps and cap box parts were found in the yard areas, the greatest number to the north of the kitchen yard fence (fig. 10.7).

The strongest argument for the use of the kitchen as an aid station is the quantity of clothing parts and buckles of types from knapsacks, haversacks, and cartridge boxes (Buchanon 1989; Cromwell 1989). One hundred and eight buckles of types common to haversack and/or knapsacks, 17 clothing clasps, 117 shoe eyelets, 36 suspender buckles, and 44 metal military coat and cuff buttons attributed to both Union and Confederate forces were found in the yard areas about the kitchen (figs. 10.8, 10.9). In addition, a large number of buttons from men's underwear (n=352) and from trousers and shirts (n=98) were found, again concentrated in the yard areas enclosing the kitchen. While certain of these buttons could have been a product of Cheatham family activities, the number and military nature of many make this an unlikely sole explanation. It is more probable that the buttons reflect removal of soiled and bloodied clothing from wounded Union and Confederate troops in preparation for transport to field hospitals. Accouterments that these wounded men wore, such as haversacks, knapsacks, belts, cartridge boxes, and cap boxes also would have been discarded. The pharmaceutical and whiskey bottles described earlier also would be logical artifacts in a primary aid station.

Certain indirect evidence supports the aid-station interpretation. References from diverse sources show that structures of the sort identified often were used to shelter and treat the wounded during and following a battle (George Adams 1952; Brooks 1966; O'Dell 1983). The position of the Cheatham house at the center of the Union offensive from May 12 on, with ready access to Centralia Road and the turnpike, made it a logical center for medical aid. Troops brought to this area easily could have been transported by ambulance to hospitals at the rear. In addition, George Sickley, medical director of the 18th Army Corps, later reported that Surgeon S. A. Richardson of the 13th New Hampshire was deserving of commendation, for on several occasions he and his assistants and operating surgeons had performed capably in field hospitals during the battle (Robert Scott 1891: 118–19, 138–39). The fact that 13th New Hampshire was encamped in the vicinity of the Cheatham farm on May

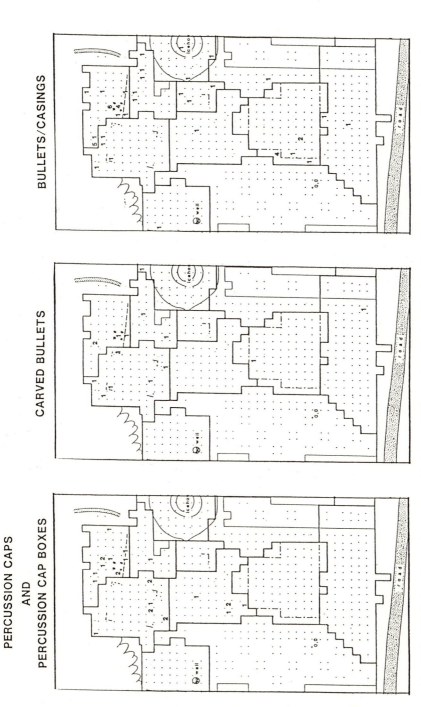

**Fig. 10.7.** *Distribution of percussion caps, carved bullets, and bullets/casings, Hatcher-Cheatham Site. Courtesy of the Department of Sociology and Anthropology, James Madison University.*

PERCUSSION CAPS
AND
PERCUSSION CAP BOXES

CARVED BULLETS

BULLETS/CASINGS

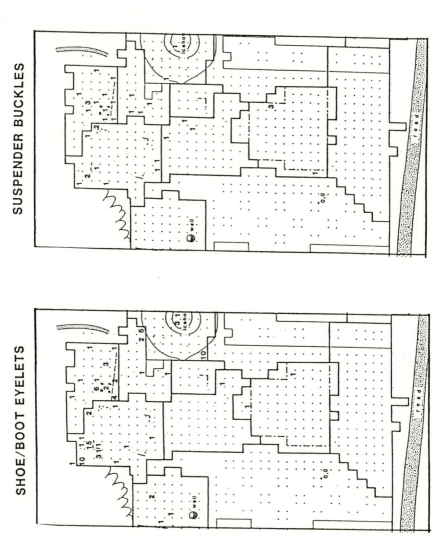

**Fig. 10.8.** *Distribution of shoe/boot eyelets and suspender buckles, Hatcher-Cheatham Site. Courtesy of the Department of Sociology and Anthropology, James Madison University.*

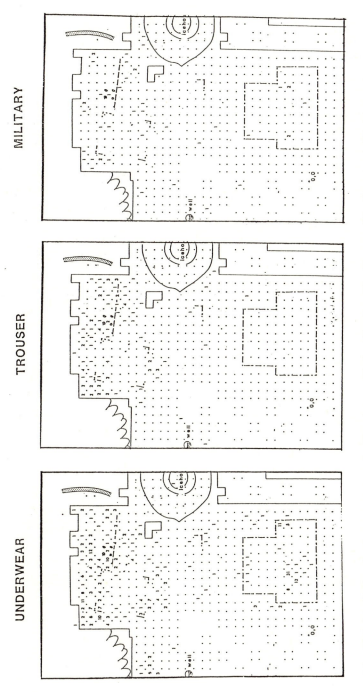

**Fig. 10.9.** *Distribution of underwear, trouser, and military buttons, Hatcher-Cheatham Site. Courtesy of the Department of Sociology and Anthropology, James Madison University.*

12 could suggest Richardson's use of the farm outbuildings. Given the fact that Cheatham was a practicing surgeon, it is possible that the medical facilities in place at the site may have made it amenable to military hospital use despite the fact that much, if not all, of Cheatham's equipment may have been removed previously.

Site excavations show that the Cheatham house had been burned and that at some later date it had been salvaged for remaining building materials. While the house is not actually reported as destroyed until 1867 (Virginia, Chesterfield County, Land Tax Lists 1861–67), it is probable that the structure was burned by Union forces either inadvertently during the battle or, just as probable, when they withdrew (McCartney 1988). Significantly, archaeological data suggest that the support buildings were not burned. Analysis of the burned/salvaged house remains show that the house stood empty, its contents removed, at the time of its destruction. This is not unreasonable in that it would be expected that Cheatham would have removed his property and family from harm's way as the threat of war loomed and the vulnerability of their position became apparent. It is also probable, given Cheatham's position as an assistant surgeon for the Confederacy, that during the engagement he would have been on call at the hospital at Fort Darling. Assuming that Union forces were aware of his service, his affiliation with the Confederate medical staff could have encouraged them to fire his house as they withdrew.

## Discussion

Given the destruction of the Cheatham home, and the continued presence of the Union troops to the south, it is unlikely that the Cheathams would have made any effort to reoccupy the farm during the ongoing hostilities. The fighting that is known to have occurred in the immediate vicinity of the house, and the use of the farm for military encampments and as a field hospital, would have reduced the farm and dwelling to a deplorable condition. The Cheathams and their neighbors, upon returning to their war-torn farmland, would have confronted insurmountable problems. The sheer devastation that would have resulted from exploding shells, trampling armies, looting, and vandalism; the stench of death; and the destruction of buildings would have been hard to overcome. Horses, livestock, and food stores left untended would have been lost to scavengers from both sides as they sought supplies. With the loss of their slaves and the death and injury of so many of their young men, the reclearing of land that had grown up from prolonged disuse, and the preparation of the land for planting, would have been difficult, if not economically impractical.

When Dr. Cheatham's list of taxable personal property is compared with similar lists of others in his district following the war, it is evident that he was more prosperous than many of his peers, despite the fact that his farm had been within the war zone. He is, for example, one of few taxpayers who report owning silver or gold plate (Virginia, Chesterfield County, Personal Property Tax Lists 1865–66). Cheatham's ability to sustain a standard of living that was at least materially comparable to that of the prewar years probably resulted from his having a readily marketable skill. As a medical professional, his expertise probably was much in demand, even more than in the prewar years. Returning soldiers recovering from the physical and emotional effects of the war, as well as the general populace, would have needed his attention (McCartney 1988: 43).

Evidence for the extent of the destruction to the Cheatham farm is the fact that on March 5, 1866, rather than reoccupying their homesite, the Cheathams relocated to a smaller property a few miles north of Chesterfield Courthouse, in a setting that may have been more favorable for Dr. Cheatham's medical practice (Virginia, Chesterfield County, Deed Book 14: 379). While the original Hatcher property continued to be farmed at a modest level, there is no evidence that the property ever was reoccupied. This conclusion is supported archaeologically, in that, while the site structures may have been salvaged after the war for use in new building, there are no artifacts to confirm a postwar occupation of the structures. In effect, what to a young couple in 1858 had been the promise of the future, was abandoned and lay in ruin less than six years later.

## Acknowledgments

The research of certain persons contributed significantly to preparation of this chapter. Martha McCartney provided the archival analysis and background on the Cheatham residence. Further, artifact analyses and interpretations provided by Rita Buchanon (clothing parts), James Cromwell (military and metal artifacts), and Paul Mullins and Susan Andrews (glasswares) were critical to the discussion.

# 11

*Joel W. Grossman*

## THE ROLE OF ESPIONAGE AND FOREIGN INTELLIGENCE IN THE DEVELOPMENT OF HEAVY ORDNANCE AT THE WEST POINT FOUNDRY, COLD SPRING, NEW YORK

Over a three-year period between 1989 and 1992, the first major federally mandated archaeological investigation of a Superfund site took place at the West Point Foundry in New York. This work led to the discovery of the well-preserved subsurface remains of R. P. Parrott's Civil War era cannon testing facilities and the otherwise unrecorded housing complex of the workers who helped produce and refine a new generation of large-caliber rifled ordnance. In addition to shedding new light on Union military research and development activities in heavy-weapons technology prior to and during the Civil War, these archaeological findings precipitated the archival discovery of a previously unrecognized aspect of Northern military history. This discovery in turn revealed the existence of a carefully orchestrated and highly effective capability in international military espionage and industrial intelligence on the part of Lincoln's executive branch and the U.S. Army and U.S. Navy ordnance bureaus which had not been addressed in past treatments of Northern Civil War history.

At times, the archaeological study of past events is consistent with available documents and published accounts of the past. When this is the case, the archaeological records provided by the surviving material remains can help augment and "flesh out" the perspectives of documented history. However, as this study has shown, the archaeological evidence also can be found to conflict with, and on occasion pointedly to contradict, the written record, in both detail and general implications. This was the case with the archaeological discoveries at West Point Foundry. Taken together, the combined archaeological and archival evidence from this first major archaeological study of Civil War era military facilities north of the Mason-Dixon Line has provided significant and unanticipated insights into the unwritten record of the Civil War and of American military and intelligence history.

This federally mandated compliance and mitigation program was performed under the jurisdiction of the U.S. Environmental Protection Agency and Army Corps of Engineers, and under contract with the lead engineering and design firm of Malcolm Pirnie, Incorporated. This large-scale, multistage site definition and data recovery effort demonstrated the feasibility of undertaking in-depth archaeological investigations within the context of potentially contaminated sites. From an archaeological and methodological standpoint alone, this effort, performed with the assistance of a range of applied-technology solutions to issues of site discovery, definition, and documentation, also clearly established that the discipline of archaeology has the ability to maintain the high standards of current federal compliance guidelines in a feasible and practical manner and time frame which do justice to both the resource and the primary mission of the Superfund environmental cleanup effort.

The West Point Foundry operated in Cold Spring, New York, across the Hudson River from the U.S. Military Academy at West Point. The archaeological remains of this significant Civil War era cannon foundry had lain dormant for the past 130 years under a nineteenth-century industrial landfill capped by modern, potentially toxic waste. This area, identified as the Marathon Battery Superfund Site, had been targeted by the U.S. Environmental Protection Agency for a major environmental cleanup effort. As part of a federally mandated planning and site evaluation conducted between 1989 and 1992, the first large-scale archaeological investigation and mitigation of a Superfund site resulted in the discovery of R. P. Parrott's Civil War era gun-testing or proofing facilities.

In addition to the exposure and documentation of the Foundry's Civil War era gun-testing facilities, computer-assisted historic map surveys also led to the discovery and excavation of an isolated cluster of unique workers' housing. These houses were located on a bluff above the foundry ruins, apart from the majority of the workers' housing situated within the town of Cold Spring. The large-scale excavation of these household remains yielded over 145,000 Civil War era artifacts, including a range of high status and technologically sophisticated artifacts. As socioeconomic and ethnic indicators, these exotic items simply did not concur with, or support, previously published historical characterizations of the workers who lived there.

The apparent inconsistencies between the material remains and the written record triggered an intensive reorientation in the ongoing archival research effort, away from a focus on the technological history of West Point Foundry proper and toward the role of foreign influences in the history of the military developments which took place there. The research then revealed the existence of a tightly controlled military research and development effort, as well as a Civil War intelligence and espionage operation, that focused on the development of large-caliber rifled cannon. This operation was funded by the Navy Ordnance Bureau and was run by some of the leading military and civilian figures of American science and technology of the time, all with direct lines of communication to President Abraham Lincoln.

## Early History of the Foundry Operations

### The Kemble Era: 1817–37

West Point Foundry began in 1817 as a private, but government-financed, establishment on the Hudson River, immediately upriver from the protective gun emplacements at West Point (figs. 11.1 and 11.2). It was one of four foundries established after the War of 1812 to produce cannon for national defense (Kemble 1916: 191–92). Save for the civilian proprietor of West Point Foundry, Gouverneur Kemble, the appointed directors of these four establishments were military officers of high standing. Kemble, however, was well connected politically, economically, and socially within New York and Washington circles. Moreover, he had proven his dedication to his country and his expertise in the area of cannon technology through his participation in "industrial espionage," first as a commercial and later as a government attaché to the Spanish court (Kemble 1916: 192–201; Raoul 1936: 463).

During his tenure in industrial and military intelligence gathering, Kemble, like many other military attachés similarly posted in foreign missions, participated in a tradition by which former attachés continued to benefit from the fruits of foreign intelligence gathering. They did so especially in the area of heavy cannon technology and manufacture. Kemble was director and proprietor of the West Point Foundry until 1837, at which time he entered the U.S. Congress, a move which induced him to invite Parrott to resign from the U.S. military and take over as director of the foundry (Raoul 1936: 466; Kemble 1916: 199–200).

While the financing, site selection, and initial construction of the foundry appears to have been adequately addressed through a combination of local resources and guarantees of government contracts, the actual technology and expertise required to develop and operate a specialized heavy-gun foundry were not available locally. The lack of skilled labor during the 1820s was both a reflection of the incipient state of industry in America and the result of explicit efforts on the part of the advanced nations of Europe to maintain their strategic technological superiority (Raoul 1936: 464–65; Kemble 1916: 195). In England as well as other European countries, export restrictions were explicitly applied to the products, plans, and technology of artillery manufacture and testing. Further, restraints limited access to workers (founders, molders, mechanics, and ordnance specialists) who were involved in the manufacture and testing of heavy ordnance.

Although the terms may have varied, the skills of iron making in general, and heavy-cannon manufacturing in particular, then were viewed as proprietary areas of national security which were tightly controlled;

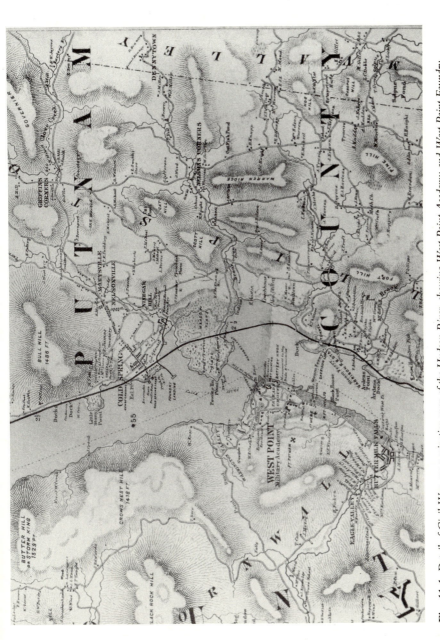

**Fig. 11.1.** *Detail of Civil War–era navigation map of the Hudson River, showing West Point Academy and West Point Foundry. Courtesy of Grossman and Associates, Inc.*

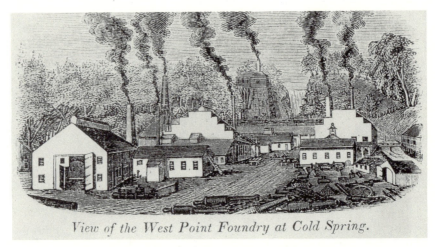

View of the West Point Foundry at Cold Spring.

**Fig. 11.2.** *Pre–Civil War Currier and Ives lithograph of the West Point Foundry, showing area immediately to the north of the Superfund Remediation Zone (Area 1). The inclusion of the elevated iron furnace at the rear suggests a pre-1837 date for the illustration. Courtesy of the Putnam County Historical Society.*

transgressors were subject to severe punishment. Thus, in violating these laws, either an Englishman or a foreigner knowingly embarked on what was defined and clearly understood as a crime against England. Such a transgression was something not to be undertaken lightly as a private commercial venture.

Against this backdrop, what Kemble and his foundry partners subsequently undertook reads as a carefully coordinated subterfuge, with all the flair of a modern spy novel. Kemble, apparently with the assistance of the U.S. military, addressed the problem of an insufficient number of foundry workers and ordnance technicians with a simple but dangerous tactic. Despite the legal and diplomatic barriers, he stole them away from England, and possibly other European countries, with a carefully formulated series of international operations, undertaken with subterfuge and with naval logistical support. According to Kemble's later account, transatlantic trips to secure British and Irish iron founders, molders, and craftsmen occurred on at least two occasions. This pattern of "borrowing" men and technology from Europe, and from England in particular, appears to have been a long-standing tradition in the technological development of both the West Point Foundry and the American military throughout the nineteenth century (Raoul 1936: 465–66).

The first such documented voyage took place between 1818 and 1825 and the second, on or about 1825. On the first trip, a Captain Graham of New York docked at Liverpool and announced that he was sailing with a work force of unskilled laborers. After setting sail, he then docked at Queenstown and, with the help of Mr. Young (a skilled ironmaster and brother of an Irish foundry owner who served under Kemble as the first superintendent at the West Point Foundry), replaced the laborers with a group of passengers who turned out to be skilled mechanics, most probably including iron founders and molders. The British got wind of the subterfuge and sent a warship in pursuit, but Captain Graham escaped, and a half-dozen men arrived in New York (Raoul 1936: 466).

The second trip, in 1825, involved an even more elaborate example of international subterfuge. Captain Graham and Mr. Young returned to the British Isles, presumably on normal business. However, upon sailing from Liverpool, they reportedly experienced a mutiny which forced them to dock at a small Irish port to unload the rebellious crew. When they returned to New York, the new crew members were found to consist of foundry specialists and "first class molders" (Kemble 1916: 195–96; Raoul 1936: 465–66). Aside from this documentary footnote to history, these special immigrants, brought to Cold Spring as part of a surreptitious quasimilitary operation, essentially disappeared from the historical record. Their existence, and the significance of their role in the development of armaments for the American Civil War, came to light only in 1990, as a result of the West Point Foundry archaeological investigations.

## The Parrott Era: 1837–67

Robert Parrott, an ordnance officer at West Point Academy, became director of the West Point Foundry in 1837. With his arrival, the establishment both consolidated and expanded its production facilities to enhance its regional security and self-sufficiency. At its peak, the West Point Foundry employed seven hundred workers and had the capacity to produce ten thousand tons of cast iron per year. The production of cast iron in turn required support facilities, which included six mines and eleven thousand acres of timberland. The latter utilized fifteen hundred workers, who produced ten thousand cords of wood for fuel per annum (Naylor 1961: 14–15; Parrott 1921; Raoul 1936: 469; Tyrell 1962; M. Wilson 1886).

Under Parrott's tenure, the foundry was a major research and development center. In addition, as a regional center of heavy cannon production, and as the sole source supplier of the Parrott rifled cannon, the West Point Foundry played a central role in establishing the military superiority of the Union land and naval forces during the Civil War. By the second and third year of the war, Parrott's facility had developed several sizes of large reinforced cast-iron rifled cannon, capable of repeatedly hitting targets at a distance of five miles or more and with an armor-piercing velocity of 1,200 feet per second (Bruce 1989: 230; Holley 1865: 487). This combined accuracy, range, and throw weight not only rendered traditional masonry fortifications and wooden ships obsolete, but also brought a new element of large-scale warfare to urban centers by providing reliable mechanisms for accurate long-distance explosive and incendiary bombardment (Bruce 1989). By the end of the war, Parrott's foundry had produced nearly two thousand cannon of various calibers, and in excess of three million shells (U.S. 40th Congress, 2d Session, 1868, volume 99: 915; Naylor 1961: 14–15).

Traditional accounts of the foundry's history have highlighted Parrott's singular role in developing his version of the rifled cannon. The picture presented by these accounts suggests that Parrott developed his version of the rifled cannon in relative technical and intellectual isolation. They also imply that he received little financial support or involvement from the government in general, or from the army and navy ordnance bureaus in particular (Kemble 1916: 199; Raoul 1936: 467; Parrott 1865; Tyrell 1962: 6). Archaeological discoveries at the West Point Foundry, however, combined with the detailed archival investigation that followed, suggest otherwise. In fact, the independent lines of archaeological and documentary evidence come together to create a very different characterization of the history of the foundry, the course of heavy-cannon development there, and Parrott's status as the "inventor" of the "Parrott" cannon. Furthermore, this evidence suggests that the Union military's role in weapons development before and during the Civil War was heavily influenced by foreign intelligence sources and was tightly controlled as an aspect of federal military policy. Finally, the combined research reveals that the military, particularly the U.S. Navy Ordnance Bureau in Washington, D.C., heavily financed and monitored Parrott's research and development activities throughout the war.

In contrast to previous portrayals, this investigation strongly indicated that the origin and development of Parrott's cast-iron rifled cannon were heavily influenced by, if not the direct result of, an elaborate government-sponsored program of foreign intelligence gathering and military and industrial espionage, both before and during the Civil War. Furthermore, archival records and congressional testimony suggested a high probability that key elements of Parrott's rifled gun actually were derived from confidential European designs and prototypes, which the American ordnance officers knew about long before Parrott's announced "invention" in 1860–61.

## The Archaeological Discovery of Parrott's
## Gun-Testing Facility and Workers' Housing

Beginning in 1989, the archaeological investigation of the West Point Foundry National Register District evolved over a three-year period, as a multistage identification, definition, and documentation effort performed in compliance with the National Historic Preservation Act, as amended. A combined approach of historic map analysis, subsurface testing, and remote sensing was applied to document the presence and extent of buried historic remains within the project impact areas that could not be avoided through construction redesign (Grossman et al. 1991). Based on the discovery of deeply stratified and otherwise undocumented nineteenth-century remains, the U.S. Environmental Protection Agency mandated a concentrated data recovery program aimed at the exposure and scientific documentation of the buried Civil War era remains located within the Superfund cleanup area.

The level of potential heavy-metal contamination within the historic shoreline landfill, as well as deep-winter conditions at the site, dictated that the field team work in protective gear, under inflated and heated domes, with all essential laboratory activities incorporated into on-site facilities outfitted with the appropriate decontamination equipment. Heavy dewatering pumps operated on a twenty-four-hour basis to maintain the excavation site in a dry, workable condition. All field personnel worked in sealed protective suits which were decontaminated and disposed of daily. All crew members were trained and certified for Hazardous Waste Material Handling (HAZMAT), and all were medically monitored before, during, and after the field effort.

The site testing and data recovery program used an assortment of applied technology procedures to expedite the excavation and recording process, and to limit the field crew's exposure to potentially toxic conditions. These tools included computer-integrated, total-station survey and mapping equipment which facilitated rapid, computer-based historic map correlations and site survey. In addition to the installation of on-site processing, inventory, decontamination, and conservation procedures, portable X-ray equipment was used to expedite the evaluation and selection of often heavily corroded metallic diagnostic artifacts. Once exposed through controlled natural stratigraphic excavation, the Civil War era gun-testing facilities also were rapidly recorded using the recently developed Rolleimetric photogrammetric three-dimensional camera system, which reduced the time and labor of the documentation effort of the exposed features and profiles by a factor as much as ten to one.

The field program was conducted in three stages between 1989 and 1992, covering three distinct areas of the site complex (fig. 11.3). The first stage consisted of a Phase I–II site identification and evaluation study of the historic foundry "Rail Spur," which ran out of the foundry along East Foundry Cove. These initial tests were important because they revealed a deep stratigraphic sequence of nineteenth-century fill layers which suggested the potential presence of deeply buried Civil War era deposits elsewhere on the site.

The second phase, and the main focus of the 1989–90 investigation, took place within what was referred to as the Area 1 remediation zone. This work consisted of a broader site definition, evaluation, and data recovery program within the former marsh and shoreline area forming the core of the Superfund cleanup zone. The deep-winter excavation utilized computer-scaled historic map projections and area-wide remote sensing survey procedures to identify and delimit the location and ex-

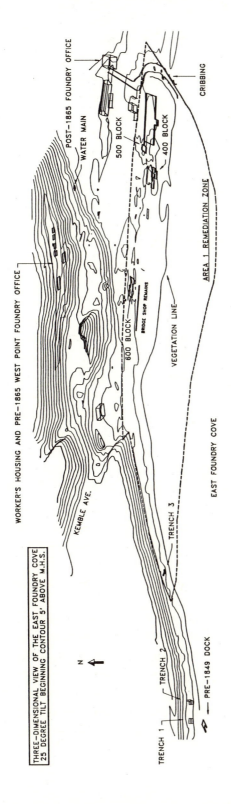

**Fig. 11.3.** *Three-dimensional perspective of the historic West Point Foundry shoreline, showing the project limits of the Area 1 Superfund Remediation Zone and locus of 1989–92 archaeological investigations. This bird's-eye view also depicts the historic rail spur bordering East Foundry Cove, the area of the gun platform and tower excavation (Block 400), and the historic workers' housing on the bluff overlooking the foundry. Courtesy of Grossman and Associates, Inc.*

tent of the buried and preserved remains of R. P. Parrot's Civil War–era gun-testing facilities. These facilities lay sealed five feet below the modern surface, and three feet below the modern water table, sandwiched within a ten-foot-deep sequence of pre– and post–Civil War historic fill deposits of foundry slag and ash which had been dumped along the shore of the former marsh beginning at least a decade before the onset of the Civil War (Grossman et al. 1991).

Finally, the third phase of the investigation began with the initial identification in 1990 of historic masonry foundation depressions adjacent to a modern dirt utility road, "The Haul Road," which overlooked and led down to the foundry in the valley below. Upon closer examination, these depressions were found to contain the well-preserved structural remains of the Civil War era complex of foundry workers' housing (fig. 11.3). This housing complex formed a group of six duplex structures which were separate and apart from the majority of the workers' housing located outside the foundry proper in Cold Spring. Initial testing revealed evidence of a buried stone foundation two to four feet thick, associated with undisturbed interior and exterior living floors, together with well-preserved hearths, artifact-filled refuse pits, and cisterns. The excavation of the naturally stratified occupation and destruction layers yielded in excess of 140,000 historic artifacts, with large proportions of diagnostic, high-status, imported, and domestic specimens. Below the historic deposits, the excavation also documented the well-preserved living surfaces, hearths, and pits of prehistoric occupants of the site (Grossman et al. 1991).

## The Shoreline Civil War Gun-Testing Facilities

The discovery of the gun-testing facilities was accomplished through the combined use of computer-assisted historic map correlation studies and grid-based magnetometer remote sensing across a rectangular shoreline area (designated Area 1), two hundred feet by seven hundred feet, where heavy disturbance was to occur from construction associated with the Superfund remediation effort. Prior to beginning the field investigations, the historic map analysis involved the compilation and digitized transfer

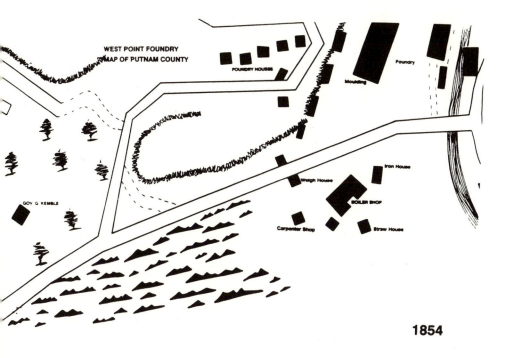

WEST POINT FOUNDRY
MAP OF PUTNAM COUNTY

FOUNDRY HOUSES

Foundry

Moulding

Iron House

Weigh House

BOILER SHOP

Carpenter Shop

Straw House

GOV G KEMBLE

1854

**Fig. 11.4.** *Detail of 1854 Bevan Map of Putnam County, showing West Point Foundry prior to development of the shoreline gun-testing facilities. Courtesy of Grossman and Associates, Inc.*

of all pertinent historic maps as scaled overlays onto the most current engineering site plans. Using these scaled historic map overlays, an attempt was made to locate specific structures and activity areas, as a basis for selecting zones for focused archaeological testing. Three mid-nineteenth-century maps were utilized, dating from 1854, 1867, and 1876, which showed sufficient detail to project the approximate location, relative to modern features, of earlier structures and foundry-related activity areas. The earliest of these, the 1854 Bevan map, showed six pre–Civil War structures in the shoreline impact zone of East Foundry Cove (fig. 11.4). Though detailed in its depictions, the 1854 map proved impossible to enlarge and scale accurately relative to any current topographic or structural remains. Nevertheless, despite these problems of scale and correlation, this prewar map was significant because it provided evidence that the shoreline area facing the cove (west of the core of the foundry complex further inland) was being used for secondary storage structures at least as early as 1854, and, by implication, that this former cove area had been partially landfilled by this date.

In contrast to the ambiguities of the 1854 Bevan map, two maps from the decade immediately following the Civil War proved considerably more accurate in scale and detail. When overlaid on the modern site map, the 1867 Beers, Ellis, and Soule (fig. 11.5) and the 1876 Reed (fig. 11.6) maps provided important new clues about the Civil War era activities that took place along the marsh. In addition to documenting a general pattern of expansion for the foundry complex itself, the maps depicted the removal of previously recorded structures, and the appearance of new structures along the shoreline zone of historic landfill. Most important, the 1867 map (fig. 11.5) showed the earliest rendering of the location, alignment, and extent of what had been labeled as the "Testing Guns" area, which was depicted at the end of a rail line used to roll out and test-fire new cannon being produced by Parrott. Jointly, given the wide latitude in the precision and consistency of the historic map coverage, these studies placed the projected gun-testing area somewhere within a corridor 80 to 100 feet wide by 200 feet long and perpendicular to the modern shoreline of East Foundry Cove.

The level of definition provided by the map data was refined through the use of a grid-based magnetometer survey of the entire 700-foot-long shoreline Superfund Remediation Zone. The actual magnetic survey of the historic industrial landfill area was conducted using two EG&G 860 magnetometers linked to portable data collectors, one to survey the site and the other as a control station to measure diurnal variations in the earth's magnetic field. A total of 4,884 data points were sampled at ten-foot intervals across the site. At the completion of the magnetic survey, the entire data set was electronically transferred into a desktop system equipped with two- and three-dimensional surface modeling programs that scaled the averaged, and coordinate-based, magnetic values relative to the site grid, to create contour or "terrain" maps. These maps illustrated the relative highs and lows in the recorded magnetic readings as color-coded peaks and valleys, each color representing a specific range of magnetic values. A total of thirty-five magnetic anomalies, or significant "dipolar" highs and lows, were rendered by the color-coded magnetic contour and mesh-surface maps (fig. 11.7). The buried Civil War era facilities were located as two major areas of extreme dipolar magnetic variation in the southeast corner of the site, and both fell

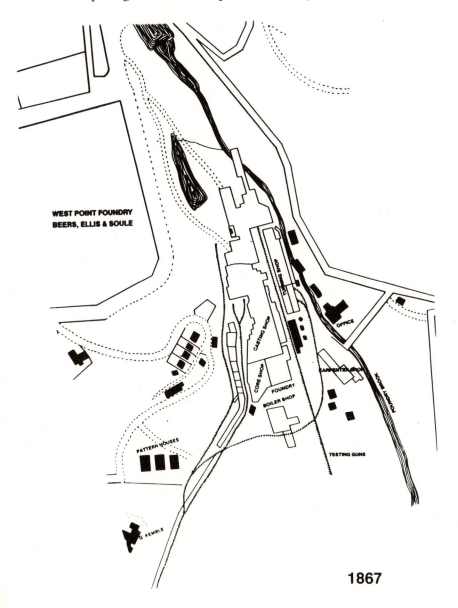

**1867**

**Fig. 11.5.** *Detail of 1867 Beers, Ellis, & Soule Map showing the "testing guns" rail line leading out of the gun casting and turning shops of the foundry and down to the shoreline area of the cannon-testing facility. Courtesy of Grossman and Associates, Inc.*

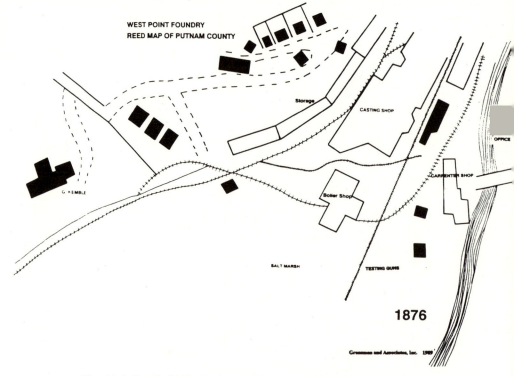

**Fig. 11.6.** *Detail of 1876 Reed Map of Putnam County, showing continued presence of the "testing guns" area a decade after the Civil War. Courtesy of Grossman and Associates, Inc.*

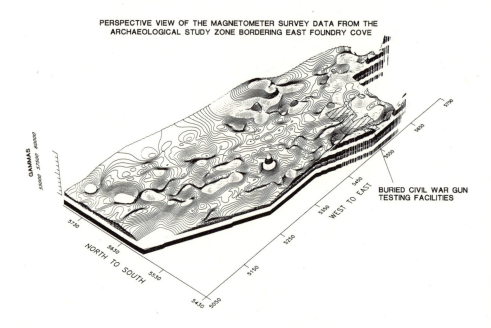

**Fig. 11.7.** *Three-dimensional perspective of topographic map showing the location and magnetic range (gammas) of all identified magnetometer anomalies. The creation of this map led to discovery of the buried Civil War gun-testing facility within the historical landfill zone of archaeological study (Area 1), ca. 700 feet by 350 feet. Courtesy of Grossman and Associates, Inc.*

# BLOCK 400 AND EXT. : COMPOSITE EAST WALL PROFILE

N ↓

POD #5

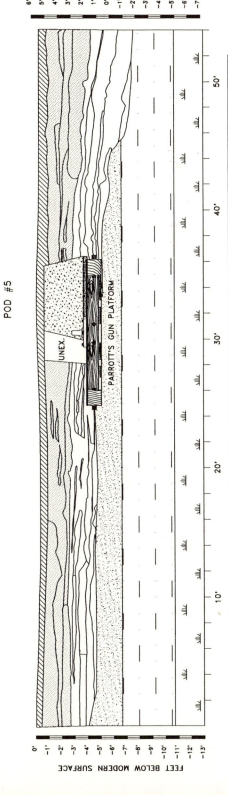

FT. ABOVE OR BELOW MEAN HIGH SEA LEVEL

FEET BELOW MODERN SURFACE

UNEX.

PARROTT'S GUN PLATFORM

▨ 401   20TH CENTURY ROOT MAT, (SURFACE DEBRIS).

▧ 402   POST-CIVIL WAR FILL AND MODERN DEBRIS.

□ 403   POST-CIVIL WAR COAL, SLAG AND DEMOLITION DEBRIS.

▥ 404   COMPOSITE CIVIL WAR SURFACE, (GREEN CLAY AND TIMBERS).

□ PRE-CIVIL WAR FILL, (COAL, ASH AND SLAG).

▦ OLD MARSH BOTTOM.

*Fig. 11.8. Stratigraphic profile of the R. P. Parrott gun platform and collapsed hoist tower under nineteenth-century fill deposits. Courtesy of Grossman and Associates, Inc.*

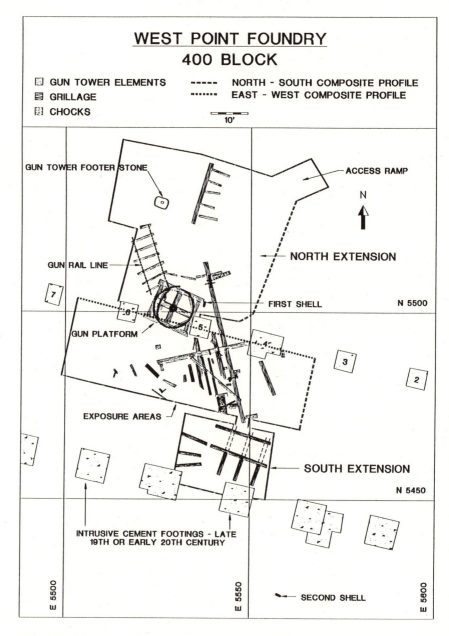

**Fig. 11.9.** *Plan of excavated Civil War gun-testing platform, tower hoist, rail line, and underlying grillage elements (Block 400). Courtesy of Grossman and Associates, Inc.*

within the sensitivity corridor defined by the computer-based historic map projections.

Parrott's Civil War era gun-testing facilities were found buried five feet below modern grade. Dated historic artifacts from the lowest level of fill below the buried Civil War surface indicated that the fill process had begun in this portion of the site at least a decade prior to the Civil War. The actual Civil War surface appears to have been laid down as an artificial layer sometime after 1857 and used throughout the war and possibly as late as the 1870s. The overlying fill consisted primarily of a four-foot accumulation of postwar ash and debris deposited between about 1880 and 1903.

In winter 1989–90, research teams identified, exposed, and recorded the well-preserved wartime cannon-testing facilities. These features included the wooden structural remains of R. P. Parrott's gun-testing platform, a rail delivery line used to move the cannon from the foundry, and the base and structural elements of a large cannon-hoisting crane topped by an observation tower. This cannon hoist tower had been used to lift the new class of heavy rifled cannons to the platform for testing, or "proofing" (Grossman et al. 1991: 58; figs. 11.8, 11.9, 11.10).

The wooden gun platform, about twelve feet square, with a cast-iron center pintle to hold the heavy cannon in place, was used in proofing the durability, accuracy, range, and shell velocity of Parrott's larger, eight- and ten-inch rifled cannon and projectiles. The identification and function of the gun-testing platform were confirmed by the archival discovery (after the excavation had been completed) of two original hand-colored plans and profiles rendered by Parrott of his ten-inch, 300-pounder, rifled cannon (fig. 11.11). This same platform was shown in a wartime photograph of the foundry's civilian gun "proofing" crew standing beside a 300-pounder rifled cannon and chassis (figs. 11.12). Another photograph from this era depicted the cannon hoist tower (fig. 11.13).

Once the buried Civil War surface had been defined, it was exposed horizontally with an area-wide control system of five-foot grid excavation units (fig. 11.10). This controlled excavation resulted in the recovery of 4,184 historical artifacts, of which 70.2 percent were stratigraphically associated with the surface supporting the gun-testing platform. Of these, 897, or nearly 25 percent, were associated with military activities.

**Fig. 11.10.** *Excavated gun platform and stone base of hoist tower, looking north. Courtesy of Grossman and Associates, Inc.*

They consisted of friction primer pins, tubes, safeties, iron pintle shear pins, vent picks, reamers for loading the shells, lead ammunition seals, and a variety of shells and exploded shell parts. The shells included two 100-pounders. One of these was a standard exploding piece, while the other appears to have been an example of Parrott's little-discussed binary incendiary shell, deployed in 1863, on the orders of President Lincoln, to burn Charleston, South Carolina (Bruce 1989).

The generation of computer-based density plots of each artifact class across this buried Civil War surface permitted the reconstruction of the former location and distribution of gun-crew positions. These plots, particularly the large numbers of friction primers found to the side and rear of the platform, could be correlated with historic Civil War era photographs of the gun crews at work testing and "proofing" a rifled cannon (fig. 11.14).

The artificial floor on which the cannon platform and hoist tower rested was built over a waterlogged historic landfill of ash and slag. The gun-testing or proofing surface was composed of a crisscrossed grillage of oak beams, which in turn was packed with a matrix of brown and green clay. When these structural details were compared with surviving

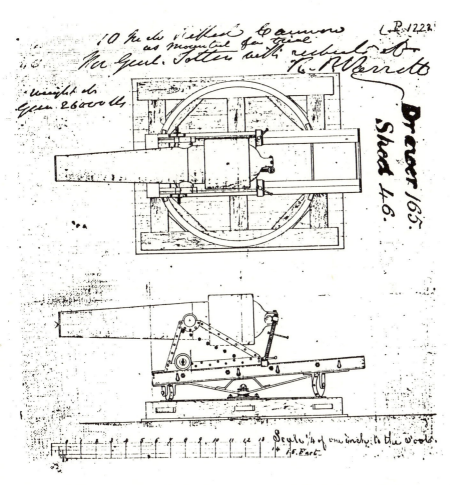

*Fig. 11.11. Sketch plan and profile of platform support system for R. P. Parrott's rifled 300-pounder, sent by Parrott to General Totten at the Washington Arsenal. Courtesy of the National Archives.*

military engineering reports on the construction of batteries from the Battle of Charleston, South Carolina, it became apparent that this West Point Foundry structure was similar to the famous Marsh Angel gun battery, built far out into the tidal flats of Charleston Harbor. The field records and engineering plans from this battle illustrate the use of a horizontal wooden platform supported by deep vertical pylons. These reports also documented that Alfred Mordeccai, the engineer in charge of

**Fig. 11.12.** *Post-1863 Civil War era photograph of gun-testing crew around a Parrott 300-pounder rifled cannon at the West Point Foundry gun-testing site. Courtesy of the Putnam County Historical Society, Cold Spring.*

constructing the Union gun batteries on Morris Island in Charleston Harbor, also had been stationed as an ordnance officer at West Point Foundry before and during the war. The parallels in construction and the presence of the same officer in both posts suggest that this engineering capability for the support of long-distance, heavy-cannon emplacements in bog or marsh environments may have been developed first at West Point Foundry.

## The Foundry Workers' Housing Complex

Following the excavation and photogrammetric recording of the gun proofing area, the field investigation shifted to the evaluation of the proposed haul road alignment along the flank of the bluff. Archaeological evidence uncovered here indicated that the composition of the workers' community was more economically complex, technically sophisticated, and ethnically distinct than had been suggested by traditional historical accounts. Previously the workers had been described as predominantly poor Irish and English laborers. However, analysis of the Civil War era artifacts from the workers' homes suggested instead the presence of

*Fig. 11.13.* *Enlarged half of a Civil War era stereograph of the West Point Foundry cannon hoist tower, observation cupola, and gun hoist crane. Courtesy of the Putnam County Historical Society, Cold Spring.*

skilled and materially well-off workers from England, France, Germany, and Austria—countries that then were actively involved with the research and development of heavy rifled ordnance (Grossman et al. 1990: 6–7; Grossman et al. 1993; Raoul 1936: 464–65; Kemble 1916: 195).

Analysis of the archaeological data from the large-scale excavation of the structures at the Haul Road revealed the presence of a large assortment of imported high-status technical and scientific tools, many of them associated with military technology. These artifacts did not fit the established characterization of supposedly poor laborers. In addition, a

*Fig. 11.14. Friction primer tubes, with attached primer wires, which were found concentrated in an oval area about ten feet at its widest point, located southwest of the gun platform. Courtesy of Grossman and Associates, Inc.*

variety of children's toys, "collector's" china figurines, miniature dollhouse furnishings, utensils, and jewelry (a cufflink stud, a watch chain, and several crosses: one gold and one with a Celtic motif) were recovered, many of these are luxury items by any standard. Identified ceramics included exotic imported types from China and Europe (including specimens from England, France, and Austria), many of which can be viewed only as high-status items, both today and during the Civil War period. This diversity in ceramic origins was paralleled by the presence of identifiable coins and tokens from France, England, and Venezuela, as well as several specimens of Spanish imperial *reales* minted in Mexico. Furthermore, the excavation revealed a diverse assortment of gentlemen's smoking pipes from England, France (Paris), Ireland, Scotland (Glasgow), Austria, and Germany, and glass artifacts from France, England, Hungary, and Bohemia (Grossman et al. 1993).

Military items specifically associated with the testing and manufacture of large-caliber guns and shells were recovered from the interior floors and features associated with the houses. These military-related items included friction primers, fuses, fuse strikers, fuse adapters, fuse caps, gun sight pendulums, and examples of shot from large-caliber shells, many of which were identical to examples from the previously excavated gun-testing facilities in the marsh. This archaeological evidence strongly suggests that at least some of the Civil War era inhabitants were involved specifically in the testing of 100- to 300-pounder rifled cannon, instead of simply doing general work at the foundry.

Finally, in addition to imported domestic household items of ceramic, glass, and metal, the artifact analysis revealed a number of unique scientific tools and instruments, including microscopes, gauges, a thermometer, calipers, battery jars, electrical contacts, carbon arcs, and timing devices. These artifacts in turn suggest that this group of residents very possibly was involved not only in the testing, but also in research and laboratory activities associated with testing the materials which went into the manufacture of the rifled guns.

## Foreign Influences and Antecedents

Based on the archaeological discoveries outlined above, the archival research was expanded and redirected to include sources relating to foreign gun technology, foreign workers, and foreign influences on Parrott's operations. This change in direction yielded unanticipated results. The research (primarily in the National Archives in Washington, D.C.) indicated that the origin and development of Parrott's cast-iron rifled cannon was heavily influenced by, if it was not the result of, an elaborate government-sponsored program of foreign military and industrial espionage before and during the Civil War. This interpretation, supported by private correspondence, records of the Navy Ordnance Bureau, and Civil War era congressional testimony, suggests the probability that key elements of Parrott's rifled gun actually were derived from confidential European designs and antecedents.

In fact, the 1862 date of Parrott's first patent was preceded by an 1860 visit from a Russian officer, or agent, who supplied Parrott with covertly obtained copies of the secret, and tightly guarded, plans for the production of the banded reinforced British Armstrong rifled cannon (Paulding 1879: 265–66). In 1879, Parrott's successor wrote that, in January 1860, twenty-two months before the date of Parrott's first patent, a Captain Schwartz of the Imperial Russian Navy had appeared at West Point Foundry and asked Parrott to make him a British Armstrong cannon. When Parrott said he was unable to because the designs were secret, Schwartz responded by providing detailed plans and specifications of the British gun. The Russian's gun was completed in March 1860, and a few weeks later Parrott produced what was described as "the first experimental gun on his own system" (Paulding 1879: 265–66).

What stands out from the archival research is that the visit of the Russian agent to Parrott's facility was not an isolated event, nor one inconsistent with broader policy and actions by the Russians toward the beleaguered Union cause. In contrast to the pro-Confederate and often pro-interventionist attitudes and actions of Britain and France during the Civil War, the special assistance provided by Captain Schwartz to Parrott was entirely consistent with Russian foreign policy in the mid-nineteenth century. This policy subsequently was manifested openly by the 1863 supportive appearance of the Russian fleet at Northern ports, in a show of force.

The Russian Czar wanted friendly relations with the U.S. for a variety of reasons. At the most mundane level, both countries consisted of large, isolated land masses; both were ethnic melting pots; both had, almost at the same time, emancipated large blocks of minorities, the slaves in America and the serfs in Russia; and, significantly, as the Czar stated in 1866, "The two peoples have no injuries to remember" (Bailey 1958: 363). Another, more immediately pressing, reason existed for a Russian officer to breach British security to help the American defense efforts. As T. A. Bailey pointed out in his *Diplomatic History of the American People*, "The overwhelming sea power of Britain had proved highly offensive to both nations. From an early date the Czar's government had deliberately undertaken to cultivate the U.S. in the hope of building up a New World rival that would curb England's power and pride" (Bailey 1958: 364).

In addition to the Czar's favorable attitude towards Lincoln's domestic policies, the Russian emperor viewed a strong, unified U.S. as a much-needed political, economic, and military counterweight to Russia's recent enemies in the Crimean War. During that war, England and France had thrown their combined military might behind the Turks against Russia (Adamov 1930; Tyrner-Tyrnauer 1962; Woldman 1952).

In actuality, "Russia's pro-Union sentiment prevented participation in any policy alien to the Lincoln administration's wishes" (Howard Jones 1992: 229). Against this larger Russian policy, Captain Schwartz's contribution can be seen as simply representing a clandestine military manifestation of a larger pattern of Russian diplomatic largesse to the North. In addition, this initial input provided by the Russian officer appears to have represented only the smallest tip of what apparently was a much larger pattern of information flow on the state of British and European cannon technology and metallurgy that continued even after the Civil War ended (Wise to Parrott, Dec. 12, 1865, National Archives RG74 E4; Mission 1865; Martin n.d.).

It is also highly probable, judging from official Ordnance Department records and reports, that both the Union military establishment and Parrott, as a former ordnance officer, had detailed knowledge of the status of European research and development efforts concerning heavy rifled cannon in particular, not only prior to the onset of the Civil War, but as much as three years before the visit of the Russian officer in 1860. One early key source was provided in an official report by Major Alfred Mordeccai of the Ordnance Department on the field observations of the U.S. Military Commission to Europe during the Crimean War between 1855 and 1856, a report written in 1856 and published in 1861. In addition to detailed field observations on the efficiency of various heavy cannon, including the early British Lancaster rifled cannon (which initially was deployed in the battles of Sebastopol), Mordeccai's report included detailed accounts on the layout, workings, and production procedures of armories and foundries in Russia, Prussia, Austria, France, England, and Belgium. Among the primary engineering reports and drawings collected by the commission, Mordeccai highlighted the acquisition, from Colonel Frederix of the Belgian foundry works at Liège, of drawings and plans of cannon produced for thirteen foreign countries under contract by that facility.

Of greatest relevance to the issue of early influences on Parrott's
work, the study included a special section (part 5) dedicated specifically
to the treatment of rifled cannon and shell technology. In addition to
describing early trials of the British (Lancaster), Swedish, and Italian
rifled canon and shells of various designs, Mordeccai's report included a
summary of Colonel Cavalli's research monograph "Memoire sur Sivers
Perfectionnemens Militaires," which had been translated from Italian in
1856 and included the 1854 test results on the accuracy and range of
Cavelli's experimental rifled guns and shells. The translation documented
that the Italians had developed a heavy rifled cannon capable of firing an
81-pound shell over a distance of between 3,140 and 5,627 yards, or
nearly three miles, with an accuracy of fifteen to thirty feet (Mordeccai
1861: 110).

In general outline, the overall report summarized past European accomplishments and failures and weaknesses in the design and manufacture of cast-iron rifled cannon, and of cast- and wrought-iron rifled
shells, with special attention to those used for the British Lancaster and
Whitworth rifled prototypes (Mordeccai 1861: 111). Finally, Mordeccai's
intelligence document also included what appears to represent the first
American technical description of the design details and initial failures
of Krupp's early cast-steel cannon and rifled shells. The Prussian rifled
gun, originally manufactured under contract for the British, fired a 259-
pound shell, twenty inches long, which was made to spin in the rifled
gun barrel through the application of a wrought-iron expansion ring, or
sabot, which was later paralleled in design by the first Parrott shells over
the same period (Mordeccai 1861: 115).

## The Role of the Navy Ordnance Bureau

It is now apparent that the Russian officer's input was not a unique or
isolated event; nor was the flow of information across the Atlantic con-
fined to Russian sources. Reports and correspondence by ordnance bureau officers document that, throughout the war, many technical decisions involving the production of Parrott's cannon were made with the
approval and oversight of the Navy Ordnance Bureau stationed both in

Washington, D.C., and at West Point Foundry (Brandt 1862). It is also clear that the ordnance officers in Washington, D.C., and at the West Point Foundry had a keen understanding and detailed technical knowledge of the state of British and European arms technology in general, and of the secret British Lancaster, Whitworth, and Armstrong rifled cannon technology in particular (Wise 1866a–c; Padgett 1945: 38–109).

Work at West Point Foundry not only was under the control of officers of the Navy Ordnance Bureau, but also was under the direct and immediate control of its chief, Commodore Henry A. Wise. Wise, in turn, was in intimate contact with special assistants to President Lincoln, and he appears to have served on various occasions as an expediter, trouble shooter, and high-level intelligence officer for the U.S. government. As chief of the Navy Ordnance Bureau, Henry Wise often dined with John Hay, Lincoln's personal secretary. As noted in Hay's diaries, the topic of their after-dinner conversations often pertained to intelligence matters and the potential for war with England (Hay in Dennett 1939: 88, 110; Anonymous, *National Cyclopedia of American Biography* 1921: 425; Bruce 1989: 16; Grossman 1991: 148).

Wise appears to have begun his career in espionage during the Mexican-American War, with additional experience gained in Southeast Asia and Japan. He made at least one secret mission to Germany to investigate and report on Krupp's new forged-steel cannon technology (Anonymous, *National Cyclopedia of American Biography* 1921: 425). His access to foreign military secrets was illustrated by the fact that his testimony before Congress often included submission of confidential military documents from other countries, including England. Wise's involvement with issues of foreign intelligence appears to have continued throughout his dealings with the West Point Foundry. He explicitly described them to Congress in his testimony before the Joint Committee Hearings on the Conduct of the War in 1865 (Wise Testimony in U.S. Congress 1865, Joint Committee Hearings on the Conduct of the War: 22–32).

Military correspondence and official reports to and from the Navy Ordnance Bureau revealed multiple references to the status of European capabilities and technology of the period, and allusions to plans and specifications for the products of various British and European munitions centers (Mordeccai 1861; Wise Testimony in U.S. Congress 1865, Joint Committee Hearings on the Conduct of the War: 22–32; Grossman 1991; Grossman et al. 1993). Additionally, explicit references to the "giving" or "exchange" of details of American technology to foreign diplomats, with the hint of reciprocal benefits, cast in a very different light the developments documented as having taken place at Parrott's West Point Foundry. Instead of Parrott's working in isolation, the testimony by ordnance bureau officers stationed there (most with extensive overseas field experience) documented the availability of a wealth of confidential information concerning the status of foreign research and development in rifled cannon technology (Testimonies of Wise, Mordeccai, Benét, and Benton in U.S. Congress 1865, Joint Committee Hearings on the Conduct of the War).

As documented in Senate testimony at the time, the American officers knew, press accounts to the contrary notwithstanding, that the carefully engineered and finely tooled British Armstrong cannon was unreliable and was being withdrawn from service. They knew that the European bronze guns were too soft to withstand the pressures of rifled shells, and that the heavily promoted Prussian forged-steel Krupp cannons were unreliable and tended to explode with grenade-like force (Benton Testimony in U.S. Congress 1865, Joint Committee Hearings on the Conduct of the War: 62). By 1863, after the bombardment of Charleston, these officers knew that the British banded Whitworth guns (one of which was experimentally deployed at a Union battery), the successor to the Armstrong, proved too delicate in combat conditions, and was 20 percent less accurate than the cast-iron Parrott cannon (Parker in Gilmore 1865: 310). In fact, the Americans were in control of information regarding the strengths and weaknesses of almost every competing rifled cannon system, at the same time that they were testing and evaluating Parrott's reinforced cast-iron cannons (Parker in Gilmore 1865: 310; Barry and Benét Testimony in U.S. Congress 1865, Joint Committee Hearings on the Conduct of the War: 47, 62).

As an example, American and foreign officials had detailed knowledge of Krupp's Prussian experiments with cast-steel rifled cannon. Although many early histories of Parrott and the West Point Foundry have alluded repeatedly to Parrott's initial awareness of Krupp's 1849 experiments in Prussia as the impetus for his own research and development efforts in rifled cannon, the weight of surviving archival evidence suggests that this description of his inspiration is inaccurate. Both the British and the Americans, while impressed with the cast-steel technology as a concept, were aware of a pattern of mortal failures of Krupp's steel guns. In addition, as General John G. Barnard, chief engineer for the defense of Washington, D.C., revealed in his Senate testimony, the Americans had developed their own opinion of the Krupp guns through hands-on experimentation, and were not overly impressed:

> In Prussia, Krupp has made rifled guns of 9-inch caliber (about 200 pounders) of cast-steel, which is probably the strongest of all materials, the steel being cast upon a core and later forged. The Russian government have [sic] given him extensive orders, and I have recommended the Governor of Massachusetts to import a few of them. It is a very expensive material, and the process of forging large masses seems yet to be uncertain. I have since observed that one of them recently burst at St. Petersburg. (Barnard Testimony in U.S. Congress 1865, Joint Committee Hearings on the Conduct of the War: 173–82)

In addition to well-informed naval ordnance officers, Commodore Wise's network of informants during the Civil War included a number of special civilian agents who had sufficient standing in Europe to gain access to otherwise restricted installations. Two such special agents who played key roles in the acquisition of detailed technical information on the manufacture, performance, and reliability of British and German rifled cannon and shell prototypes were Abram S. Hewitt and Henry S. Sanford, who at the time were publicly perceived as, respectively, an industrialist and a diplomat.

As Lincoln's diplomat-at-large in Europe, Sanford is credited with playing an important role in undermining Confederate maneuvers in France and England (Wriston 1929: 779). Sanford's diplomatic career began with his appointment as attaché to the Russian court in Saint Petersburg, followed by a posting in Paris, and then, with the inauguration of President Lincoln, as minister to Belgium. Sanford has been recognized for his skill in undertaking delicate missions. Of immediate relevance to the Union's weapons development program, he single-

handedly supplied the North with otherwise unavailable stores of salt-
peter, the key ingredient of gunpowder, and also played a key role in
conducting back-channel negotiations with the British over the Trent
Affair (Anonymous, *National Cyclopedia of American Biography* 1921: 140;
Axelrod 1992: 194).

Sanford reported directly to Commodore Wise when his activities involved the acquisition of information and hardware relevant to the
bureau's weapons development program. His clandestine activities also
included acquisition of difficult-to-obtain examples of production prototypes of European ordnance. Unpublished letters from Sanford to Wise
in 1863 also document in detail his role in acquiring and sending an
example of Krupp's cast-steel cannon to the U.S. for testing. In this instance he was beseeching Wise to help direct the piece to suitable authorities so that it could be tested properly and "given to our Yankee
inventors to look at and endeavor to imitate its metal." He went on to
say that "Gen. Chazal, the Minister of War here [Belgium], told me that
he had tested one by 10,000 discharges in every conceivable form . . .
and he considers it indestructible" (Sanford to Wise, Aug. 7, 1863, Wise
Papers, LB 5, No. 6.5, New York Historical Society, New York).

In contrast to Henry Sanford, Abram Hewitt's wartime exploits and
ties to Wise have not been recognized previously. His firm, Cooper and
Hewitt, was the first to produce iron girders and supports to be used in
fireproof buildings and bridges in New York. Utilizing the reputation
(and access to facilities which may have been closed to others) gained by
his innovations in cast-iron structures and molded facades, in 1862
Hewitt "visited England in order to learn the process of making gun-
barrel iron, and was enabled to supply the gun-barrel material needed
by the U.S. government during the continuance of the civil war"
(Anonymous, *National Cyclopedia of American Biography* 1921: 295). This
fact, as well as his critical involvement in the production of Union mor-
tars, also under the direction of Wise, became public record after the
war (Nevins 1935; Bruce 1989: 159).

What was not known, however, is that, when Abram Hewitt reported
back to unnamed members of the U.S. government, he reported directly
to Commodore Wise of the Navy Ordnance Bureau, a relationship
documented in a series of unpublished letters from Hewitt to Wise. Of

immediate pertinence to Parrott's work with rifled cannon development is one particular letter which details the technological history and production techniques of the British precursor to the Armstrong cannon. The description is revealing because it highlights the technical parallels between the British methods of production and those ultimately adopted by Parrott for making the reinforced element around the breach of his cast-iron rifled cannon. Hewitt wrote:

> Capt Blakeley commenced with a wrought iron tube, with wrought iron jackets in rings. His next step was to abandon the rings and substitute a continuous jacket. This was shrunk on hot, while the inner ring was kept cool with a stream of water [the very procedure that Parrot characterized as being a key element of his "invention"]. . . . His next step was to make the initial tube of cast iron, and to shrink on it a jacket of wrought iron. (Hewitt to Wise, Apr. 22, 1862, Wise Papers, LB1, No. 9, New York Historical Society, New York)

This unpublished source suggests that, given his ties to the Ordnance Bureau in general and to men under the command of Wise in particular, it is highly probable that Parrott was well aware of the essential details of ongoing European research.

## Lincoln and Executive Branch Involvement

Several newly discovered primary sources document that President Abraham Lincoln was intimately involved with rifled cannon technology early in its developmental history. Perhaps the most overt example of industrial espionage by the Federal defense establishment involved the purchase and trans-shipment of a battery of British Whitworth cannon for testing and combat deployment through private sources during the Civil War. The details of this acquisition and the resulting evaluation of the gun's worthiness were first brought to light in an unpublished letter to Lincoln from his first secretary of war, Simon Cameron, dated July 1, 1861; and in detail later, in 1864, during hearings held by the U.S. Joint Committee on the Conduct of the War.

This unpublished letter documents that President Lincoln knew of the ongoing efforts by the War Department to acquire heavy gun technology and details of rifled shell technology by as early as July 1861, several months after the war had begun. On July 1, 1861, Secretary of War Simon Cameron reported that efforts were being made to acquire and test current models of European heavy ordnance from England and on the continent, including France and Austria:

> Some patriotic American citizens resident in Europe, fearing that the country might not have a sufficient supply, purchased on their own responsibility, through co-operation with the United States Ministers to England and France, a number of improved cannon and muskets, and at your [Lincoln's] insistence, this department accepted the drafts drawn to defray the outlay thus assumed.
> A perfect battery of the six Whitworth 12 pounder rifled cannon, with three thousand rounds of ammunition, the magnificent donation of sympathizing friends in Europe, has also been received from England (Cameron to Lincoln, July 1, 1861, National Archives RG107 E5).

The wording and date of this report to the president are important for three reasons. First, the report documents that, early in 1861, Lincoln was aware of the U.S. efforts to acquire and benefit from European research and development accomplishments in large-caliber rifled cannon. Second, this document shows that the U.S. was keenly aware of the superior fire power, accuracy, distance, and penetration capabilities of rifled ordnance as early as 1861, and already was converting its existing 32- and 42-pounder smooth-bore cannon into rifled versions. Third, this report documents that, prior to July 1861, during the first months after the outbreak of the Civil War, Lincoln had sanctioned and paid for the importation and testing not only of British Whitworth rifled cannon, but also of other new systems from England and France.

Access by the Navy Ordnance Bureau and the executive branch to many of the most carefully guarded secrets of the European arsenals was forcefully illustrated by the discovery in the National Archives of a previously unknown numerical table found folded with an 1863 personal note to President Lincoln from Admiral Dahlgren. This handwritten listing was titled "Tables of Comparative Power of American and European Heavy Rifled Ordnance" (Dahlgren to Lincoln, Jan. 24, 1863, National

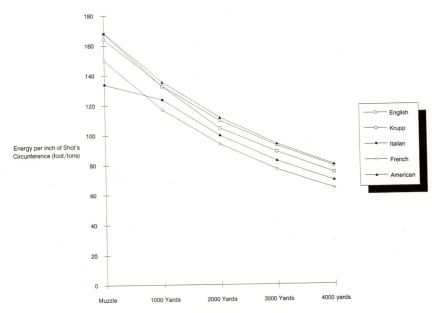

**Fig. 11.15.** *Line graph derived from classified Civil War memo and data table presented to President Lincoln by Admiral Dahlgren. It compares the energy per inch of short circumference (potential penetration in foot/tons), between American and European ten-inch rifled cannon. Despite public misconceptions to the contrary, this confidential briefing document illustrated the superiority of American rifled cannon relative to European heavy ordnance. Derived from Navy Ordnance Department Records, National Archives.*

Archives RG156 E200). The comparative table was a detailed technical report, of the most confidential nature, on the relative shell velocity of American versus English, German, Italian, and French rifled shells of various calibers (fig. 11.15).

This data comparing domestic and foreign shell velocity showed Lincoln that the inexpensive American rifled guns produced by Parrott at West Point Foundry were, in fact, 5 to 20 percent superior in velocity and fire power, depending on the caliber and country in question. What the data indicated to the president was that, by 1863, Parrott's rifled cannon and shells, at close range, could outgun a British or French ironclad. This would have been critical information for a commander-in-chief faced with the possibility of a sea-based conflict with foreign ships. The discovery of this document was important because it clearly indicated that both the Union War Department and President Lincoln controlled, and had timely access to, tactically specific hard data on the strengths and weaknesses of European weapons systems of the time. Given the volume of foreign, predominantly British, weapons that were being shipped to and used by the Confederacy, this document indicates that Lincoln and his inner cabinet of military advisors were making wartime decisions based upon intimate knowledge of the tactical and technological capabilities and weaknesses of their adversaries (Hay in Dennett 1939: 76; Anonymous, *National Cyclopedia of American Biography* 1921: 425; Grossman 1991: 147).

While no explicit mandate for the development of a foreign intelligence gathering program was found in any of the surviving archival sources, the existence of such a program was alluded to in an official 1864 report for the U.S. Navy (initially presented before Congress in 1864 but not published until after the War), concerning the status of heavy ordnance. In the report Wise stated, "The bureau has sought in vain among the systems of European nations and the improvements of our own country for a better gun, taken as a whole, than the Parrott rifle" (U.S. Congress 1869: 156–57).

This oblique yet explicit reference and other comments by high-ranking officers and staff of the Navy Ordnance Bureau, speaking before U.S. Senate investigators during and after the war, clearly document that this stream of confidential information flowed through the offices of the Navy Ordnance Bureau, both to the executive branch of President Lincoln and to U.S. producers of heavy ordnance.

## Parrott's Accomplishments in Retrospect

Given the fact that Parrott's work during the Civil War was supervised and predominantly funded through contracts with the Ordnance Department, it now appears highly probable that Parrott actively utilized data on the most promising experimental systems and techniques of manufacture coming from Europe. Only when this broader international context of fluid transatlantic information exchange and access to foreign sources is taken into account can we accurately evaluate the details of

Parrott's foundry operations, production procedures, and accomplishments in the area of heavy rifled ordnance.

Parrott's public image was that of a lone inventor who developed his new cannon at his own expense and in isolation, with little government support. He helped to cultivate this impression. In 1862 Parrott wrote, "I was led to the construction of my gun wholly by my own experiments and conclusions." The originality of Parrott's design and patent was officially questioned, however, in 1864 and 1865, during confidential Senate investigations following the repeated occurrence of premature explosions of his shells and cannon in both land and sea combat (Grossman 1991: 222–23; Turner in Gilmore 1865: 151). In 1865, while testifying under oath before the U.S. Joint Committee on the Conduct of the War, Parrott initially reiterated his claim to invention by stating: "In 1860, I made the first of these guns. I made it from my own ideas upon the subject of what would make a gun of moderate cost and of good strength." Chairman Wade pushed the point and asked, "You were the inventor of these guns, were you?" Parrott responded in the affirmative, but with a little more caution: "Yes, sir. I do not pretend to be the inventor of the idea of putting a band on the gun because that thing has been tried before; but I believe my gun is the first banded gun that was ever actually introduced into the service of any country as part of its armament" (Parrott Testimony in U.S. Congress 1865, Joint Committee Hearings on the Conduct of the War: 139). With these words Parrott essentially negated his earlier claims for invention of the gun, and instead emphasized only the production and incorporation of this technology into the American arsenal.

Thus, the idea of a banded or "hooped" rifled cannon was not new, either in Europe or the U.S. It was the details of design and methods of production for the Armstrong cannon that provided the critical technological elements for Parrott at Cold Spring. The proprietary aspect of the Armstrong cannon involved the use of a heavy, steam-powered trip hammer to weld a wrought-iron coil, or band element, and the use of heat and controlled cooling to evenly shrink the band onto the barrel of the gun. If the Russian officer indeed provided Captain Parrott with the details of the British system of making rifled cannon with wrought-iron hoops as reinforcement around the breach, then he had the essential elements to make a highly accurate, high-velocity, long-distance cast-iron gun which would not break apart when fired with a heavy charge and sluggish rifled shell. By adopting this one element of a coiled wrought iron band over the breach of the gun, Parrott would have been able to develop an inexpensive and easily produced rifled cannon, at one-half to one-quarter the cost of contemporary British guns (Grossman 1991). Thus, from an engineering perspective alone, the development of Parrott's rifled ordnance appears to have reflected awareness of, access to, and familiarity with the latest military developments in weapons technology in Europe at the time.

## Discussion

The discovery of historically inconsistent high-status and "high-technology" Civil War era artifacts in the isolated complex of "workers housing" above the foundry precipitated the focused archival investigation of formerly confidential primary sources. These sources cast a different light on the status of American heavy weapons technology relative to contemporary developments in England, France, Germany, Belgium, and Russia. They provide new evidence that Parrott was not working in isolation and that the foundry which he administered rather was, from its inception, controlled, supervised, and financially supported by the ordnance bureaus of the military. The developments which took place there were not isolated phenomena, but instead formed part of a concerted effort involving the assimilation of the most current developments in the European arms industry, through extensive borrowing and outright espionage.

Taken together, these data now suggest that the Union was actively and covertly working to gain access to, and to apply, the results of costly European research efforts in heavy rifled cannon development, which had been under way since the 1850s. This policy of industrial and military espionage, and its manifestation in the products of the West Point Foundry, in effect saved the Union millions of dollars and years of development time—time that, at the onset of hostilities in April 1861, the

North did not have. What took the British over a decade and over $12 million dollars to develop, with questionable success, was accomplished at Parrott's facility in a matter of months and at a fraction of the cost (Holley 1865: 80). While the North was five years behind Europe in heavy ordnance technology at the beginning of the war, by 1863 it had matched if not surpassed its European counterparts in what was, in fact, a transatlantic arms race.

This archaeological and archival investigation also highlighted the existence of an effective foreign intelligence gathering capability which operated out of the Navy Ordnance Bureau, with direct lines of communication to both the president and Parrott. This information network appears to have operated under the direct control of Commodore Henry A. Wise, who served first as assistant to Adm. John A. Dahlgren, chief of the Navy Ordnance Bureau, and then, as of 1863, as Dahlgren's successor in the position (Hay in Dennett 1939: 108–10). As the archaeological and archival investigations have documented, Wise directed the flow of ongoing research and testing work for the development of heavy weapons systems for the Navy, at the West Point Foundry and other munitions centers. He did so based on an extensive knowledge of the status of research and development efforts in heavy rifled cannon systems throughout mid-nineteenth-century Europe (U.S. Congress 1865, Joint Committee Hearings on the Conduct of the War: 22–32).

Thus, during the war, the Navy Ordnance Bureau was not limited to merely administering and tracking government purchases and acquisitions. Instead, it also was intimately involved with larger issues surrounding foreign technological advances and ongoing government efforts aimed at benefiting from access to, and utilization of, these European accomplishments in rifled cannon and shell technology. It was in this context, and in direct response to acquired insights into the status of European weapons technology, that the Union military establishment managed its domestic cannon and shell development program in heavy ordnance. Against this backdrop, as chief of the bureau, Wise, and his officers stationed at West Point Foundry, appear to have controlled information on almost every aspect and detail of Parrott's foundry operation, including access to, and flow of, foreign technological and military secrets to the foundry and to Parrott.

In addition, Commodore Wise worked in intimate contact with Lincoln, as well as with members of the president's "kitchen cabinet" which met with little or no public visibility and worked with Lincoln throughout the war (Hay in Dennett 1939: 76; Bruce 1989: 159). Because of the president's 1862 visit to the foundry, his constant association with Wise, and his direct involvement in the first field experiments with rifled incendiary shells, Lincoln was aware of the capabilities and tactical implications of heavy rifled cannon technology for both domestic and transatlantic conflicts at least as early as summer 1862, if not before (Benét in Bruce 1989: 97; Grossman et al 1991). Cameron's letter to the president in 1861 suggests that Lincoln's personal involvement with heavy rifled cannon may have been established by 1861.

Furthermore, American developments in heavy ordnance took place with a dual focus—on preparing for potential threats to the Union not only from the South but from the transatlantic naval powers of England and France. Much of the concern for developing an effective rifled cannon centered on countering, and preparing for conflict with, one of these latter two maritime powers, most urgently during the first half of the war, between 1861 and 1863, when the threat was greatest. It was during this time that Parrott's efforts to develop and produce his 200- and 300-pounder rifled cannon were at their peak.

These insights from the West Point Foundry investigation are presented not to derogate Parrott or detract from his accomplishments, but instead to place the role of Parrott, the West Point Foundry, and the Union military establishment in a new perspective. The archaeological and archival evidence strongly suggests that Parrott, rather than being an example of "Yankee ingenuity" in a regionally and technologically isolated context, was a player in a sophisticated international and national program of military intelligence and espionage. The foundry itself, rather than being an example of fledgling capitalism at its best, rising to meet the technical demands of the government in times of need, in fact functioned as a "proprietary" operation, heavily underwritten by the government, much like the "Flying Tigers" in China during World War II or "Air America" during the Vietnam War era.

This data recovery program, mandated by the U.S. Environmental Protection Agency, has resulted in the discovery of what appears to rep-

resent the unique remains of Civil War era military technology not otherwise preserved at any known mid-nineteenth-century site or institu-
tional repository. In terms of its contribution to Civil War history, the
physical and archival discoveries which emerged from the West Point
Foundry investigation shed new light on the history of Parrott's invention in particular, and on the development of American military technology in general. The documentary investigation of Civil War foreign
intelligence efforts triggered by the archaeological discoveries has written a new chapter in Civil War history. What has emerged is a story of
nationally- and internationally-based intelligence operations which
flourished under the sanction of President Lincoln and his inner circle
of military advisors. The historical implications are complimentary to
Lincoln's administration and suggest a level of technological and geopo-
litical sophistication which appears not to have been recognized in past
treatments of Lincoln's executive branch structure and operations.

*Paul A. Shackel*

# 12

# MEMORIALIZING LANDSCAPES AND THE CIVIL WAR IN HARPERS FERRY

Harpers Ferry National Historical Park receives about half a million visitors a year, many with an interest in Civil War history. Although the war devastated the town's industrial and social fabric, most of the town's commercial and residential sections redeveloped in the 1870s and 1880s. Industrial ruins of private and government factories were allowed to stand and decay. The ruins became part of a vernacular landscape that memorialized early industry. Allowing ruins to stand in a decaying state is a form of preservation that memorializes past events. As historian Richard Sellars (1987: 19) notes, "Even without monuments, [preservation] is an act of memorializing. Preservation acknowledges that something so important happened that it must be remembered and at least some terrain set aside."

The armory and industrial ruins created by the Civil War in Harpers Ferry served to memorialize the war's industrial context. The Civil War served as a sharp dividing line in the town's history. Industrial ruins functioned as a conduit to the past by creating monuments to the early industrial era. They also placed the Civil War within an industrial context, showing it as the first major conflict of the modern era. During the hostilities, both sides exploited new factory technologies. Armies used the railroads extensively; new technologies developed fast-firing weapons; and people and machines mass-produced guns, uniforms, and other equipment. The commemoration of these new industrial phenomena in Harpers Ferry, as well as other areas throughout the country, helped to reinforce an industrial consciousness and still serves as a reminder of the "immutable" traditions of industrialization.

Only recently have landscape issues been addressed and questions asked about the changing dynamic cultural landscapes and the built environment in this historic town (Gilbert et al. 1991; Joseph et al. 1993; Shackel 1992). Here I examine how private and government industries developed in early-nineteenth-century Harpers Ferry and how entrepreneurs and federal agencies used the built environment to encourage a particular ideology. After the Civil War, northern industrialists constructed a memorializing landscape that established and reinforced an industrial ideology through the remainder of the nineteenth and into the twentieth centuries.

## Social Context of an Industrializing Town

After the end of the French and Indian War, George Washington began to speculate in land along the lower Potomac River (Robert Mitchell 1977: 59, 127). Washington dedicated himself to improving navigation along the river and invested in the Potowmack Company, a corporation involved in constructing canals along the Potomac. Such improvements, he believed, would attract trade to the ports of Alexandria and Georgetown and create economic growth in the new Federal City and the Potomac Valley region (Merritt Smith 1977: 27–28).

In 1794, the United States Congress proclaimed it necessary to establish armories for the manufacture and storage of arms. As part of his plan to develop the Potomac Valley, President Washington was determined to build an armory at Harpers Ferry, located at the confluence of the Shenandoah and Potomac rivers. He received endorsements from Georgetown and Alexandria merchants who stood to profit from hinterland trade (Merritt Smith 1977: 29–30). The Wagers, heirs to the founder of Harpers Ferry, Robert Harper, owned the lands that contained the community, a small cluster of buildings with several water-powered mills. Acquisition of all lands in Harpers Ferry necessary for construction of the armory had been completed by 1796. By agreement, the proprietary family kept a six-acre reserve for commercial development, a ferry concession of three-quarters of an acre, and rights to monopolized mercantile trade (Merritt Smith 1977: 147). Additional lands deemed to be unworthy of development were excluded from the agreement. Among the lands excluded was Virginius Island, which later developed into a thriving industrial community.

Construction of the armory began in 1799, and the first guns were produced by 1801. The armory's initial management and labor force centered on Northern gunsmiths, but by the 1810s native Virginians controlled the installation's daily functions. Complex social networks and intermarriages allowed four families to dominate the armory as well as the social and economic affairs of the community. Under the native civilian management, labor practices consistently followed a craft ethos. Armorers were involved with many of the steps related to the guns' production. Workers could enter the manufacturing facility whenever they chose, as long as they met monthly quotas. Armorers prided themselves on being craftsmen, and the industrial complex was slow to adopt any new form of work discipline. Outsiders with new industrial ideals were ostracized and sometimes chased out of town (Merritt Smith 1977).

The town developed slowly, in a rather haphazard fashion (fig. 12.1). An 1805 observer described the town as consisting of a post office and about fifteen houses (Joseph Scott 1805). By 1810 it had "a good tavern, several large stores for goods, a library, one physician, and a professor of the English language" (Vale in Noffsinger 1958: 20).

The development of new forms of transportation in the 1830s heightened Harpers Ferry's importance as a center between the Ohio and Shenandoah valleys and the East. In 1834, the Chesapeake and Ohio Canal connected the town to the coastal ports of Georgetown and Alexandria, and in 1837, the Baltimore and Ohio (B&O) Railroad linked

**Fig. 12.1.** *1803 Patoumack Company map of Harpers Ferry. Courtesy of Harpers Ferry National Historical Park.*

Harpers Ferry to Baltimore and more distant hinterlands. Connecting Harpers Ferry to regional and national networks was essential to its continued economic growth (Everhart 1952: 22). This new infrastructure stimulated private industry on Virginius Island in the Shenandoah River, an area excluded from the original 1796 agreement between the federal government and the Wager family. The island contained a variety of mills by the early nineteenth century. One of the larger enterprises began as a custom gristmill, called Peacher's Mill after the first proprietor of the island (*Harper's Ferry Mill Co. v. Thos. H. Savery et al.* 1887: 17). In the 1830s, the machinery was upgraded by Fontaine Beckham, enabling the mill to produce refined flour for export rather than only grinding grains for local farmers who marketed their own meal (*Virginia Free Press*, Aug. 18, 1831: 3). The mill burned in 1839, only to be rebuilt the following year. The owners of the mill, which stood adjacent to the recently installed Winchester and Potomac Railroad line, rebuilt the structure to about twice its original size and capitalized on the new transportation network. By 1844, the mill was purchased by Abraham and John Herr (*Virginia Free Press,* Feb. 7, 1839: 2; *Virginia Free Press,* June 15, 1843: 3; Virginia, Jefferson County, Deed Book 28, Sept. 2, 1846: 292–93) and its production volume reached thirteen times the national average (Bergstresser 1988: 22).

The railroad's development also generated other industrial investment on Virginius Island, including a cotton factory (*Virginia Free Press*, Apr. 2, 1846: 2; Johnson and Barker 1993: 41). A spur from the main line connected the factory with national markets. However, the factory went bankrupt in the 1850s, and it was converted to a flour mill after the Civil War (*Spirit of Jefferson*, July 30, 1867: 2; Johnson and Barker 1993: 44–46).

As Harpers Ferry increasingly relied on industrial networks, workers were forced to conform to many of the routines associated with the new capitalist infrastructure. In the 1840s, the armory labor system and physical plant underwent major revision. Before that time, most of the armory buildings were unsuited to the implementation of a division of labor, as they lacked architectural and functional unity. Factories were usually constructed when needed, without regard to manufacturing discipline or the routines needed for mass production. The Harpers Ferry facilities contrasted sharply with the orderly layout commonly associated with the New England factory system.

In 1844, Superintendent Major John Symington, an engineer, created a plan for the armory's renovation. Government factory buildings were reconstructed in a homogeneous architectural plan that facilitated the mass production of weapons. Architectural style became consistent throughout the armory, conforming to a Gothic Revival style. Symington also imposed a grid pattern over the existing town street plan (fig. 12.2). The new plan facilitated industrial development and provided a sense of order and uniformity.

Government supervisors also reorganized the workers' daily routines. Workers became increasingly alienated from their labor and became responsible for only one part of the manufacturing process. A poem appeared in the *Virginia Free Press* (Mar. 31, 1842: 3) denouncing this new work discipline. The author condemned the new "oppression" and likened it to wearing the "chains of servile slavery." The armory workers went on strike, rented a canal boat, and marched to President Tyler. In Washington, the president noted that he was sympathetic to the workers' cause but told them that they must "hammer out their own salvation" (Barry 1903). Armory workers were forced to accept the new work discipline or lose their jobs.

By 1854, twenty-five new government industrial structures were built, all within a unified architectural plan (Merritt Smith 1977: 275–76). Harpers Ferry, including Virginius Island, became a sprawling industrial town containing the United States Armory and Arsenal. Private manufacturing establishments also thrived, including a textile mill, flour mill, sawmill, iron foundry, machine shop, and carriage manufactory, as well as over forty mercantile shops (Gilbert 1984: 1). An 1855 account described the town:

> The village is compactly, though irregularly built around the base of a hill, and is the center of considerable trade. It contains four or five churches, several manufactories and flour mills, a United States armory in which about 250 hands are employed, producing, among other articles, some 10,000 muskets annually, and a national arsenal. In the latter are continually stored from 80,000 to 90,000 stand of arms. (Edwards in Noffsinger 1958: 43)

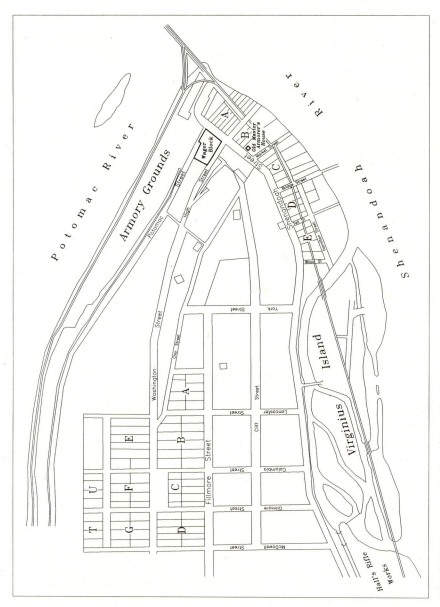

**Fig. 12.2.** *Symington's 1840s grid design for Harpers Ferry. Courtesy of Harpers Ferry National Historical Park. (Compiled by John Ravenhurst)*

## The Civil War and the Creation of a Memorializing Landscape

After the bombardment of Fort Sumter and Lincoln's call to raise 75,000 troops in April 1861, Virginia seceded from the Union. Seizing the armory and arsenal at Harpers Ferry became a major objective for the Confederacy. Lieutenant Roger Jones, stationed at Harpers Ferry with fifty regulars and fifteen volunteers, feared that an advancing force of 360 Confederates would capture the town. Before these forces arrived on May 18, 1861, Jones set fire to the federal factory buildings and abandoned the town. The arsenal, along with seventeen thousand guns, was destroyed, although the townspeople, in an attempt to salvage their livelihood, saved the machinery. The Confederates shipped the armory machinery to Richmond, where it was used to make arms for the South (Noffsinger 1958: 45–46; Snell 1960b: 5). The musket factory on the Potomac River and the rifle factory on Halls Island in the Shenandoah River also were rendered inoperable during the war.

Private industry suffered as well. Even though Abraham Herr, the flour mill's main proprietor, owned four slaves in 1860, he supported Union troops when they arrived in Harpers Ferry in 1861. The commanding officer ordered the partial destruction of the flour mill to prevent Confederate troops from using the facility. When the Confederates arrived several weeks later, they forced Herr's partner, James Welch, to torch the mill. This action, they claimed, was retaliation for wheat donated by Herr to the Union army (Barry 1903: 131–34; Johnson and Barker 1993).

During the Civil War, Harpers Ferry changed hands eight times. From 1861 to 1863, Harpers Ferry was occupied alternately by Union and Confederate troops. At times the town was left unoccupied; Joseph Barry, a local historian, characterized the town as a "no-man's land" (Barry 1903; also see Snell 1960b). The town was mostly deserted, and portions were in a ruinous state (Drickamer and Drickamer 1987: 124; Ward 1985: 63). Annie P. Marmion, a resident of Harpers Ferry, stated that the town's population during unoccupied times declined from a prewar total of 2,500 to "less than 20 families" (Marmion 1959: 4). Food and safety during these periods were the major concerns: "The great objects in life were to procure something to eat and keep yourself out of sight by day, and your lamps or rather candle light hidden by night, lights of every kind being regarded as signals to the Rebels were usually rewarded by a volley of guns" (Marmion 1959: 7).

In 1863, Union forces returned to Harpers Ferry for the duration of the war and revived the town's economy. Many offices, boardinghouses, restaurants, and other businesses opened to serve the expanding population (Drickamer and Drickamer 1987: 130). Feeling that they were safe, civilians flocked to Harpers Ferry (Marmion 1959: 11). During the last year of the war, General Philip Sheridan fortified Harpers Ferry to secure his supplies. His army reroofed the burned musket factory buildings and established a supply depot at Harpers Ferry (Snell 1960a: 39). From August 1864 through February 1865, Sheridan's army used Harpers Ferry as a base of operations to attack the Confederate stronghold in the Shenandoah Valley. Trains of up to one thousand wagons left town to supply troops and returned carrying prisoners and wounded. John Mosby, a Confederate committed to guerrilla warfare in the Harpers Ferry region, constantly harassed these wagon trains. Such actions necessitated the deployment of large numbers of Union troops to Harpers Ferry to protect shipments from further harassment (Snell 1960a: 3, 38).

Union clerk Charles Moulton noted in 1864, "While the supply depot was stationed here, there was nothing but a perfect jam all day and night in the streets, army wagons blocking up the streets and large number of soldiers were coming in continually and goodly share of them getting drunk" (Drickamer and Drickamer 1987: 213). This military occupation produced a thriving but unstable economy that was responsible for the majority of the Civil War era archaeological deposits found throughout Harpers Ferry.

## An Archaeology of the Civil War and the Memorializing Landscape

Soon after the war, the military withdrew from war-torn Harpers Ferry. The government decided not to rebuild the armory and sold most of its property holdings at auction. Many of the townspeople were left in a desperate situation, as the industrial viability of prewar Harpers Ferry became nothing more than a memory. Archaeological investigations found a hiatus of mass-produced material goods in the postwar community. This hiatus may be attributed to the slow reoccupation of the town and to disastrous floods in 1870 and 1877 which accelerated the town's deterioration.

Water power had been the catalyst for much of the industrial growth prior to the Civil War. By the 1870s, there was little movement to reexploit this natural resource. Steam power gained importance as its cost decreased, and water power came to be perceived as inadequate and more expensive. As a result, Harpers Ferry never regained the economic prominence it had had during the 1840s and 1850s (Gilbert 1984).

In the 1880s and 1890s, touring battlefields and other areas of historical importance became a popular recreational activity among Americans. Harpers Ferry became a popular tourist spot along the B&O Railroad and the Chesapeake and Ohio Canal. Citizens developed and rebuilt the main business district in the lower town area. New enterprises, such as restaurants, hotels, and boardinghouses flourished (Shackel 1993; Fenicle 1993; Winter in press). Many portions of the early- and mid-nineteenth-century commercial district were either renovated or replaced by new and imposing Victorian structures. In some cases the materials used for renovation were "salvaged" from the town's industrial ruins (Fisher, Chickering, and Jenkins 1991).

Visitors to Harpers Ferry were either day travelers or those who owned or rented cottages in the community. Tourist brochures described several important landmarks, including the site of John Brown's fort (the original armory engine house) and the ruins of the United States Armory (Anonymous 1910; Anonymous n.d.; Taft 1898). The United States Armory grounds along the Potomac River were purchased by William Savery, a Delaware entrepreneur interested in reexploiting the river's water power potential. He constructed a pulp mill that stood adjacent to the armory ruins and the John Brown fort. In 1891, a group of entrepreneurs purchased the fort from Savery and moved it by rail to the Chicago Exposition. Several years later, the fort was relocated on a farm outside Harpers Ferry. In the first decade of the twentieth century, it was purchased by Storer College and transported to its campus in upper Harpers Ferry.

Savery sold a right-of-way to the B&O Railroad, and after 1891 ten feet of railroad berm fill covered the original engine house foundation, as the railroad line through Harpers Ferry was realigned. The first thing tourists saw as they entered town was an obelisk monument erected by the railroad marking the fort's original location (fig. 12.3). Adjacent to this feature, the federal government placed iron tablets commemorating the Confederates' 1862 siege of the town, in which 12,500 Union troops had surrendered. The tablets were mounted there for "the enlightenment of travelers concerning the fighting that took place in the capture of Harpers Ferry by the Confederate Army in September, 1862" (qtd. in Gilbert et al. 1991: 3.88) Also visible from the tracks were several remaining foundations of the former musket factory. In 1916, the B&O Railroad landscaped the grounds around the musket factory foundations with trees and flower beds. By 1923, a large garden filled the remains of the old armory grounds (*Spirit of Jefferson* May 16, 1896: 2; Gilbert et al. 1991: 3.95). The garden's design "incorporated the embankment, the matured trees and ornamental shrubs planted along the old river wall, and the rectangular outlines of old building foundations, creating a distinctive gateway of monuments, history, and ornamental landscape" (Gilbert et al. 1991: 3.95–3.96; *Spirit of Jefferson* May 16, 1916: 2) (fig. 12.4). Many of these landscape changes made by the railroad were celebrated by the town, as they were incorporated into an unofficial "public square."

While the Potomac River side of Harpers Ferry was slow to redevelop, the railroad explicitly recognized the town's early industry, John Brown's raid, and the Civil War. On the Shenandoah River portion of Harpers Ferry, northern entrepreneurs eagerly invested in Virginius Island's industrial revitalization. Jonathan Child and John McCreight, industrialists from Ohio, purchased Virginius Island and made repairs to the old cotton factory and converted it into a flour mill. Even though they renovated the worker's domestic dwellings and surrounding grounds, Child and McCreight allowed the substantial ruins of Herr's flour mill to stand and incorporated them into the vernacular landscape of the island (fig. 12.5). In the late nineteenth century, William Savery, owner of the pulp mill on the Potomac River, purchased Virginius Island and developed a second pulp mill on Hall's Island. Hall's Rifle Works and later armory buildings were submerged when the pulp mill created a holding pond for its industry. Herr's flour mill ruins continued to stand

*Fig. 12.3.* The "John Brown Fort" obelisk monument and the five commemorative tablets, ca. 1900. Courtesy of Harpers Ferry National Historical Park, HF 1149.

*Fig. 12.4.* The outlining of armory buildings and the creation of an ornamental landscape, ca. 1936. Courtesy of Harpers Ferry National Historical Park, HF 1049.

**Fig. 12.5.** *Herr's flour mill (lower building), domestic structures (center buildings), and recently abandoned Child and McCreight flour mill (top building), ca. 1900. Courtesy of Harpers Ferry National Historical Park, HF 895.*

on Virginius Island and often were mistaken as the "Rifle Factory ruins" of Hall's Island (Taft 1898). A 1941 guidebook describes the island as containing Herr's mill and the rifle factory (Anonymous 1941: 234; Joseph et al. 1993). Virginius Island never contained the rifle factory, which was located to the north on Hall's Island.

## Discussion

The meanings and uses of ruins in the American landscape have only recently been discussed by archaeologists (see King 1994a, 1994b). Different groups have had varying degrees of success in preserving ruins or saving graphic reminders of the past. Many working-class people view the preservation of old buildings and ruins as an attempt to save the memory of a degrading phase of human history. Robert Vogel of the

Smithsonian Institution notes, "The dirt, noise, bad smell, hard labor and other forms of exploitation associated with these kinds of places make preservation ludicrous. 'Preserve a steel mill?' People say, 'It killed my father. Who wants to preserve that?'" (qtd. in Lowenthal 1985: 403). While ruins may stir unfavorable emotions for some people, other groups may implicitly or explicitly perceive these material culture remains in different ways. Those who prescribe to an industrial decay may see the preservation of ruins as a symbolic link to the past that provides a sense of continuity between past and present. Ruins show the impact of time and lend credibility to the long-term establishment of any particular institution that occupied that ruin.

In the case of Harpers Ferry, the Civil War created these industrial ruins. After the war, local entrepreneurs renovated their community using various construction materials, including those salvaged from industries found on the armory grounds and on Virginius Island. These actions dismembered many prominent standing industrial structures and symbolically dismantled the industrial ideals that the community had resisted throughout the armory's occupation of the town. While local entrepreneurs dismantled the town's industries, northern capitalists, including Savery, Child, and McCreight, purchased industrial sites and kept the armory and flour mill ruins intact and visible to the community and tourists. By the end of the nineteenth century, Savery owned both the armory and Virginius Island lands. These northern entrepreneurs developed or redeveloped industries according to northern industrial ideals. Their enterprises stood adjacent to the decaying ruins that demonstrated the long-term establishment of industrialization. David Lowenthal reminds us that "precedence legitimates action on the assumption, explicit or implicit, that what has been should continue to be or be again" (Lowenthal 1985: 40).

The armory and flour mill ruins stood as graphic reminders to Harpers Ferry citizens of their town's former industrial prowess. The armory ruins remained through the nineteenth century and soon became a popular attraction during the postbellum fad for visiting Civil War sites. After the railroad realignment covered the original site of the John Brown fort and part of the armory grounds, the B&O Railroad created a monumental landscape with trees, shrubs, bushes, and terraces that memorialized the former industry that once had existed on B&O Railroad property. At Harpers Ferry, ruins and relics of industrialization and of the Civil War became intertwined with commemoration and visitation; they remain so today.

Historian J. H. Plumb argues that industrial society, unlike agrarian communities, does not need the past. He states that "scientific and industrial society have no sanction in the past and no roots in it; we now look back only as a matter of curiosity, of nostalgia, a sentimentality . . . the strength of the past in all aspects of life is far, far weaker than it was a generation ago" (qtd. in Lowenthal 1985: 364).

While Plumb sees the past in industrial society as not serving any moral or educational value, and some claim that preserving ruins may run counter to the spirit of modern enterprise (see Lowenthal 1985: 402–3), I believe that preservation serves a major function in industrial society. While the Civil War left much of Harpers Ferry's industry in ruins, these remains served as a symbol of historical precedent, bolstering a claim to roots in an industrial past. The existence of decaying ruins amplifies the age of industrial institutions and grounds their symbolic meanings in a legitimate past. Decay secures antiquity, even if that "antiquity" is only a few decades old. Ruins help to inspire reflections on institutions that once had been proud or strong. As Lowenthal (1985: 197) again reminds us, "Remembering the past is crucial for our sense of identity . . . to know what we were confirms that we are."

## Acknowledgments

I am grateful to Clarence Geier and Susan Winter for inviting me to contribute to this volume, and for their helpful comments. I also thank Barbara Little for her suggestions during the writing of the manuscript. Stephen Potter made me aware of Richard Sellars's work. Maureen Joseph is responsible for much of the recent landscape development in Harpers Ferry National Historical Park. Her research, along with Perry Wheelock's work, has significantly enhanced the park's data base regarding the changing cultural landscape.

# GLOSSARY

*Abatis:* An obstacle formed of felled trees with trimmed and sharpened branches facing the enemy. Generally placed to enhance the defensibility of a fortified position against enemy attack. (Hogg n.d.: 155–58)

*Battery:* A group of artillery pieces and associated parapet arrangements which allow the guns to fire over them (barbette) or through openings (embrasures). (Mahan 1862: 52)

*Entrenchment:* Any temporary or permanent fortification. Ideally, such structures provide shelter from hostile fire, serve as obstacles to a hostile advance, and allow maximum use of fire power by the defenders. To meet expectations, entrenchments typically possess a covering mass or embankment (parapet) which protects the occupying troops from enemy fire and attack yet allows maximum return fire. Entrenchments commonly possess an exterior ditch which constitutes an obstacle to enemy attack, and whose construction provides the earth for the embankment. (Mahan 1862: 1, 2)

*Fortification:* Any disposition made to enable an armed force to resist, with advantage, the attack of another armed force superior to it in numbers. (Mahan 1862: 1)

*Howitzer:* Shorter-barreled artillery piece with "chambers" in the bore for smaller powder charges. These were designed to fire shells at higher elevations over shorter range. (Thomas 1985: 2–33)

*Lunette:* A redan to which flanks or lateral wings have been added to enhance defense. (Hogg n.d.: 155–58)

*Parapet:* Raised mass of earth, rubble, or other material which creates an embankment serving to protect occupying troops from enemy fire and attack, and yet allowing maximum return fire. (Mahan 1862: 1, 2)

*Powder Magazine:* A facility constructed to store and maintain demolition equipment and ammunition. Such structures were necessary for entrenched artillery positions and commonly were associated with earthworks and batteries. When constructing a powder magazine, it was important to place it in a position neither exposed to enemy fire and nor close to the force of men manning the facility. Such structures were constructed to be "shot proof" and also to keep moisture from affecting the powder. (Mahan 1862: 58)

*Redan:* An entrenchment or fortification with two faces which form an angle or salient. (Hogg n.d.: 155–58)

*Redoubt:* A closed, independent entrenchment or fortification with a square or polygonal plan or shape. (Hogg n.d.: 155–58)

*Salient:* The horizontal plan of a fortification is designed to provide mutual defense for its component parts. To accomplish this, certain parts are placed towards the enemy to encounter their attack, while other parts are removed from the hostile forces to create an effective field of fire to cover and protect the advanced parts. Because of this basic scheme, fortification plans typically exhibit outlines which include a system of angular points called salients. (Mahan 1862: 3, 4)

# BIBLIOGRAPHY

Abel, Annie H.
1919    *The American Indian as Participant in the Civil War.* Rpt. 1970. New York: Johnson Reprint.

Adamov, E. A.
1930    Russia and the United States at the Time of the Civil War. *Journal of Modern History* 2: 586–602.

Adams, George W.
1952    *Doctors in Blue: The Medical History of the Union Army in the Civil War.* New York: Henry Schuman.

Adams, William Hampton
1976    Trade Networks and Interaction Spheres: A View from Silcott. *Historical Archaeology* 10: 99–112.

1977    Silcott, Washington: Ethnoarchaeology of a Rural American Community. *Reports of Investigations* 54. Pulman: Washington State Univ., Laboratory of Anthropology.

1990    Landscape Archaeology, Landscape History, and the American Farmstead. In Historical Archaeology of Southern Plantations and Farms, ed. Charles E. Orser, Jr. *Historical Archaeology* 24, no. 4: 92–101.

Ames, Kenneth M.
1991    The Archaeology of the *Longue Duree:* Temporal and Spatial Scale in the Evolution of Social Complexity on the Southern Northwest Coast. *Antiquity* 65: 935–45.

Anderson, Bern
1962        *By Sea and River: The Naval History of the Civil War.* New York: Alfred A. Knopf.

Anderson, David G., and Jenalee Muse
1982        The Archaeology of Tenancy in the Southeast: A View from the South Carolina Low Country. *South Carolina Antiquities* 14: 71–82.

Anderson, Fred
1984        *A People's Army: Massachusetts Soldiers and Society in the Seven Years' War.* Chapel Hill: Univ. of North Carolina Press.

Anderson, Jay
1984        *Time Machines: The World of Living History.* Nashville, Tenn.: American Association for State and Local History.

Anderson, Russell Howard
1929        Agriculture in Illinois During the Civil War Period, 1850–1870. Ph.D. diss., Univ. of Illinois, Urbana.

Andrews, Susan, and Paul Mullins
1989        "Table Ware and Bottle Glass Assemblages." The Hatcher-Cheatham Site (44CF258): A Multicomponent Historic Site in Chesterfield County, Virginia. Vol. 4. Report prepared by James Madison Univ. Archaeological Research Center, Harrisonburg, Va. Submitted to the Virginia Dept. of Highways and Transportation, Richmond.

Anonymous
N.d.        In John Brown's Country. On file, McDonald Collection, Harpers Ferry National Historical Park, Harpers Ferry, W.Va.

1910        Hilltop House brochure. On file, HFB 305, Harpers Ferry National Historical Park, Harpers Ferry, W.Va.

1921        Hewitt, Adams Stevens. In *National Cyclopedia of American Biography* 3: 140–295.

1941        West Virginia: A Guide to the Mountain State. WPA Guide. Brochure Collection. Harpers Ferry National Historical Park, Harpers Ferry, W.Va.

Associated Press.
1990        The Blue, the Gray, and the Souvenirs. *State Newspaper,* Columbia, S.C. Nov. 25: 2.

Atack, Jeremy, and Fred Bateman
1987        *To Their Own Soil: Agriculture in the Antebellum North.* Ames: Iowa State Univ. Press.

Axelrod, Alan
 1992        *The War Between the Spies: A History of Espionage During the Civil War.* New York: Atlantic Monthly Press.

Babits, Lawrence E.
 1988        Military Records and Historical Archaeology. In *Documentary Archaeology in the New World,* ed. Mary C. Beaudry, 119–25. New York: Cambridge Univ. Press.

Bailey, Thomas
 1958        *A Diplomatic History of the American People.* 6th ed.. New York: Appleton-Century-Crofts.

Baker, Oliver E.
 1926        Agricultural Regions of North America, Part I: The Basis of Classification. *Economic Geography* 2: 459–93.

Ball, Horace
 1863        Horace Ball to his father, July 13, 1863. In *Civil War Letters of Horace Ball, 34th Massachusetts Regiment, 1862–1863.* Bound photocopies on file, Harpers Ferry National Historical Park, Harpers Ferry, W.Va.

Barnes, J. A.
 1954        Class and Committees in a Norwegian Island Parish. *Human Relations* 7: 39–58.

Barnes, John S.
 1896        *Submarine Warfare, Offensive and Defensive, Including a Discussion of the Offensive Torpedo System.* New York: Van Nostrand.

Barry, Joseph
 1903        *The Strange Story of Harpers Ferry, With Legends of the Surrounding Country.* Rpt. 1959. Shepherdstown, W.Va.: Shepherdstown Register.

Bartnik, George P.
 1976        A Cultural-Historical Overview of Camp Nelson, Concentrating on Its Main Line of Defense. Frankfort: Kentucky Dept. of Transportation.

Bass, George F.
 1983        A Plea for Historical Particularism in Nautical Archaeology. In *Shipwreck Anthropology,* ed. Richard A. Gould, 91–104. Albuquerque: Univ. of New Mexico Press.

Baxter, Nancy N.
 1980        *Gallant Fourteenth: The Story of an Indiana Regiment.* Traverse City, Mich.: Pioneer Study Center Press.

Beard, Evelyn Y.
1969        Reminiscences of Civil War Days. *Magazine of History and Biography* 13: 32–35. Randolph County Historical Society, Elkins, W.Va.

Beatty, John
1879        *The Citizen Soldier, Or Memoirs of a Volunteer.* Cincinnati: Wilsatch, Baldwin and Co.

Bennett, Frank M.
1896        *The Steam Navy of the United States.* Pittsburgh: W. T. Nicholson.

Bergstresser, Jack
1988        Virginius Island: Water Powered Industrial Village. Report prepared for Historic American Engineering Record (no. WV-35), National Park Service. Report on file, Harpers Ferry National Historical Park, Harpers Ferry, W.Va.

Berlin, Ira, ed.
1982        The Black Military Experience. *Freedom: A Documentary History of Emancipation, 1861–1865.* Ser. 2. Cambridge: Cambridge Univ. Press.

Bevan, Bruce, David G. Orr, and Brooke S. Blades
1984        The Discovery of the Taylor House at the Petersburg National Battlefield. *Historical Archaeology* 18, no. 2: 64–74.

Binford, Lewis
1968        *New Perspectives in Archaeology.* Chicago: Aldine.

Blades, Brooke S.
1981        Excavations at the Confederate Picket Line, Crater Area, Petersburg National Battlefield. Unpublished manuscript on file in the Mid-Atlantic Regional Office, National Park Service, Philadelphia.

Blades, Brooke S., and John L. Cotter
1978        Archaeological Test Excavations at the Hare House Site, Petersburg National Battlefield. Unpublished manuscript on file in the Mid-Atlantic Regional Office, National Park Service, Philadelphia.

Blank-Roper, Laurie
1990a       *Historical Archaeology on the Central Illinois Expressway, 1986 Season.* Normal: Illinois Univ., Midwestern Archaeological Research Center.

1990b      *Historical Archaeology on the Central Illinois Expressway, 1987 Season*. Normal: Illinois Univ., Midwestern Archaeological Research Center.

Bloch, Maurice

1985      *Marxism and Anthropology: The History of a Relationship*. Oxford: Oxford Univ. Press.

Bogue, Allan G.

1963      *From Prairie to Corn Belt: Farming on the Illinois and Iowa Prairies in the Nineteenth Century*. Chicago: Univ. of Chicago Press.

Bogue, Margaret Beattie

1959      *Patterns from the Sod: Land Use and Tenure in the Grand Prairie, 1850–1900*. Springfield: Illinois State Historical Library.

Braley, Chad O.

1987      *The Battle of Gilgal Church: An Archaeological and Historical Study of Mid-Nineteenth-Century Warfare in Georgia*. Athens, Ga.: Southeastern Archaeological Services, Inc.

Brandt, D.

1862      Record of the Firing of a 100-pdr Rifled Parrott Gun. . . . July 29, 1862. Record Group 74, Entry 191. National Archives, Washington, D.C.

Breitburg, Emanuel

1983      An Analysis of Faunal Remains from Wynnewood State Historic Site, Sumner County, Tennessee, and Its Implications for Tennessee Plantation Site Archaeology in the Central Basin. *Tennessee Anthropologist* 8: 182–99.

Brooks, Stewart

1966      *Civil War Medicine*. Springfield, Ill.: C. C. Thomas.

Bruce, Robert V.

1989      *Lincoln and the Tools of War*. Chicago: Univ. of Illinois Press.

Bruins, Derk

1987      Technology and the Military: The Impact of Technological Change on Social Structure in the United States Navy. In *Technology, The Economy, and Society: The American Experience,* ed. Joel Colton and Stuart Bruchey. New York: Columbia Univ. Press.

Buchanan, Franklin

N.d.      *Official Report of the Battle Between the C.S.S. Virginia (formerly the U.S.S. Merrimack) and the U.S.S. Monitor on March 9, 1862*. Naval Historical Foundation.

Buchanon, Rita
    1989      "Buttons." The Hatcher-Cheatham Site (44CF258): A Multi-component Historic Site in Chesterfield County, Virginia. Vol. 4. Report prepared by James Madison Univ. Archaeological Research Center, Harrisonburg, Va. Submitted to the Virginia Dept. of Highways and Transportation, Richmond.

Buresh, Lumir
    1977      *October 25th and the Battle of Mine Creek.* Kansas City, Mo.: Lowell Press.

Burns, James McGreggor
    1982      *The Vineyard of Liberty.* New York: Alfred A. Knopf.

Butler, Benjamin F.
    1892      *Butler's Book.* Boston: A. M. Thayer.

Cameron, Simon
    1861      Correspondence to Abraham Lincoln. July, 1, 1861. Record Group 107, Entry 4. National Archives, Washington, D.C.

Carter, Rosalie
    1972      *A Visit to the Carter House, Franklin, Tennessee.* Nashville, Tenn.: Blue & Gray Press.

Catton, Bruce
    1965      *A Stillness at Appomattox.* New York: Pocket Books.

Clark, Christopher
    1979      The Household Economy, Market Exchange, and the Rise of Capitalism in the Connecticut Valley, 1800–1860. *Journal of Social History* 13: 169–89.

Clay, R. Berle
    1990      Office of State Archaeology News. *Kentucky Archaeology Newsletter* 7, no. 2: 3.

Cleland, Charles E.
    1988      Questions of Substance, Questions that Count. *Historical Archaeology* 22, no. 1: 13–17.

Clinton, Catherine, and Nina Silber, eds.
    1992      *Divided Houses: Gender and the Civil War.* New York: Oxford Univ. Press.

Clopton, William T.
    1905      Account Written by Samuel A. Mann on December 2, 1898, to William I. Clopton, Describing Drewry's Bluff in 1862. *Southern Historical Society Journal* 34: 82–98. Richmond, Va.: Southern Historical Society.

Coates, Earl J., and Dean S. Thomas
   1990          *An Introduction to Civil War Small Arms.* Gettysburg, Pa.: Thomas
                 Publications.

Cochran, Thomas C.
   1961          Did the Civil War Retard Industrialization? *Mississippi Valley His-
                 torical Review* 48: 197–210.

Cohen, G. A.
   1978          *Karl Marx's Theory of History: A Defense.* Princeton, N.J.:
                 Princeton Univ. Press.

Confederate States of America
   1862–1863  Confederate Pay Vouchers. Microfilm on file at National Ar-
                 chives, Washington, D.C.

Conzen, Michael P.
   1971          *Frontier Farming in an Urban Shadow: The Influence of Madison's
                 Proximity on the Agricultural Development of Blooming Grove, Wis-
                 consin.* Madison: State Historical Society of Wisconsin.

Cotter, John L., Daniel G. Roberts, and Michael Parrington
   1992          *The Buried Past: An Archaeological History of Philadelphia.* Phila-
                 delphia: Univ. of Pennsylvania Press.

Courbin, Paul
   1988          *What Is Archaeology?* Trans. Paul Bahn. Chicago: Univ. of Chi-
                 cago Press.

Cox, Jacob D.
   1897          *The Battle of Franklin Tennessee, November 30, 1864.* New York:
                 Charles Scribner's Sons.

Crass, David Colin
   1990          Economic Interaction on the New Mexican Military Frontier.
                 *Volumes in Historical Archaeology* 13. Ed. Stanley South. South
                 Carolina Institute of Archaeology and Anthropology, Univ. of
                 South Carolina, Columbia.

Cromwell, James R., Jr.
   1989          "Non-Architectural Metal Artifacts." The Hatcher-Cheatham
                 Site (44CF258): A Multicomponent Historic Site in Chester-
                 field County, Virginia. Vol. 4. Report prepared by James Madi-
                 son Univ. Archaeological Research Center, Harrisonburg, Va.
                 Report Submitted to Virginia Dept. of Transportation, Rich-
                 mond.

Crumley, Carole L.
1979        Three Locational Models: A Epistemological Assessment for An-
            thropology and Archaeology. In *Advances in Archaeological Method
            and Theory* 2, ed. Michael B. Schiffer, 141–73. New York: Aca-
            demic Press.

Crumley, Carole L., and William H. Marquardt, eds.
1987        *Regional Dynamics: Burgundian Landscapes in Historical Perspective.*
            San Diego, Calif.: Academic Press.

Curtis, Richard
1957        *History of the Great Naval Engagement Between the Iron-Clad
            Merrimack C.S.N. and Cumberland Congress and the Iron-Clad
            Monitor U.S.N. March the 8th and 9th 1862 as Seen by a Man at
            the Gun.* Rpt. Hampton, Va.: Houston Publishing House.

Dabney, Virginius
1971        *Virginia: The New Dominion.* New York: Doubleday.

Dahlgren, John A.
1863        Correspondence to Abraham Lincoln. Jan. 24, 1863. Record
            Group 156, Entry 200. National Archives, Washington D.C.

Daly, Robert W.
1957        *How the Merrimack Won: The Strategic Story of the C.S.S. Virginia.*
            New York: Crowell.

Dalzell, George W.
1940        *The Flight from the Flag: The Continuing Effect of the Civil War Upon
            the American Carrying Trade.* Chapel Hill: Univ. of North Caro-
            lina Press.

Danziger, Edmund J., Jr.
1969        The Office of Indian Affairs and the Problem of Civil War In-
            dian Refugees in Kansas. *Kansas Historical Quarterly* 35: 257–75.

Davis, Maj. George B., Leslie J. Perry, and Joseph Kirkley, eds.
1881        *The War of the Rebellion: A Compilation of the Official Records of the
            Union and Confederate Armies.* Ser. I, vol. 46. Washington, D.C.:
            Govt. Printing Office.

1892        *The War of the Rebellion: A Compilation of the Official Records of the
            Union and Confederate Armies.* Ser. I, vol. 39, pt. 2. Washington,
            D.C.: Govt. Printing Office.

1894        *The War of the Rebellion: A Compilation of the Official Records of the
            Union and Confederate Armies.* Ser. I, vol. 46, pt. 1. Washington,
            D.C.: Govt. Printing Office.

1896        *The War of the Rebellion: A Compilation of the Official Records of the Union and Confederate Armies.* Ser. I, vol. 48, pt. 2. Washington, D.C.: Govt. Printing Office.

1978        *Atlas to Accompany the Official Records of the Union and Confederate Armies.* Compiled by Capt. Calvin D. Cowles. Rpt. of 1891–95 U.S. Government Publication. New York: Arno Press.

Davis, William C.
1989        *The Fighting Men of the Civil War.* New York: Gallery.

Deegan, Kathleen A.
1988        Neither History nor Prehistory: The Questions that Count in Historical Archaeology. *Historical Archaeology* 22, no. 1: 7–12.

Deetz, James
1967        *Invitation to Archaeology.* Garden City, N.Y.: Natural History Press.

1977        *In Small Things Forgotten: The Archaeology of Early American Life.* New York: Anchor Books.

Dennett, Tyler
1939        *Lincoln and the Civil War in the Diaries and Letters of John Hay.* New York: DaCapo.

Dickens, Roy S., and Linda H. Worthy
1984        *Archaeological Investigations at Picketts Mill Historic Site, Paulding County, Georgia.* Atlanta: Georgia Dept. of Natural Resources, Parks and Historic Sites Division.

Dilliplane, Timothy L.
1975        *Exploratory Excavations at Fort Granger.* Printed for limited distribution by the Jaycees, Franklin, Tenn., with assistance from the National Park Service.

Drickamer, Lee C., and Karen D. Drickamer, eds.
1987        *Fort Lyon to Harpers Ferry: On the Border of North and South with "Rambling Jour": The Civil War Letters and Newspaper Dispatches of Charles H. Moulton (34th Mass. Vol. Inf.).* Shippensburg, Pa.: White Mane Publishing Co.

Dyer, Frederick Henry
1908        *A Compendium of the War of the Rebellion* 1. New York: Thomas Yoseloff.

1959        *A Compendium of the War of the Rebellion.* New York: Thomas Yoseloff.

Early, Jubal A.
1960        *War Memoirs.* Indianapolis: Indiana Univ. Press.

Edwards, Captain
1908    *A Condensed History of the Seventeenth Regiment S.C.V., C.S.A., from
        Its Organization to the Close of the War.* Columbia, S.C.: R. L. Bryan
        Co.

Elder, Betty Doak
1981    War Games: Recruits and Their Critics Draw Battle Lines over
        Authenticity. *History News* 36, no. 8: 8–12.

Esarey, Mark E., Frederick W. Lange, Floyd R. Mansberger, and William D.
        Walters, Jr.
1985    A Report on Phase I Reconnaissance Historic Archaeological
        Investigations on Four Segments of the F.A.P. 408 Highway Cor-
        ridor, Adams and Pike Counties, Illinois. Report submitted to
        Illinois Dept. of Transportation, Springfield.

Everhart, William C.
1952    A History of Harpers Ferry. Manuscript on file at Harpers Ferry
        National Historical Park, Harpers Ferry, W.Va.

Farrar, Hayward
1991    Black Freedmen at City Point, 1864–65. Unpublished manu-
        script on file in the Mid-Atlantic Regional Office, National Park
        Service, Philadelphia.

Faust, Drew Gilpin
1990    Altars of Sacrifice: Confederate Women and the Narratives of
        War. *Journal of American History* 76: 1200–1228.

Faust, Patricia, ed.
1986    *Historical Times Illustrated Encyclopedia of the Civil War.* New York:
        Harper and Row.

February, Jack M.
1987    Archaeological Testing of Civil War Sites 15Js96 and 15Js97. A
        Supplement to the Original Survey Report for the Relocation of
        Highway 27 South of Nicholasville in Jessamine County, Kentucky.
        Kentucky Transportation Cabinet, Division of Environmental
        Analysis, Frankfort.

Fenicle, Diane L.
1993    The Ties that Bind: A Social History of Block B, Lots 2 and 3
        Families. In *Interdisciplinary Investigations of Domestic Life in Gov-
        ernment Block B: Perspectives on Harpers Ferry's Armory and Com-
        mercial District*, Occasional Report 6, ed. Paul A. Shackel, 3.1–
        22. National Capital Region, National Park Service.

Fiegel, Kurt H.

1989    Stingy Ridge: An Archaeological and Historical Mitigation Report of the John Luther Richards Farm Complex, Jamestown, Russell County, Kentucky. Transportation Cabinet, Frankfort.

1990    Stingy Ridge: A Study of Twentieth-Century Rural Kentucky Farm Organization. Paper presented at Kentucky Heritage Council Annual Archaeology Conference, Bowling Green, Ky.

Fisher, Perry G., Patricia Chickering, and Michael Jenkins

1991    Historical Structures Report, Package 116, History Section, 1865–1952: Lots 2 and 3, Block B, Shenandoah Street, Park Buildings 32, 33, 33A, 34–35, 34, and 36, Harpers Ferry National Historical Park, W.Va. Historical Research Report, Cooperative Agreement, National Park Service and Univ. of Maryland.

Fite, Gilbert C.

1984    *Cotton Fields No More: Southern Agriculture, 1865–1980*. Lexington: Univ. Press of Kentucky.

Flannery, Kent V.

1974    Culture History Versus Cultural Process: A Debate in American Archaeology. In *New World Archaeology: Theoretical and Cultural Transformations,* compiled by Ezra B. W. Zubrow, Margaret C. Fritz, and John M. Fritz, 5–8. Rpt. from *Scientific American,* Aug. 1967. San Francisco: W. H. Freeman.

Fontana, Bernard L., and John C. Greenleaf

1962    Johnny Ward's Ranch. *Kiva* 28, no. 1–2.

Foote, Shelby

1974    *The Civil War: A Narrative* 3. New York: Random House.

Fowler, Robert H.

1986    Preface. In *Historical Times Illustrated Encyclopedia of the Civil War,* ed. Patricia Faust, xix–xxi. New York: Harper and Row.

Fox, Richard Allan, Jr.

1993    *Archaeology, History, and Custer's Last Battle*. Norman: Univ. of Oklahoma Press.

Fox, Steven J.

1978    Archaeology of Fortress Rosecrans: A Civil War Garrison in Middle Tennessee. Report prepared for National Park Service, Tennessee Historical Commission, and City of Murfreesboro, Tenn.

Frassanito, William

 1983   *Grant and Lee: The Virginia Campaigns, 1864–1865.* New York: Charles Scribner's Sons.

Fredrickson, George M.

 1965   *The Inner Civil War: Northern Intellectuals and the Crisis of the Union.* New York: Harper and Row.

Friedlander, Amy

 1990   Beyond Regionalism: History, Archaeology, and the Future. *Historical Archaeology* 24, no. 4: 102–9.

Frye, Susan W., and Dennis E. Frye

 1989   Maryland Heights: Archeological and Historical Resources Study. Occasional Report 2, Regional Archeology Program, National Capital Region, National Park Service. On file, Harpers Ferry National Historical Park, Harpers Ferry, W.Va.

Fussell, Paul

 1975   *The Great War and Modern Memory.* New York: Oxford Univ. Press.

 1991   *The Norton Book of Modern War.* New York: Norton.

Gates, Paul W.

 1941   Land Policy and Tenancy in the Prairie States. *Journal of Economic History* 1: 60–82.

 1945   Frontier Landlords and Pioneer Tenants. *Journal of the Illinois State Historical Society* 38: 143–206.

 1965   *Agriculture and the Civil War.* New York: Alfred A. Knopf.

Geier, Clarence R., Jr.

 1989   "Faunal Analysis." In The Hatcher-Cheatham Site (44CR258): A Multicomponent Historic Site in Chesterfield County, Virginia, Vol. 4. Prepared by James Madison Univ. Archaeological Research Center. Report Submitted to Virginia Dept. of Highways and Transportation, Richmond.

Geier, Clarence R., Jr., Martha M. McCartney, and James R. Cromwell, Jr.

 1989   "Volume I: Methodology, Culture History, and Interpretations." In The Hatcher-Cheatham Site (44CF258): A Multicomponent Historic Site in Chesterfield County, Virginia. Prepared by James Madison Univ. Archaeological Research Center. Report Submitted to Virginia Dept. of Transportation, Richmond.

Geier, Clarence R., David White, Stephen Thompson, Bernadette T. Whitney,

 1989   and Thomas R. Whyte

"Volume II: Description and Interpretation of the Site Architecture and Cemetery." In The Hatcher-Cheatham Site (44CF258): A Multicomponent Historic Site in Chesterfield County, Virginia. Prepared by James Madison Univ. Archaeological Research Center. Report Submitted to Virginia Dept. of Transportation, Richmond.

Gerard, Jeremy

  1990        Civil War Documentary Scores Big Victory for Public Television. *State Newspaper,* Columbia, S.C. Vol. 29: 1.

Gilbert, Cathy, Maureen DeLay Joseph, and Perry Carpenter Wheelock

  1991        Cultural Landscape Report: Lower Town, Harpers Ferry National Historical Park. Harpers Ferry National Historical Park, National Capital Region, National Park Service.

Gilbert, Dave

  1984        *Where Industry Failed: Water-Powered Mills at Harpers Ferry, West Virginia.* Charleston, W.Va.: Pictorial Histories Publishing Co.

Gilmore, Q. A.

  1865        Engineer and Artillery Operations Against the Defenses of Charleston Harbor in 1863; Comprising the Descent upon Morris Island, the Demolition of Fort Sumter, the Reduction of Forts Wagner and Gregg with Observations on Heavy Ordnance, Fortifications, etc. New York: D. Van Nostrand.

Glassie, Henry

  1977        Archaeology and Folklore: Common Anxieties, Common Hopes. In *Historical Archaeology and the Importance of Material Things,* ed. Leland Ferguson. Special Publication Ser. no. 2, 23–35. California, Pa.: Society for Historical Archaeology.

Godelier, Maurice

  1986        *The Mental and the Material: Thought, Economy, and Society.* Trans. Martin Thom. London: Verso.

Gould, Richard A., ed.

  1983        *Shipwreck Anthropology.* Albuquerque: Univ. of New Mexico Press.

Grantz, Denise L.

  1984        *Final Report: Nineteenth-Century Farmstead Model Development and Testing Project.* Report submitted to Pennsylvania Historical and Museum Commission, Harrisburg.

Gray, Lewis Cecil

  1933        *History of Agriculture in the Southern United States to 1860.* Washington, D.C.: Carnegie Institution.

Griffin, John W.

1978    End Products of Historic Sites Archaeology. In *Historical Archae-ology: A Guide to Substantive and Theoretical Contributions,* ed. Rob-ert Schuyler. Farmingdale, N.Y.: Baywood Publishing.

Grossman, Joel W.

1991    Civil War Era in the Age of Superfund: The Role of Espionage and Foreign Intelligence in the Development of Heavy Ordnance at the West Point Foundry, Cold Spring, New York. Paper presented at 1991 Annual Meeting of Society for Historical Archaeology, Richmond, Va.

Grossman, Joel W., et al.

1990    The Archaeology of Rascal Hill: Phase I Sensitivity Evaluation and Subsurface Testing for the Proposed Haul Road Impact Cor-ridor (Area I), Marathon Battery Remediation Project. Report for Malcolm Pirnie, Inc., New York.

1991    The Archaeological Discovery and Excavation of R. P. Parrott's Civil War Era Gun-Testing Facility at West Point Foundry. The Ex-panded Stage II Site Definition and Data Recovery of Remediation Area I, and Stage IB–II Sensitivity Evaluation of the Western Rail Road Spur for the Marathon Battery Project. Vols. 1 and 2. New York: Grossman and Associates, Inc.

1993    The Archaeology and Economic History of the Civil War Era Workers Housing Complex at West Point Foundry, Cold Spring, New York. Prepared for Malcolm Pirnie, Inc. On file with USEPA Region II, New York, U.S. Army COE, Kansas City.

Hagerman, Edward

1988    *The American Civil War and the Origins of Modern Warfare: Ideas, Orga-nization and Field Command.* Bloomington: Indiana Univ. Press.

Haggett, Peter

1990    *The Geographer's Art.* Basil Blackwell, Oxford, England.

Hahn, Steven, and Jonathan Prude. eds.

1985    *The Countryside in the Age of Capitalist Transformation: Essays in the Social History of Rural America.* Chapel Hill: Univ. of North Caro-lina Press.

Hall, T. E.

1865    Letter to Gen. M. C. Meigs, Mar. 30, 1865. Record Group 92, Box 720. National Archives, Washington, D.C.

*Harper's Ferry Mill Co. v. Thos. H. Savery et al.*
1887          Certificate of Evidence and Argument of Counsel, United States
              Circuit Court, District of West Virginia. Savery Papers Collection,
              Harpers Ferry National Historical Park, Harpers Ferry, W.Va.

Harris, Charles S.
1987          *Civil War Relics of the Western Campaigns, 1861–1865.*
              Mechanicsville, Va.: Rapidan Press.

Harrison, Lowell H.
1975          *The Civil War in Kentucky.* Lexington: Univ. Press of Kentucky.

Henderson, Lillian
N.d.          *Roster of Confederate Soldiers of Georgia, 1861–1865.* Harperville,
              Ga.: Longinoi and Porter.

Henretta, James A.
1978          Families and Farms: *Mentalité* in Pre-Industrial America. *William
              and Mary Quarterly* 35: 3–32.

Herman, Bernard
1984          Slave Quarters in Virginia: The Persona behind Historic Arti-
              facts. In *The Scope of Historical Archaeology,* ed. David G. Orr and
              Daniel Crozier. Philadelphia: Temple Univ. Press.

Herskovitz, Robert M.
1978          Fort Bowie Material Culture. *Anthropological Papers of the Univer-
              sity of Arizona* 31. Tucson, Ariz.

Hewitt, A. S.
1862          Letter to H. Wise, Apr. 22, 1862. Wise Papers. LB1, no. 9. New
              York: New York Historical Society.

Hinds, James R., and Edmund Fitzgerald
1981          *Bulwark and Bastion: A Look at Musket Era Fortification with a
              Glance at Period Siegecraft.* Las Vegas, Nev.: Council on Aban-
              doned Military Posts.

Hogg, Ian V.
N.d.          *Fortress: A History of Military Defense.* New York: St. Martin's
              Press.

Holley, Alexander L.
1865          *A Treatise on Ordnance and Armor: Embracing Descriptions, Discus-
              sions, and Professional Opinions Concerning the Material, Fabrication,
              Requirements, Capabilities, and Endurance of European and American
              Guns for Naval, Sea Coast and Iron Clad Warfare and Their Rifling
              Projectiles, and Breech Loading.* New York: Van Nostrand.

Holt, Lewis

1862        Letter to his sister, Oct. 16, 1862. In Letters from Caroline: Glimpses of Life and Valor Through the Eyes of Civil War Infantrymen. Unpublished typescript on file, Harpers Ferry National Historical Park, Harpers Ferry, W.Va.

1863        Letter to his sister, Sept. 2, 1863. In Letters to Caroline: Glimpses of Life and Valor Through the Eyes of Civil War Infantrymen. Unpublished typescript on file, Harpers Ferry National Historical Park, Harpers Ferry, W.Va.

Hoobler, James A.

1986        *Cities Under the Gun: Images of Occupied Nashville and Chattanooga.* Nashville, Tenn.: Rutledge Hill Press.

Horn, Stanley F.

1957        *The Decisive Battle of Nashville.* Knoxville: Univ. of Tennessee Press.

1977        *Guides to the Civil War in Tennessee.* Nashville, Tenn.: Civil War Centennial Commission.

1987        *The Army of Tennessee.* Wilmington, N.C.: Broadfoot Publishing.

Hougen, Harvey R.

1985        The Marais des Cygnes Massacre and the Execution of William Griffith. *Kansas History* 8, no. 2: 74–94.

Huyette, Miles Clayton

1915        *The Maryland Campaign and the Battle of Antietam.* Buffalo, N.Y.: privately printed.

Ingle, John

1988        Report on Relocation and Restoration of Grant's Cabin. Unpublished Report on file in the Mid-Atlantic Regional Office, National Park Service, Philadelphia.

Jackson, William K.

1990        Reenactors at War. *Civil War* 8, no. 4: 52–57.

Jimmerson, Randall C.

1988        *The Private Civil War.* Baton Rouge: Louisiana State Univ. Press.

Johnson, Mary, and John Barker

1993        Virginius Island: The Transformation of a Small Industrial Community, 1800–1936. National Park Service and Univ. of Maryland. On file at Harpers Ferry National Historical Park, Harpers Ferry, W.Va.

Johnson, Robert U., and C. C. Buel, eds.

1884–1887  *Battles and Leaders of the Civil War.* 3 vols. New York: n.p.

Jones, Howard
1992          *Union in Peril: The Crisis Over British Intervention in the Civil War.*
              Chapel Hill: Univ. of North Carolina Press.

Jones, Pat
1939          New Thunder Along the James. *Richmond* (Va.) *Times-Dispatch
              Magazine,* Sept. 24: 8–10.

Joseph, J. W., Mary Beth Reed, and Charles E. Cantley
1991          *Agrarian Life, Romantic Death: Archaeological and Historical Testing
              and Data Recovery for the I-85 Northern Alternative, Spartanburg
              County, South Carolina.* Stone Mountain, Ga.: New South Asso-
              ciates.

Joseph, Maureen De Lay, Perry Carpenter Wheelock, Deborah Warshaw, An-
              drew Kriemelmeyer
1993          Cultural Landscape Report: Virginius Island, Harpers Ferry Na-
              tional Historical Park. On file at Harpers Ferry National His-
              torical Park, Harpers Ferry, W.Va.

Josephy, Alvin M., Jr.
1991          *The Civil War in the American West.* New York: Alfred A. Knopf.

Jurney, David H.
1987          Cut and Wire Nails: Functional and Temporal Interpretations.
              In *Historic Buildings, Material Culture, and People of the Prairie Mar-
              gin.* Richland Creek Technical Ser., vol. 5, ed. David H. Jurney
              and Randall W. Moir. Archaeology Research Program, Institute
              for the Study of Earth and Man, Southern Methodist Univ.,
              Dallas, Tex.

Jurney, David H., and Randall W. Moir, eds.
1987          *Historic Buildings, Material Culture and People of the Prairie Margin.*
              Archaeology Research Program, Institute for the Study of Earth
              and Man, Southern Methodist Univ., Dallas, Tex.

Keegan, John
1976          *The Face of Battle.* New York: Viking Press.
1988          *The Mask of Command.* New York: Penguin Books.

Kelley, Dayon
1969          *General Lee and Hood's Texas Brigade at the Battle of the Wilderness.*
              Hillsboro, Tex.: Hill Junior College Press.

Kemble, Gouverneur, III
1916          *West Point Foundry* 15: 190–203. New York: New York State His-
              torical Association.

Kemp, Thomas R.
 1990      Community and War: The Civil War Experience of Two New
           Hampshire Towns. In *Toward a Social History of the American Civil
           War: Exploratory Essays,* ed. Maris A. Vinovskis, 31–77. Cam-
           bridge: Cambridge Univ. Press.

Kennedy, Joseph C. G., compiler
 1864a     *Agriculture of the United States in 1860.* Washington, D.C.: Govt.
           Printing Office.

 1864b     *Population of the United States in 1860.* Washington, D.C.: Govt.
           Printing Office.

Kerksis, Sidney
 1974      *Plates and Buckles of the American Military, 1795–1874.* Stone
           Mountain, Ga.: Stone Mountain Press.

Ketchum, Richard M., ed.
 1960      *The American Heritage Picture Heritage of the Civil War.* New York:
           American Heritage Publishing Co.

King, Julie A.
 1994a     Rural Landscape in the Mid-Nineteenth-Century Chesapeake.
           In *Historical Archaeology of the Chesapeake,* ed. Paul A. Shackel and
           Barbara J. Little. Washington, D.C.: Smithsonian Institution
           Press.

 1994b     "The Transient Nature of All Things Sublunary": Romanticism,
           History, and Ruins in Nineteenth-Century Southern Maryland.
           In *Methods and Meanings: Case Studies in Landscape Archaeology,*
           ed. Rebecca Yamin and Karen Bescherer. Boca Raton, Fla.:
           CRC Press.

Kirkley, Joseph W.
 N.d.      History of the 7th Maryland Infantry. Manuscript in Joseph W.
           Kirkley Papers, Library of Congress, Washington D.C.

Knoke, David, and James H. Kuklinski
 1982      *Network Analysis.* Newberry Park, Calif.: Sage.

Kohl, Philip L.
 1981      Materialist Approaches in Prehistory. *Annual Reviews of Anthro-
           pology* 10: 89–118.

Kroeber, A. L.
 1917      The Superorganic. In *American Anthropologist* 19: 163–213.

Kuttruff, Carl
 1989      Excavations on Confederate Entrenchments, Nashville, Tennessee.
           Paper presented at First Joint Archaeological Congress, Baltimore.

Landon, William
   1933        The Fourteenth Indiana Regiment on Cheat Mountain: Letters
               to the Vincennes Sun. *Indiana Magazine of History* 29.

Langhorne, Henry, and Lawrence E. Babits
   1988        Anthropological Title Searches in Rockbridge County, Virginia.
               In *Documentary Archaeology in the New World,* ed. Mary C. Beaudry,
               132–37. Cambridge: Cambridge Univ. Press.

Langsdorf, Edgar
   1964        Price's Raid and the Battle of Mine Creek. *Kansas Historical
               Quarterly* 30: 281–306.

Lazelle, Henry M., ed.
   1887        *The War of the Rebellion: A Compilation of the Official Records of the
               Union and Confederate Armies.* Ser. I, vol. 19, pt. 2. Washington,
               D.C.: Govt. Printing Office.

Lees, William B.
   1990        Getting the Lead Out: Archaeological Research at the Mine
               Creek Civil War Battlefield, Kansas. Paper presented at Plains
               Conference, Oklahoma City, Okla. Conference sponsored by
               Kansas State Historical Society.

Legg, James B., and Steven D. Smith
   1989        "The Best Ever Occupied . . .": Archaeological Investigations of
               a Civil War Encampment on Folly Island, South Carolina. Re-
               search Manuscript Ser. no. 209. Columbia, S.C.: South Caro-
               lina Institute of Archaeology and Anthropology.

Leone, Mark P.
   1984        Interpreting Ideology in Historical Archaeology: Using the
               Rules of Perspective in the William Paca Garden, Annapolis,
               Maryland. In *Ideology, Power and Prehistory,* ed. Daniel Miller and
               Christopher Tilley, 25–35. New York: Cambridge Univ. Press.
   1986        Symbolic, Structural, and Critical Archaeology. In *American Archae-
               ology, Past and Future: A Celebration of the Society for American Archae-
               ology, 1935–1985,* ed. David J. Meltzer, Don D. Fowler, and Jeremy
               A. Sabloff, 415–38. Washington, D.C.: Smithsonian Institution Press.

Leone, Mark P., and Parker B. Potter, Jr., eds.
   1988        *The Recovery of Meaning: Historical Archaeology in the Eastern United
               States.* Washington, D.C.: Smithsonian Institution Press.

Lesser, Alexander
   1961        Social Fields and the Evolution of Society. *Southwestern Journal of
               Anthropology* 17: 40–48.

Lesser, W. Hunter
  1981        Preliminary Archeological and Historical Investigations of Cheat
              Summit Fort. *West Virginia Archeologist* 31: 31–37.
  1982        Cheat Summit Fort: A Status Report Concerning Eligibility for
              Nomination to the National Register of Historic Places. West Vir-
              ginia Geological and Economic Survey. 0F98. Morgantown, W.Va.

Lewis, Berkely R.
  1960        *Small Arms and Ammunition in the United States Service, 1776–*
              *1865.* Smithsonian Miscellaneous Collections, vol. 129.
              Smithsonian Institution, Washington, D.C.

Lewis, Clifford M.
  1963        Camp Allegheny: A Survey of a Confederate Winter Quarters.
              *West Virginia Archaeologist* 16: 33–45.

Little, Barbara J., and Paul A. Shackel
  1989        Scales of Historical Anthropology: An Archaeology of Colonial
              Anglo-America. *Antiquity* 63: 495–509.

Long, E. B.
  1971        *The Civil War Day by Day: An Almanac, 1861–1865.* Garden City,
              N.Y.: Doubleday.

Long, John S.
  1957        The Gosport Affair, 1861. *Journal of Southern History* 23: 157–72.

Lord, Francis A.
  1960        *They Fought for the Union.* New York: Bonanza.
  1979        *Civil War Collector's Encyclopedia.* West Columbia, S.C.: Lord
              Americana and Research.

Lord, Francis A., and Arthur Wise
  1970        *Uniforms of the Civil War.* New York: Thomas Yoseloff.

Lowenthal, David
  1985        *The Past Is a Foreign Country.* Cambridge: Cambridge Univ. Press.

Lucas, Marian B.
  1989        Camp Nelson, Kentucky, During the Civil War: Cradle of Liberty
              or Refugee Death Camp. *Filson Club History Quarterly* 63: 439–59.

Lutz, Francis Earle
  1954        *Chesterfield, an Old Virginia County.* Richmond, Va.: William Byrd Press.

Luvaas, Jay
  1988        *The Military Legacy of the Civil War: The European Inheritance.*
              Lawrence: Univ. Press of Kansas.

Mahan, D. H.
  1862        *A Treatise on Field Fortifications.* New York: John Wiley.

Mainfort, Robert C., Jr.
  1980        Archaeological Investigations at Fort Pillow State Historic Area:
              1976–1978. *Research Series* 4. Nashville: Tennessee Dept. of Con-
              servation, Division of Archaeology.

Manning, Mathew, ed.
  1990        *The Standard Periodicals Dictionary.* 13th ed.. New York: Oxbridge
              Communications.

Mansberger, Floyd
  1986        Changing Patterns of Nineteenth-Century Ceramics. In *Nineteenth-Cen-
              tury Historic Archaeology in Illinois,* ed. Thomas E. Emerson and Charles L.
              Rohrbaugh, 131–79. Springfield: Illinois Historic Preservation Agency.

Marcus, Alan I., and Howard P. Segal
  1989        *Technology in America: A Brief History.* New York: Harcourt Brace
              Jovanovich.

Margolin, Samuel G.
  1987        Civil War Legacy Beneath the James: The Discovery of the U.S.S.
              *Cumberland* and the C.S.S. *Florida. Archaeology* 40, no. 5: 50–57, 84.

Mariners' Museum Library, Newport News, Va.
  1871        "Obstructions at Drewry's Bluff James River Va. Removed in
              1871." Map. File no. VK/1273/J21.

Marmion, Annie P.
  1959        Under Fire: An Experience in the Civil War. Memoirs compiled and
              published by William Vincent Marmion, Jr. Booklet File, Park Li-
              brary, Harpers Ferry National Historical Park, Harpers Ferry, W. Va.

Marquardt, William H.
  1985        Complexity and Scale in the Study of Fisher-Gatherers-Hunters:
              An Example from the Eastern United States. In *Prehistoric Hunter-
              Gatherers: The Emergence of Cultural Complexity,* ed. T. Douglas Price
              and James A. Brown. Orlando, Fla.: Academic Press.
  1990        Dialectical Archaeology. Paper presented at Seminar on Critical Ap-
              proaches in Archaeology: Material Life, Meaning, and Power,
              Cascais, Portugal.
  1992        Dialectical Archaeology. In *Archaeological Method and Theory* 4, ed.
              Michael B. Schiffer, 104–40. Tuscon: Univ. of Arizona Press.

Marquardt, William H., and Carole L. Crumley
  1987        Theoretical Issues in the Analysis of Spatial Patterning. In *Re-
              gional Dynamics: Burgundian Landscapes in Historical Perspective,* ed.
              Carole L. Crumley and William H. Marquardt, 1–18. San Di-
              ego, Calif.: Academic Press.

Martin, J. D.

N.d. Reports of Special Agents 1865–1870: Respectively Forwarded to E. Simpson, Captain U.S. Navy. Notes on Belgium Fuses, Primers and Artillery, Including Reports by Agents of Prussian, Austrian, and Spanish Origin. Record Group 74, Entry 201, Item 15, National Archives, Washington, D.C.

Maryland, State of

1861 *Journal of the Proceedings of the House of Delegates, in Extra Session.* Frederick, Md.: Elihu S. Riley.

McBride, Kim A., and W. Stephen McBride

1989 Cheat Summit Fort: An Annotated Bibliography. *Archaeological Report* 197. Program for Cultural Resource Assessment, Univ. of Kentucky, Lexington.

1990 Camp Allegheny: An Annotated Bibliography. *Archaeological Report* 213. Program for Cultural Resource Assessment, Univ. of Kentucky, Lexington.

McBride, W. Stephen

1991 Flush Times on the Upper Tombigbee: Settlement and Economic Development in Lowndes County, Mississippi, 1833–1860. Ph.D. diss., Michigan State Univ., East Lansing.

McBride, W. Stephen, and Kim A. McBride

1987 Socioeconomic Variation in a Late Antebellum Southern Town: The View from Archaeological and Documentary Sources. In *Consumer Choice in Historical Archaeology,* ed. Suzanne Spencer-Wood, 143–61. New York: Plenum Press.

McBride, W. Stephen, and William E. Sharp

1991 *Archaeological Investigations at Camp Nelson: A Union Quartermaster Depot and Hospital in Jessamine County, Kentucky.* Archaeological Report 241. Program for Cultural Resource Assessment, Univ. of Kentucky, Lexington.

McCartney, Martha W.

1988 The Hatcher-Cheatham Site (44CF258): A Middling Farmstead in Rural Chesterfield County, Virginia. Manuscript on file, Dept. of Sociology and Anthropology, James Madison Univ., Harrisonburg, Va.

McCorvie, Mary R.

1987 *The Davis, Baldridge, and Huggins Sites: Three Nineteenth-Century Upland South Farmsteads in Perry County, Illinois.* Carbondale, Ill.: American Resources Group.

1988        Socioeconomic Ranking of Three Mid-19th-Century Farm-
            steads in Perry County, Illinois. In *Historic Archaeology in Illinois,*
            ed. Charles L. Rohrbaugh and Thomas E. Emerson, 67–80.
            Springfield: Illinois Historic Preservation Agency.

McDonough, James Lee, and Thomas L. Connelly

1983        *Five Tragic Hours: The Battle of Franklin.* Knoxville: Univ. of Ten-
            nessee Press.

McKee, W. Reid, and M. E. Mason, Jr.

1971        *Civil War Projectiles: Small Arms and Field Artillery.* Private publi-
            cation.

1980        *Civil War Projectiles II, Small Arms and Field Artillery.* Orange, Va.:
            Moss Publications.

McMurry, Sally

1988        *Families and Farmhouses in Nineteenth-Century America: Design and
            Social Change.* New York: Oxford Univ. Press.

McPherson, James M.

1988        *Battle Cry of Freedom: The Civil War Era.* New York: Oxford Univ. Press.

McWhiney, Grady, and Perry D. Jamieson

1984        *Attack and Die: Civil War Military Tactics and the Southern Heritage.*
            University: Univ. of Alabama Press.

Meigs, Gen. M. C.

1865        Letter to Secretary Edwin M. Stanton, Oct. 5, 1865. Record
            Group 92, Box 720. National Archives, Washington, D.C.

1866        Letter to Secretary Edwin M. Stanton, Jan. 12, 1866. Record
            Group 92, Box 720. National Archives, Washington, D.C.

Merrill, Michael

1977        Cash Is Good to Eat: Self-Sufficiency and Exchange in the Rural
            Economy of the United States. *Radical History Review* 3: 42–71.

1980        So What's Wrong with the 'Household Mode of Production'?
            *Radical History Review* 22: 141–46.

Miller, A. B.

1866        Map of Camp Nelson Showing the Locations of Buildings. Car-
            tographic Section, National Archives, Washington, D.C.

Miller, George L.

1980        Classification and Economic Scaling of 19th Century Ceramics.
            *Historical Archaeology* 14: 1–40.

1991        A Revised Set of CC Index Values for Classification and Economic
            Scaling of English Ceramics from 1787 to 1880. *Historical Archaeol-
            ogy* 25 no. 1: 1–25.

Mission, H.
1865        Report of Board on Rifled Ordnance. June 30, 1865. Record
            Group 74, Entry 191. National Archives, Washington, D.C.

Mitchell, Reid
1988        *Civil War Soldiers.* New York: Viking Press.

Mitchell, Robert
1977        *Commercialism and Frontier: Perspectives on the Early Shenandoah
            Valley.* Charlottesville: Univ. Press of Virginia.

Mohaghan, Jay
1955        *Civil War on the Western Border, 1854–1865.* New York: Bonanza.

Moir, Randall W., and David H. Jurney, eds.
1987        *Pioneer Settlers, Tenant Farmers, and Communities.* Dallas, Tex.:
            Southern Methodist Univ., Institute for the Study of Earth and
            Man, Archaeology Research Program.

Moore, George E., ed.
1961        The Civil War Journal of George F. Morgan. *West Virginia History*
            22: 4.

Mordeccai, Alfred
1861        *Military Commission to Europe in 1855 and 1856: Report of Major
            Alfred Mordeccai of the Ordinance Department.* Washington, D.C.:
            George W. Bowman, Printer.

Muckleroy, Keith
1978        *Maritime Archaeology.* Cambridge: Cambridge Univ. Press.

Munden, Kenneth W., and Henry P. Beers
1962        *Guide to Federal Archives Relating to the Civil War.* National Ar-
            chives and Record Service, Washington, D.C.

Nash, Howard P., Jr.
1969        *Stormy Petrel: The Life and Times of General Benjamin Butler, 1818–
            1893.* Cranberry, N.J.: Associated Univ. Presses.

Naylor, Colin T.
1961        *Civil War Days in a Country Village.* Peekskill, N.Y.: Highland Press.

Nelson, Dean
1982        Right Nice Little House[s]: Impermanent Camp Architecture
            of the American Civil War. In *Perspectives in Vernacular Architec-
            ture,* ed. Camille Wells. Annapolis, Md.: Vernacular Architecture
            Forum.

Nevins, Allan
1935        *Abram S. Hewitt with Some Account of Peter Cooper.* New York:
            Harper and Brothers.

Nevins, Allan, James I. Robertson, Jr., and Bell I. Wiley, eds.
    1970        *Civil War Books: A Critical Bibliography.* Baton Rouge: Louisiana State Univ. Press.

Nicholls, Michael L.
    1981        In the Light of Human Beings. *Virginia Magazine of History and Biography* 89, no. 1: 67–78.

Noffsinger, James P.
    1958        Harpers Ferry, West Virginia: Contributions Toward a Physical History. Eastern Office of Design and Construction, National Park Service, Philadelphia, Pennsylvania. Typescript on file at Harpers Ferry National Historical Park, Harpers Ferry, W.Va.

*Norfolk Virginian*
    1875        A Diving Feat: Safe of the *Cumberland* Recovered. June 12.

North, Douglass C.
    1974        *Growth and Welfare in the American Past: A New Economic History.* 2d ed. Englewood Cliffs, N.J.: Prentice-Hall.

Nowak, Leszek
    1983        *Property and Power: Toward a Non-Marxian Historical Materialism.* Dordrecht, Holland: D. Reidel.

O'Dell, Jeffrey
    1983        *Chesterfield County: Early Architecture and Historic Sites.* Chesterfield, Va.: Chesterfield County Board of Supervisors.

O'Malley, Nancy
    1987        *Middle-Class Farmers on the Urban Periphery.* Report 162. Program for Cultural Resource Assessment, Univ. of Kentucky, Lexington.

O'Neil, Charles
    1922        Engagement between the 'Cumberland' and the 'Merrimack.' *United States Naval Institute Proceedings* 48, no. 6: 863–93.

Orr, David G.
    1982        The City Point Headquarters Cabin of Ulysses S. Grant. In *Perspectives in Vernacular Architecture,* ed. Camille Wells. Annapolis, Md.: Vernacular Architecture Forum.

Orr, David G., Brooke S. Blades, and Douglas V. Campana
    1985        Uncovering Early Colonial City Point, Virginia. *Archaeology* 38, no. 3: 64–65, 78.

Orser, Charles E., Jr.
    1988a      *The Material Basis of the Postbellum Tenant Plantation: Historical Archaeology in the South Carolina Piedmont.* Athens: Univ. of Georgia Press.

1988b    The Archaeological Analysis of Plantation Society: Replacing Status and Caste with Economics and Power. *American Antiquity* 53: 735–51.

1989    On Plantations and Patterns. *Historical Archaeology* 23, no. 2: 28–40.

1990    Historical Archaeology on Southern Plantations and Farms: Introduction. *Historical Archaeology* 24, no. 4: 1–6.

1991    The Continued Pattern of Dominance: Landlord and Tenant on the Post-bellum Cotton Plantation. In *The Archaeology of Inequality,* ed. Robert Paynter and Randall H. McGuire, 40–54. Oxford, England: Basil Blackwell.

In press    Consumption, Consumerism, and Things from the Earth. *Historical Methods,* forthcoming.

Orser, Charles E., Jr., and Claudia C. Holland

1984    Let Us Praise Famous Men, Accurately: Toward a More Complete Understanding of Postbellum Southern Agricultural Practices. *Southeastern Archaeology* 3: 111–20.

Otto, John S.

1977    Artifacts and Status Differences: A Comparison of Ceramics from Planter, Overseer, and Slave Sites on an Antebellum Plantation. In *Research Strategies in Historical Archaeology,* ed. Stanley South, 91–118. New York: Academic Press.

Owsley, Frank L., Jr.

1987    *The C.S.S. Florida: Her Building and Operations.* Tuscaloosa: Univ. of Alabama Press.

Padgett, James A.

1945    The Life of Alfred Mordeccai as Related by Himself. *The North Carolina Historical Review* 23, no. 1.

Parker, William H.

1985    *Recollections of a Naval Officer, 1841–1865.* Rpt. of 1883 ed. Annapolis, Maryland: Naval Institute Press.

Parrott, R. D. A.

1921    *Cold Blast Charcoal Pig Iron Made at Greenwood, Orange County, New York, During the Civil War Period, 1861–1865.* Flushing, N.Y.

Parrott, Robert P.

1865    The Parrott Guns: Explanation by the Inventor. New York *Evening Post,* Jan. 28.

Paulding, J. N.
    1879        The Cannon and Projectiles Invented by Robert P. Parrott. Rpt.
                1972, in *Heavy Artillery Projectiles of the Civil War, 1861–1865,*
                ed. Sydney C. Kerksis and Thomas Dickey. Kennesaw, Ga.:
                Phoenix Press.

Paynter, Robert
    1988        Steps to an Archaeology of Capitalism: Material Change and
                Class Analysis. In *The Recovery of Meaning: Historical Archaeology*
                *in the United States,* ed. Mark P. Leone and Parker B. Potter, Jr.,
                407–33. Washington, D.C.: Smithsonian Institution Press.

Perdue, Rosa M.
    1902        The Sources of the Constitution of Kansas. *Transactions of the*
                *Kansas State Historical Society, 1901–1902.* Topeka: State of Kan-
                sas.

Perry, Milton F.
    1965        *Infernal Machines: The Story of Confederate Submarine and Mine War-*
                *fare.* Baton Rouge: Louisiana State Univ. Press.

Phelps, David S., ed.
    1979        An Archaeological-Historical Study of the Bryan Cemetery and
                Site 31Cu25, Simmons-National Airport, New Bern, North
                Carolina. *North Carolina Archaeological Council Publication* 10. Ra-
                leigh, N.C.

*Philadelphia Inquirer*
    1866        Relics of the War-General Grant's Log Cabin. Aug. 6, 1866.

Philips, Stanley S.
    1971        *Bullets Used in the Civil War, 1861–1865.* Laurel, Md.: Wilson's
                Specialty Co.
    1974        *Excavated Artifacts from Battlefields and Campsites of the Civil War,*
                *1861–1865.* Lanham, Md.: published by the author.

Phillippe, Joseph S.
    1985        *Phase II Archaeological Testing of Historic Sites for the FAP 408*
                *Highway Project, Illinois Route 79 to Hull Interchange, Pike County,*
                *Illinois.* Report submitted to Illinois Dept. of Transportation,
                Springfield.

Pool, J. T.
    1862        *Under Canvas; or, Recollections of the Fall and Summer Campaign of*
                *the 14th Regiment Indiana Volunteers: Col. Nathan Kimball in West-*
                *ern Virginia.* Terre Haute, Ind.: Oliver Bartlett Publishers.

Porter, P. A.
 1863   Unpublished Map of Maryland Heights Fortifications and
      Campgrounds, RG 393. Miscellaneous Uninventoried Records,
      1821–1920. 6th New York Heavy Artillery Regimental Letter
      and Order Book. Record Group 94, Records of the Adjutant
      General's Office. National Archives, Washington, D.C.

Raab, L. Mark, ed.
 1982   *Settlement of the Prairie Margin: Archaeology of the Richland Creek
      Reservoir, Navarro and Freestone Counties, Texas, 1980–1981. A
      Research Synopsis.* Dallas, Tex.: Southern Methodist Univ., Dept.
      of Anthropology.

Randall, J. G., and David Donald
 1969   *The Civil War and Reconstruction.* Lexington, Mass.: D. C. Heath.

Raoul, Margaret Lente
 1936   Gouverneur Kemble and the West Point Foundry. *Americana His-
      torical Magazine* 30, no. 3: 461–73.

Raper, Arthur F.
 1936   *Preface to Peasantry: A Tale of Two Black Belt Counties.* Chapel Hill:
      Univ. of North Carolina Press.

Rapoport, David C.
 1971   Foreword. In *Primitive War: Its Practice and Concepts,* by Harry
      Holbert Turney-High, v–xi. 2d ed. Columbia: Univ. of South
      Carolina Press.

Reader, Francis
 1890   *History of the 5th West Virginia Cavalry, Formerly the Second Virginia
      Infantry, and of Battery G, First West Virginia Light Artillery.* New
      Brighton, Pa.: F. S. Reader.

Resticaux, E. B. W.
 1865   Letter to Gen. Robert Allen, Mar. 20, 1865. Box 720, Record
      Group 92. National Archives, Washington, D.C.

Riordan, Timothy Benedict III
 1985   The Relative Economic Status of Black and White Regiments
      in the Pre–World War I Army: An Example from Fort Walla,
      Washington. Ph.D. diss., Dept. of Anthropology, Washington
      State Univ., Pullman.

Riordan, Timothy B., and William Hampton Adams
 1985   Commodity Flows and National Market Access. *Historical Archae-
      ology* 19, no. 2: 5–18.

Ripley, Warren
  1970      *Artillery and Ammunition of the Civil War.* New York: Van Nostrand Reinhold.

Robertson, James I., Jr.
  1984      *The Civil War: Tenting Tonight.* Alexandria, Va.: Time-Life Books.
  1988a     *Soldiers Blue and Gray.* Columbia: Univ. of South Carolina Press.
  1988b     Foreword. In *Civil War Eyewitnesses: An Annotated Bibliography of Books and Articles,* by Garold L. Cole, vii–viii. Columbia: Univ. of South Carolina Press.

Robertson, James Oliver
  1980      *American Myth, American Reality.* New York: Hill and Wang.

Robertson, Joseph Clarke
  1987      *Back Door to Richmond: The Bermuda Hundred Campaign, April-June 1864.* Newark: Univ. of Delaware Press.

Robinson, William M., Jr.
  1961      Drewry's Bluff: Naval Defense of Richmond. *Civil War History* 7: 167–75.

Rosenthal, M. L., ed.
  1966      *Selected Poems and Two Plays of William Butler Yeats.* New York: Collier Books.

Rutman, Darrett B.
  1971      *The Morning of America, 1603–1789.* Boston: Houghton Mifflin.

Sahlins, Marshall
  1976      *Culture and Practical Reason.* Chicago: Univ. of Chicago Press.

Salisbury, Stephen
  1962      The Effect of the Civil War on American Industrial Development. In *The Economic Impact of the American Civil War,* ed. Ralph Andrews, 161–68. Cambridge, Mass.: Schenkman.

Sanford, H. S.
  1863      Correspondence to H. Wise, Aug. 7, 1863. Wise Papers, LB5, no. 6.5, New York Historical Society, New York.
  1865      Correspondence to H. Wise, Feb. 16, 1865. Wise Papers, LB10, no. 67.5, New York Historical Society, New York.
  1866      Correspondence to H. Wise, Feb. 16, 1866. Wise Papers, LB12, no. 66. New York Historical Society, New York.
  1866      Correspondence to H. Wise, May 8, 1866. Wise Papers, LB12, no. 155. New York Historical Society, New York.

Schock, Jack M.

1987    Archaeological Testing of Civil War Sites 15Js96 and 15Js97: A Supplement to the Original Survey Report for the Relocation of Highway 27 South of Nicholasville in Jessamine County, Kentucky. Kentucky Transportation Cabinet, Division of Environmental Analysis, Frankfurt.

Schuyler, Robert

1977    The Spoken Word, the Written Word, Observed Behavior and Preserved Behavior: The Contexts Available to the Archeologist. *Conference on Historic Sites Archaeology Papers* 10, no. 2: 99–120.

1988    Archaeological Remains, Documents, and Anthropology: A Call for a New Cultural History. *Historical Archaeology* 22, no. 1: 36–42.

Scofield, Levi T.

1888    The Retreat from Pulaski to Nashville. In *Sketches of War History, 1861–1865,* vol. 2. Published by the Commandery of the Military Order of the Loyal Legion of the United States. Cincinnati: Robert Clarke & Co.

Scott, Douglas D., and Richard A. Fox, Jr.

1987    *Archaeological Insights into the Custer Battle: An Assessment of the 1984 Field Season.* Norman: Univ. of Oklahoma Press.

Scott, Douglas D., Richard A. Fox, Jr., Melissa A. Conner, and Dick Harmon

1989    *Archaeological Perspectives on the Battle of the Little Big Horn.* Norman: Univ. of Oklahoma Press.

Scott, Joseph

1805    *A Geographical Dictionary of the United States of North America.* Philadelphia: Archibald Bartram.

Scott, Robert N., ed.

1880    *The War of the Rebellion: A Compilation of the Official Records of the Union and Confederate Armies.* Ser. I, vol. 2. Washington, D.C.: Govt. Printing Office.

1881    *The War of the Rebellion: A Compilation of the Official Records of the Union and Confederate Armies.* Ser. I, vol. 5. Washington, D.C.: Govt. Printing Office.

1889    *The War of the Rebellion: A Compilation of the Official Records of the Union and Confederate Armies.* Ser. I, vol. 27, pt. 2. Washington, D.C.: Govt. Printing Office.

1891    *The War of the Rebellion: A Compilation of the Official Records of the Union and Confederate Armies.* Ser. I, vol. 36, pt. 2. Washington, D.C.: Govt. Printing Office.

Sears, Richard D.

1986        *A Practical Recognition of the Brotherhood of Man: John G. Fee and the Camp Nelson Experience.* Berea, Ky.: Berea College.

1987        John G. Fee, Camp Nelson, and Kentucky Blacks, 1864–1865. *Register of the Kentucky Historical Society* 85: 29–45.

Seasholes, Nancy S.

1990        "Opinion." In History for Archaeologists: Interpretation Rather than Particularism. *Society for Historical Archaeology Newsletter* 23, no. 3: 17–19.

Selfridge, Thomas O., Jr.

1893        The Merrimac and the Cumberland. *Cosmopolitan* 15: 176–84.

1924        *Memoirs of Thomas O. Selfridge, Jr.* New York: Putnam's Sons.

Sellars, Richard

1987        Vigil of Silence: The Civil War Memorials. *Courier.* National Park Service. Mar.: 18–19.

Sellers, John R.

1986        *A Guide to Collections in the Manuscript Division of the Library of Congress.* Library of Congress, Washington, D.C.

Semmes, Raphael

1893        *Service Afloat; Or, The Remarkable Career of the Confederate Cruisers Sumter and Alabama, During the War Between the States.* New York: P. J. Kenedy.

Shackel, Paul A.

1992        The Material Reification of Factory Discipline and Resistance in Early Industrial Society. Paper presented at April meeting of Society for American Archaeology, Pittsburgh, Pa.

1993        A Social History of Harpers Ferry and Block B, Lot 3 and 2, Lower Town. In Interdisciplinary Investigations of Domestic Life in Government Block B: Perspectives on Harpers Ferry's Armory and Commercial District. *Occasional Report* 6, ed. Paul A. Shackel, 2.1–12. National Capital Region: National Park Service.

Simon, John Y., ed.

1982        *The Papers of Ulysses S. Grant* 10: *January 1–May 31, 1864.* Carbondale: Southern Illinois Univ. Press.

Simpson, Lt. Col. J. H.

1864        Camp Nelson and Its Defenses, Jessamine County, Kentucky. Office of U.S. Engineers, Cincinnati. Cartographic Section, National Archives, Washington, D.C.

Sinclair, G. Terry
  1898        The Eventful Cruise of the "Florida." *Century Magazine* 57: 417–27.
Smith, Charles R., and Shawn K. Bonath (Compilers)
  1982        A Report on Phase I and Phase II Historical Archaeological In-
               vestigations on Three Segments of the FAP 408 Corridor,
               Adams, Pike, and Scott Counties, Illinois (1979–1981). Report
               submitted to Illinois Dept. of Transportation, Springfield.
Smith, Gerald P.
  1985        Fort Germantown Historic Park: Historic Background, Archaeo-
               logical Investigations, and Recommendations. Prepared for City of
               Germantown, Tenn.
  1987        Fort Germantown: 1986 Excavations. Prepared for City of
               Germantown, Tenn.
Smith, Merritt Roe
  1977        *Harpers Ferry Armory and the New Technology: The Challenge of
               Change.* Ithaca, N.Y.: Cornell Univ. Press.
Smith, Page
  1982        *Trial by Fire: A People's History of the Civil War and Reconstruction.*
               New York: McGraw-Hill.
Smith, Samuel D.
  1990        Site Survey as a Method for Determining Historic Site Signifi-
               cance. *Historical Archaeology* 24, no. 2: 26–33.
  1991        Excavation Data for Civil War Period Military Sites in Middle
               Tennessee. Paper presented at Annual Meeting of Society for
               Historical Archaeology, Richmond, Va.
Smith, Samuel D., Fred M. Prouty, and Benjamin C. Nance
  1990        A Survey of Civil War Period Military Sites in Middle Tennes-
               see. *Report of Investigations* 7. Nashville: Tennessee Dept. of Con-
               servation, Division of Archaeology.
Smith, Steven D.
  1991        A Comparison of the Documentary Evidence of Material Cul-
               ture and the Archaeological Record: Store Ledgers and Two
               Black Tenant Sites, Waverly, Mississippi. In *Volumes in Historical
               Archaeology* 12, ed. Stanley South. Columbia: South Carolina In-
               stitute of Archaeology and Anthropology.
Snell, Charles W.
  1959        Harpers Ferry Becomes a Fortress: September 21, 1862–Octo-
               ber 6, 1863. Report on file, Harpers Ferry National Historical
               Park, Harpers Ferry, W. Va.

1960a   Harpers Ferry Repels an Attack and Becomes the Major Base of Operations for Sheridan's Army, July 4, 1864–July 27, 1865. Report on file, Harpers Ferry National Historical Park, Harpers Ferry, W.Va.

1960b   The Fortifications at Harpers Ferry, Virginia, in 1861, and Jackson's Attack, May 1862. Report on File, Harpers Ferry National Historical Park, Harpers Ferry, W.Va.

Snyder, Lynn M.

1989   Vertebrate Faunal Remains from Sites 38CH964 and 38CH965, Folly Island, Charleston County, South Carolina, 1988 Excavations. In "The Best Ever Occupied . . . " Archaeological Investigations of a Civil War Encampment on Folly Island, South Carolina, by James B. Legg and Steven D. Smith, B.1–23. *Research Manuscript Series* 209. Columbia: South Carolina Institute of Archaeology and Anthropology.

Socolofsky, Homer E.

1979   *Landlord William Scully.* Lawrence: Regents Press of Kansas.

1985   American Land Policies and William Scully. In *Working the Range: Essays on the History of Western Land Management and the Environment,* ed. John R. Wunder, 129–37. Westport, Conn.: Greenwood.

South, Stanley

1977   *Method and Theory in Historical Archaeology.* New York: Academic Press.

Spillman, W. J.

1919   The Agricultural Ladder. *Papers on Tenancy* 2: 29–38. Office of the Secretary, American Association for Agricultural Legislation, Univ. of Wisconsin, Madison.

*Spirit of Jefferson.* Newspaper on microfilm at Harpers Ferry National Historical Park, Harpers Ferry, W.Va.

Stampp, Kenneth M.

1956   *The Peculiar Institution.* New York: Vintage Books.

Stern, Philip Van Doren

1959   *They Were There: The Civil War in Action as Seen by Its Combat Artists.* New York: Crown.

Still, William N., Jr.

1971   *Iron Afloat: The Story of the Confederate Armorclads.* Columbia, S.C.: Vanderbilt Univ. Press.

Stine, Linda F.

1989 Archaeological Inventory Survey and National Register Evaluations: Military Ocean Terminal, Sunny Point, New Hanover County, North Carolina. *Resource Studies Series* 137, ed. Lesley Drucker. Columbia, S.C.: Carolina Archaeological Services.

Street, James

1985 *The Struggle for Tennessee: Tupelo to Stones River.* Alexandria, Va.: Time-Life Books.

Sword, Wiley

1992 *Embrace an Angry Wind (The Confederacy's Last Hurrah: Spring Hill, Franklin and Nashville).* New York: Harper Collins Publishers.

Sylvia, Stephen W., and Michael J. O'Donnell

1978 *The Illustrated History of American Civil War Relics.* Orange, Va.: Moss Publications.

Taft, Grace Jennings

1898 A Trip to Harpers Ferry. Manuscript on file at Harpers Ferry National Historical Park, Harpers Ferry, W.Va.

Thomas, Dean

1981 *Ready . . . Aim . . . Fire! Small Arms Ammunition in the Battle of Gettysburg.* Biglerville, Pa.: Osborn Printing Co.

1985 *Cannons: An Introduction to Civil War Artillery.* Arendtsville, Pa.: Thomas Publications.

Todd, Frederick P.

1974 *American Military Equipage, 1851–1872.* Providence, R.I.: Company of Military Historians.

1980 *American Military Equipage, 1851–1872.* New York: Charles Scribner's Sons.

Trefousse, Hans L.

1957 *Ben Butler: The South Called Him Beast!* New York: Twayne.

Tune, Teresa W.

1991 Appendix B: Camp Nelson Vertebrate Fauna. In *Archaeological Investigations at Camp Nelson: A Union Quartermaster Depot and Hospital in Jessamine County, Kentucky,* by W. Stephen McBride and William E. Sharp, 187–92. Report 241. Lexington: Univ. of Kentucky, Program for Cultural Resource Assessment.

Turney-High, Harry Holbert

1971 *Primitive War: Its Practice and Concepts.* 2d ed. Columbia: Univ. of South Carolina Press.

Tyler, General.

1863      Letter to General Morris, June 23, 1863, 6th New York Heavy Artillery Regimental Letter and Order Book, Record Group 94, Records of the Adjutant General's Office. National Archives, Washington, D.C.

Tyrell, William G.

1962      Parrott's Famed Cannon Perfected and Produced at the Cold Spring Foundry. In *New York State and the Civil War* 1, no. 11: 3–8.

Tyrner-Tyrnauer, A. R.

1962      *Lincoln and the Emperors.* New York: Harcourt Brace Jovanovich.

Underwater Archaeological Joint Ventures [UAJV]

1982      James River Survey: The Last of the Confederate Navy. Unpublished report on file, State Historic Preservation Office, Richmond, Va.

U.S. Congress

1865      Joint Committee Hearings on the Conduct of War. Report on the Character and Efficiency of Heavy Ordnance . . . The Mode of Fabrication; the Amount of Royalty Paid, the Tests to Which These Guns Are Subjected . . . When Rifled Guns Were Introduced . . . January 25, 1864. 38th Congress, 2d Session, Report 121, Library of Congress, Washington, D.C.

U. S. Congress, Senate Joint Committee on Ordnance

1868      Report on the 1867 Investigation of Purchases, Contracts, and Experiments of the Ordnance Department, on March 30, 1867. 40th Congress, 3d Session, Report no. 266. Library of Congress, Washington, D.C.

U.S. Dept. of Defense, Army

1860      *Regulations Concerning Barracks and Quarters for the Army of the United States.* Washington, D.C.: George W. Bowman.

1862      *The Ordnance Manual for the Use of the Officers of the United States Army.* Philadelphia: Lippincott and Co.

U.S. Dept. of the Interior, National Park Service

1986      *National Park Statistical Abstract.* Statistical Office, Denver Service Center, National Park Service.

U.S. Geological Survey

1981      Chester, Virginia Quadrangle. 7.5 minute ser. U.S. Geological Survey, Washington, D.C.

1974      Drewry's Bluff, Virginia Quadrangle. 7.5 minute ser. U.S. Geological Survey, Washington, D.C.

U.S. Govt. Printing Office

1863        *Revised United States Army Regulations of 1861.* Washington, D.C.: Govt. Printing Office.

1880–1901   *The War of the Rebellion: A Compilation of the Official Records of the Union and Confederate Armies.* Washington, D.C.: Govt. Printing Office.

1883        *Report of the Productions of Agriculture as Returned at the Tenth Census.* Washington, D.C.: Govt. Printing Office.

U.S. National Archives, Washington, D.C.

N.d.        Returns of Military Posts. M-617, Microfilm Roll 1527.

1863–1866   Camp Nelson, Quartermaster Dept. Records. Record Group 92, Box 720.

U.S. Naval History Division

1961–1966   *Civil War Naval Chronology, 1861–1865.* 5 vols. Washington, D.C.: Govt. Printing Office.

U.S. Office of Naval War Records

1901        *Official Records of the Union and Confederate Navies in the War of the Rebellion.* 31 vols., 1894–1927. Washington, D.C.: Govt. Printing Office.

Universal Pictures Corporation

1930        *All Quiet on the Western Front.* Script by Erich Maria Remarque; Directed by Lewis Milestone; produced by Carl Laemmle, Jr.

Vance, Rupert B.

1929        *Human Factors in Cotton Culture: A Study of the Social Geography of the American South.* Chapel Hill: Univ. of North Carolina Press.

Van Dyke, Augustus M.

1903        Early Days: Or, the School of the Soldier. In *Sketches of War History 1861–1865.* Military Order of the Loyal Legion of the United States, Ohio Commandery.

Vinovskis, Maris A.

1989        Have Social Historians Lost the Civil War? *Journal of American History* 76: 34–58.

1990a       Introduction. In *Toward a Social History of the American Civil War: Explanatory Essays,* ed. Maris A. Vinovskis, vii–xii. Cambridge: Cambridge Univ. Press.

1990b       Have Social Historians Lost the Civil War? Some Preliminary Demographic Speculations. In *Toward a Social History of the American Civil War: Exploratory Essays,* ed. Maris A. Vinovskis, 1–30. Cambridge: Cambridge Univ. Press.

*Virginia Free Press.* Newspaper on microfilm at Harpers Ferry National Historical Park, Harpers Ferry, W.Va.

Virginia, Chesterfield County. Court Records.

1860  Agricultural Census Records. Chesterfield County Courthouse, Chester, Va.

N.d.  Deed Books 14, 42, 43. Chesterfield County Courthouse, Chester, Va.

1850–1865 Personal Property Tax Lists. Chesterfield County Courthouse, Chester, Va.

1858  Slave Schedules. Chesterfield County Courthouse, Chester, Va.

1860  Slave Schedules. Chesterfield County Courthouse, Chester, Va.

Virginia, Jefferson County. Court Records.

1846  Deed Book 28, 2 Sept. 1846: 292–93

Walker, John W.

1971  Excavations of the Arkansas Post Branch of the Bank of the State of Arkansas, Arkansas Post National Monument. Lincoln, Nebr.: National Park Service, Midwest District.

Ward, Joseph F.

1985  Civil War Letters of J. E. Ward, 34th Regiment, Massachusetts Volunteers, Company B. Typescript on file, Harpers Ferry National Historical Park, Harpers Ferry, W.Va.

Watson, Patty Jo, Steven A. LeBlanc, and Charles Redman

1971  *Explanation in Archaeology.* New York: Columbia Univ. Press.

Wayne, Michael

1983  *The Reshaping of Plantation Society. The Natchez District, 1860–1880.* Baton Rouge: Louisiana State Univ. Press.

West, George B.

1977  *When the Yankees Came: Civil War and Reconstruction on the Virginia Peninsula,* ed. Parke Rouse, Jr. Richmond, Va.: Dietz Press.

Wiener, Jonathan M.

1959  *They Who Fought Here.* New York: Macmillan.

1978  *Social Origins of the New South: Alabama, 1860–1885.* Baton Rouge: Louisiana State Univ. Press.

Wild, Frederick W.

1989  *The Household Economy: Reconsidering the Domestic Mode of Production.* Boulder, Colo.: Westview.

Wild, Frederick W., ed.

1912  *Memoirs and History of Capt. F.W. Alexander's Baltimore Battery of Light Artillery.* Loch Raven, Md.: Press of Maryland School for Boys.

Wiley, Bell I.
1959        *They Who Fought Here.* New York: Macmillan.
1984        *The Life of Billy Yank: The Common Soldier of the Union.* Baton Rouge: Louisiana State Univ. Press.

Willey, Gordon R., and Philip Phillips
1958        *Method and Theory in American Archaeology.* Chicago: Univ. of Chicago Press.

Williams, T. Harry
1983a       That Sad Strange War. In *The Selected Essays of T. Harry Williams,* by T. Harry Williams, 31–42. Baton Rouge: Louisiana State Univ. Press.

1983b       Freeman, Historian of the Civil War: An Appraisal. In *The Selected Essays of T. Harry Williams,* by T. Harry Williams, 185–94. Baton Rouge: Louisiana State Univ. Press.

Wilson, Edmund
1962        *Patriotic Gore.* New York: Oxford Univ. Press.

Wilson, M.
1886        *Thirty Years of Early History of Cold Spring and Vicinity with Incidents. By One Who Has Been a Resident Since 1819.* Newburgh, N.Y.: Schram Printing House.

Wingate, George W.
1896        *History of the Twenty-Second Regiment of the National Guard of the State of New York.* New York: Edwin W. Dayton.

Winter, Susan E.
In press     "The Changing Social Structure of Lower-Town Harpers Ferry." An Archaeology of Harpers Ferry's Commercial and Residential District, ed. Paul A. Shackel and Susan E. Winter. *Historical Archaeology,* forthcoming.

Winters, Donald L.
1978        *Farmers Without Farms: Agricultural Tenancy in Nineteenth-Century Iowa.* Westport, Conn.: Greenwood.

Wise, Henry A.
Wise Papers, LB 5, no. 6.5, New York Historical Society, New York.
1865        Correspondence to Robert P. Parrott, Dec. 12, 1865. Record Group 74, Entry 4. National Archives, Washington, D.C.
1866a       Correspondence to Proprietor of West Point Foundry, Cold Spring, New York, Oct. 10, 1866. Record Group 74, Entry 4. National Archives, Washington, D.C.

1866b        Correspondence to Robert P. Parrott, Oct. 11, 1866. Record
             Group 74, Entry 4. National Archives, Washington, D.C.

1866c        Correspondence to Robert P. Parrott, Nov. 8, 1866, Record
             Group 74, Entry 4, National Archives, Washington, D.C.

1867         Correspondence to Robert P. Parrott, Nov. 8, 1867. Record
             Group 74, Entry 4. National Archives, Washington, D.C.

Woldman, Albert A.

1952         *Lincoln and the Russians.* Cleveland, Ohio: World.

Wolf, Eric K.

1984         Culture: Panacea or Problem? *American Antiquity* 49: 393–400.

Wood, Raymond

1990         Ethnohistory and Historical Method. In *Archaeological Method and
             Theory* 2, ed. Michael B. Schiffer. Tucson: Univ. of Arizona Press.

Worden, John L., S. D. Greene, and H. Ashton Ramsay

1912         *The Monitor and the Merrimack: Both Sides of the Story.* New York:
             Harper & Brothers.

Work, Henry Clay

1862         Grafted into the Army. Published song.

Wright, David R.

1982         Civil War Field Fortifications: An Analysis of Theory and Practi-
             cal Application. M.A. thesis, Middle Tennessee State Univ.,
             Murfreesboro, Tenn.

Wriston, H. M.

1929         *Executive Agents in American Foreign Relations.* Baltimore: Johns
             Hopkins Univ. Press.

Young, Amy L., and Phillip J. Carr

1989         Building Middle Range Research for Historical Archaeology
             with Nails. Paper presented at the Seventh Proceedings on Ohio
             Valley Urban and Historic Archaeology, Cincinnati, Mar. 17–
             19, 1989.

Young, Franklin K.

1897         A Tale of Two Frigates. *Nickell Magazine* (May): 269–78.

# CONTRIBUTORS

JANET G. BRASHLER is associate professor of anthropology at Grand Valley State University. She holds a Ph.D. degree from Michigan State University at Lansing. She has been active in both prehistoric and historical archaeology for twenty-five years. Her experience with Civil War period sites includes the recording and preservation of encampments and other military sites on the eastern Allegheny front in West Virginia.

CLARENCE R. GEIER, Jr. is professor of anthropology at James Madison University in Harrisonburg, Virginia. He holds a Ph.D. degree from the University of Missouri-Columbia. He is author of numerous articles on the prehistory and history of Virginia. He served as senior director for excavations at the Hatcher-Cheatham site south of Richmond, Virginia, and was involved with the preservation of elements of the Magruder defensive perimeter in Newport News, Virginia. Recently he has been involved with the analysis of Civil War sites in the lower Valley of the Shenandoah, particularly those associated with the Battle of Third Winchester and Cedar Creek.

JOEL W. GROSSMAN is founder and president of Grossman & Associates, Inc., of New York. He received his Ph.D. as a Fulbright and Special Career Fellow from the University of California at Berkeley. His archaeological experience is international in scope. His activity in historical archaeology has included discovery and excavation of the first seventeenth-century Dutch West India Company remains in Lower Manhattan, and excavations at eighteenth-century Fort Henry on the Hudson River in Washington County, New York. He was selected by the USEPA to direct the first large-scale data recovery program of a Superfund site at the Civil War era testing facilities and workers site at the West Point Foundry in Cold Spring, New York.

WILLIAM B. LEES is director of the Historic Sites Division of the Oklahoma Historical Society. He received his Ph.D. in anthropology from Michigan State University at Lansing. His research has covered diverse areas of historical archaeology. With respect to the Civil War in the western United States, his historical interests have focused on the reinterpretation of battlefields and battlefield events using broad-scale archaeological information. As illustrated by his presentation on the Battle of Mine Creek, Kansas, he is interested in the use of archaeology to search for meaningful artifact patterns resulting from a battle. He seeks to use these data in a critical evaluation of established interpretations of specific battles and battle events.

W. HUNTER LESSER is an archaeologist with the USDA Forest Service, Monongahela National Forest, based in Elkins, West Virginia. He has a B.S. degree in anthropology and natural science from Shorter College in Rome, Georgia. He has been involved with extensive prehistoric and historical archaeological research, and has been particularly active in studying the 1861 Civil War campaigns in the Allegheny Mountains of West Virginia. He serves on the West Virginia Archives and History Commission and on the board of directors of the Rich Mountain Battlefield History Commission.

SAMUEL G. MARGOLIN is president of Virginia Archaeological Services of Newport News, Virginia. He holds a Ph.D. in American history from the College of William and Mary at Williamsburg, Virginia. He has had extensive experience in the investigation of underwater archaeological sites within Virginia and was directly involved with the discovery, evaluation, and analysis of data from the C.S.S. *Florida,* a Confederate raider, and the U.S.S. *Cumberland,* a Union warship.

KIM A. MCBRIDE is staff historical archaeologist for the Program for Cultural Resource Management at the University of Kentucky in Lexington. She received her Ph.D. in anthropology from Michigan State University at Lansing. Her archaeological experience has focused on the Ohio Valley and the southeastern United States. She has had extensive experience in nineteenth-century historical archaeology, including work at Civil War period military sites.

W. STEVEN MCBRIDE is staff historical archaeologist for the Program for Cultural Resource Management at the University of Kentucky in Lexington. He received his Ph.D. in anthropology from Michigan State University at Lansing. His archaeological experience focuses on the Ohio Valley and the southeastern United States. He has had extensive experience in nineteenth-century historical archaeology, including work at diverse Civil War period military sites.

DAVID G. ORR is regional archaeologist for the Middle Atlantic Region of the National Park Service. He received his Ph.D. in history, with an emphasis in classical archaeology, from the University of Maryland at College Park. Research interests include nineteenth-century American historical archaeology. As regional archaeologist, he oversees the cultural resources housed within numerous battlefields in the eastern theater of the Civil War. He is coeditor of a work on Delaware prehistory and of the John Cotter Festschrift, *Scope of Historic Archaeology.*

CHARLES E. ORSER, JR., is associate professor of anthropology and director of the Midwestern Archaeological Research Center at Illinois State University. He received his Ph.D. in anthropology from Southern Illinois University. He has worked in historical archaeology since 1971, with particular experience on sites in Illinois, Indiana, Michigan, Georgia, Louisiana, and South Carolina. He has published widely on the archaeology of agricultural systems during the Civil War period. Perhaps most notable is his *The Material Basis of the Postbellum Tenant Plantation: Historical Archaeology in the South Carolina Piedmont* (University of Georgia Press, 1988) and his edited volume for the Society of Historical Archaeology, *Historical Archaeology on Southern Plantations and Farms* (1990).

PAUL A. SHACKEL is park archaeologist for Harpers Ferry National Historical Park in West Virginia. He received his Ph.D. in anthropology from the State University of New York at Buffalo. His research focuses on the interpretation of the meanings and uses of Civil War era material artifacts and landscapes. He is currently active in the study of the industrial and domestic components of Harpers Ferry. Paul is coeditor, with Susan Winter, of a special volume to be published by the Society for Historical Archaeology, on archaeological research at Harpers Ferry.

SAMUEL D. SMITH is historical archaeologist for the Tennessee Division of Archaeology. He holds an M.A. degree from the University of Florida. He is the author of numerous reports and publications concerning historical archaeology in Tennessee. He has directed two major site survey projects involving Civil War period military sites in Tennessee, and directed the excavation of the Carter House in Franklin, Tennessee, which was involved in the 1864 Battle of Franklin.

STEVEN D. SMITH is consulting archaeologist with the South Carolina Institute of Archaeology and Anthropology at the University of South Carolina. He holds an M.A. from the University of Kentucky. With seventeen years of field experience, Steven has been involved with the excavation of Civil War military sites in South Carolina, including the camp and cemetery of the 55th Massachusetts at Folly Island.

SUSAN E. WINTER is chief of the Branch of Cultural Resources at the C & O Canal National Historical Park in Maryland. She received her M.A. degree in anthropology from the College of William and Mary in Williamsburg, Virginia. Prior to assuming her present position, she was park archaeologist at Harpers Ferry National Historical Park, where she directed the evaluation of Civil War remains within the park, in particular the fortifications, encampments, and cultural features on Maryland and Loudoun Heights. She is coeditor, with Paul Shackel, of a special volume to be published by the Society for Historical Archaeology, on archaeological research at Harpers Ferry.

# INDEX